Arkansas in Ink

T0289219

Arkansas in Ink

Gunslingers, Ghosts, and Other Graphic Tales

Illustrated by Ron Wolfe
Edited by Guy Lancaster

BUTLER
CENTER
BOOKS

Copyright © 2014 by The Encyclopedia of Arkansas History & Culture

All rights reserved. Published by Butler Center Books, part of the Butler Center for Arkansas Studies, a division of the Central Arkansas Library System. No part of this book may be reproduced in any form, except for brief passages quoted within reviews, without the express written consent of Butler Center Books.

The Butler Center for Arkansas Studies
Central Arkansas Library System
100 Rock Street
Little Rock, Arkansas 72201

www.butlercenter.org

First edition: September 2014

Manager: Rod Lorenzen
Book and cover design: Mike Keckhaver
Copyeditor: Ali Welky

ISBN 978-1-935106-73-9
e-ISBN 978-1-935106-74-6

Library of Congress Cataloging-in-Publication Data

Arkansas in ink : gunslingers, ghosts, and other graphic tales / illustrated by Ron Wolfe ; edited by Guy Lancaster. – First edition.
pages cm
Summary: "Interesting stories from Arkansas history, illustrated with cartoons"-- Provided by publisher.
ISBN 978-1-935106-73-9 (paperback : alkaline paper) – ISBN 978-1-935106-74-6 (e-book) 1. Arkansas--History--Anecdotes. 2. Arkansas--Social life and customs--Anecdotes. 3. Arkansas--History--Pictorial works. 4. Arkansas--History--Caricatures and cartoons. I. Wolfe, Ron. II. Lancaster, Guy, 1976-

F411.6.A75 2014
976.7--dc23

2014026392

The publishing division of the Butler Center for Arkansas Studies
was made possible by the generosity of Dora Johnson Ragsdale and John G. Ragsdale Jr.

Printed in the United States of America

This book is printed on archival-quality paper that meets requirements of the American National Standard for Information Sciences, Permanence of Paper, Printed Library Materials, ANSI Z39.48-1984.

Table of Contents

About the Encyclopedia of Arkansas 4

Introduction 5

Politics

Arkansas Loan and Thrift 8

Arkansas Negro Democratic Association 10

Arkansas Real Estate Bank and
Arkansas State Bank 12

Big Lake Wars. 14

Brooks-Baxter War 16

Hattie Caraway 20

Convict Lease System 22

Crittenden County Expulsion of 1888. 24

Election Fraud 26

"The Family" 29

Featherstone v. Cate. 30

GI Revolt. 32

Marlin Hawkins. .34

John Law's Concession. 36

Virginia Johnson .38

Guy Hamilton "Mutt" Jones 40

Little Rock Censor Board. 42

McLean v. Arkansas Board of Education 44

Martha Mitchell. .46

Carrie Nation 48

Plumerville Conflict of 1886–1892. 50

V. V. Smith. 52

Union Labor Party. 54

Paul Van Dalsem. .56

Waldron War 58

Wilson-Anthony Duel. 60

Women of the Ku Klux Klan 62

Law and Outlaws

Arkansas State Police 64

Barker-Karpis Gang 66

West Bogan (Trial of). 68

Bullfrog Valley Gang 70

Edward Coy (Lynching of). 72

Maud Crawford (Disappearance of). 74

Bill Doolin. 76

Connie Franklin (Alleged Murder of) 78

Hot Springs Shootout. 80

Island 37 82

Maxine Jones. 84

Owney Madden. .86

Olyphant Train Robbery. 88

Isaac Parker. 90

Parley P. Pratt (Murder of) 92

Prohibition 94

Howell A. "Doc" Rayburn. 98

Bass Reeves 100

Tom Slaughter 102

Helen Spence. 104

Belle Star. 106

Texarkana Moonlight Murders. 108

Tucker-Parnell Feud. 110

Vapors. 112

Sidney Wallace 114

Oddities

The Amazing Adventures of My Dog Sheppy . . 116

Atkins Pickle Company. 118

Black Bears 120

Cobbites. 122

Crater of Diamonds State Park 124

Crescent Hotel 126

Dardanelle Pontoon Bridge 128

Eureka Springs Baby. 130

"The Fayetteville Polka" 132

Fouke Monster 134

Ghost Legends 136

Gowrow 138

Gurdon Light 140

Harmonial Vegetarian Society. 141

Incoming Kingdom Missionary Unit 142

Ivory-billed Woodpeckers. 144

King Crowley 146

Old Mike. 148

Tarantulas. 149

Turkey Trot Festival. 150

White River Monster 151

Celebrities

Julie Adams 152

"Broncho Billy" Anderson. 154

Rodger Bumpass. 156

Johnny Cash 158

Gail Davis. 162

Bob Dorough 164

"Aunt Caroline" Dye. 166

Gil Gerard. 168

Kenny Johnson 170

Louis Jordan 172

Lum and Abner. 174

Douglas MacArthur 176

Robert McFerrin Sr.. 178

Patsy Montana 180

Hal Needham 182

Kate Phillips. 184

Anita Pointer 186

Jimmy Wakely. 188

Elton and Betty White 190

About the Encyclopedia of Arkansas History & Culture

The Encyclopedia of Arkansas History & Culture (EOA) is a project of the Butler Center for Arkansas Studies at the Central Arkansas Library System (CALS) in Little Rock, Arkansas. It is the only state encyclopedia in the country to be produced by a library system. The EOA strives to offer a definitive, comprehensive, and accurate record of America's twenty-fifth state. The mission of this free online encyclopedia is to collect and disseminate information on all aspects of the state's history and culture and to provide a comprehensive reference work for historians, teachers, students, and others seeking to understand and appreciate Arkansas's heritage.

The EOA debuted online to the public in May 2006 as a work in progress. At that time, it contained approximately 700 entries and 900 pieces of media; as of 2014, the site offers more than 3,600 entries and more than 4,800 pieces of media.

Users have come from every continent (including Antarctica) and more than 230 countries. During its first month online, the EOA had about 47,000 visits; the EOA now receives nearly two million visits each year.

Major funding for the establishment of the EOA was provided by the Winthrop Rockefeller Foundation. Over the years, the EOA has also received funding from the Department of Arkansas Heritage, the Arkansas General Assembly, the Arkansas Humanities Council, and the National Endowment for the Humanities, as well as donations from individuals, foundations, and organizations. CALS has pledged to keep the EOA in operation in perpetuity.

EOA staff members:

Guy Lancaster, Editor

Mike Keckhaver, Media Editor

Mike Polston, Staff Historian

Ali Welky, Assistant Editor

Kay Bland, Education Coordinator

Jasmine Jobe, Editorial Assistant

Former EOA staff members:

Tom W. Dillard, Founding Editor

Jill Curran, Project Manager

Nathania Sawyer, Senior Editor and Project Manager

Tim Nutt, Special Projects Editor

Steven Teske, Fact Checker

Anna Lancaster, Editorial Assistant

Shirley Schuette, Editorial Assistant

For more information, visit the EOA online at www.encyclopediaofarkansas.net.

Introduction

By Guy Lancaster, editor of the Encyclopedia of Arkansas History & Culture

I still remember the first comic book I ever purchased—*G.I. Joe* no. 39, bought at Books Plus in Jonesboro, Arkansas, in 1985, when I was nine years old. Most kids probably pick up their first issues a bit younger than that, sometimes encouraged by a parent who had fond memories of superheroes and soldiers. But my father was still nursing a grudge against his own mother, who—because he wouldn't clean his room one day—tossed away his copies of *Fantastic Four* no. 1, *Namor the Sub-Mariner* no. 1, and *Sgt. Fury and His Howling Commandos* no. 1. Poor dad. My discovery of comic books probably brought back some painful memories for him.

That was nearly thirty years ago, when comic books were 75 cents, which seemed expensive back then but seems like almost nothing now, in this era when single issues have long since broken the three-dollar mark. Despite the passage of almost three decades, I can still easily call to mind some of the visuals in those comic books, such as the high cliff our heroes must descend in order to approach the enemy base unawares. And I remember being confused by military time. "Let's rendezvous at 2300 hours." I could do the math and knew that 2300 hours was nearly 100 days—just how long *were* these missions? Until my father explained the twenty-four-hour clock to me, I thought our eponymous "Real American Hero" had more free time on his hands than he really should.

Why do I remember all of this? Why is a *G.I. Joe* comic book of three decades' vintage in the forefront of my mind while certain novels I've read much more recently do not strike the same chord? I think the combination of visuals and text goes a long way toward explaining that. Comics theorist Scott McCloud, in his 1993 book *Understanding Comics*, cites several antecedents to the comic book form—for example, Egyptian hieroglyphics and illuminated Bible manuscripts—to prove that this combination

of word and image has long standing in human culture. In fact, human beings evolved as visual creatures, so it's no accident that certain visual cues resonate with our memories more than text. Rock art in European caves dates back to 40,000 or so years ago and may have been produced for religious ceremonies. Written language is much newer, showing up in the world only in the Bronze Age, having perhaps evolved from the marks used to count goods received. But while it's amazing that this trades-man's shorthand eventually developed to give us such magnificent works as George Eliot's *Middlemarch*, it doesn't change the fact that a random *G.I. Joe* issue still ranks higher in my memory, annoying as that is.

There is power in the combination of media, in word and image brought together. That is why we wanted to do this book. We here at the Encyclopedia of Arkansas project wanted to make a book presenting some of the more interesting facets of Arkansas history in a manner that would resonate in a unique way. The online Encyclopedia of Arkansas History & Culture—portions of which are presented in this volume—went live to the public on May 2, 2006. It now includes more than 3,600 entries and 4,800 pieces of media, and it continues to grow at an astonishing rate, adding more with each passing year. As closely as I work on the text day in and day out, these days, when I think about the Barker-Karpis Gang (p. 66), what first comes to mind is Ron Wolfe's drawing of that sweet old granny version of Ma Barker, armed with a bomb, a knife, two guns, and a cake. It captures something that words can't, as does his picture of a mischievous Helen Spence (p. 104) escaping from custody in her checkered dress. (And what's with her smile, by the way? Isn't it amazing how a crooked line like that can load a figure down with ambiguity?)

Our illustrator Ron Wolfe has been kicking around the comics scene for some time, from writing duties on *Clive Barker's Hellraiser* in the early 1990s down to the present day with his own series, *Knights of the Living Dead*. He also writes and illustrates for the state's most widely circulated newspaper, the *Arkansas*

Democrat-Gazette. Ron has that cartoonist's knack of caricature, of capturing the emotional gamut from absurdity to horror in a few spare lines, and his talents are on full display in this book. No one has yet caught on film the "monster" that allegedly haunts the White River, but even if someone did tomorrow, I'll bet you will still find that Ron's drawing of a smiling, Nessie-like creature (p. 151) holds first place in your brain. I'm thrilled that he has turned his talents to illustrating these vignettes of our state's history. Arkansas has a rich heritage, and believe me when I say that you won't be forgetting the stories presented herein anytime soon, for Ron's style perfectly captures the often lunatic twists and turns our state has taken through the years.

Maybe, just maybe, thirty years from now, you'll be thankful that you can talk with some expertise about the Brooks-Baxter War or the shadier history of Hot Springs. That will have made this whole project worthwhile.

If, after reading this book, you want to delve a little further into Arkansas history, the best place to start is the online Encyclopedia of Arkansas History & Culture, from which these entries were pulled. Each entry is not only illustrated with historical media and hyperlinked to other entries, it also has a bibliography at the bottom that will guide you to more specific resources on that particular subject. In addition, there are overview entries covering specific time periods, from prehistory to the present, as well as larger themes, such as "Religion," "Environment," and "Literature and Authors." The Encyclopedia of Arkansas is the perfect starting point for any introduction to the state's history and culture, and the staff of the EOA works diligently to keep all its information up to date.

The Encyclopedia of Arkansas has been made possible by the hard work of hundreds of authors from not only Arkansas but also around the country and the world. Some of their work is represented here in this volume. We thank each and every one of them for working to bring so many interesting facets of state and local history to light.

If you want to delve even further into the state's history, the University of Arkansas Press has published several general volumes on Arkansas history. Two have recently been released in second editions: *Arkansas: A Narrative History* by Jeannie M. Whayne, Thomas A. DeBlack, George Sabo, and Morris S. Arnold (2013) and *A Documentary History of Arkansas*, edited by C. Fred Williams, S. Charles Bolton, Carl H. Moneyhon, and LeRoy T. Williams (2013). UA Press also published the four-volume "Histories of Arkansas" series covering particular time periods in greater detail: *Arkansas, 1800–1860: Remote and Restless* by S. Charles Bolton (1998), *With Fire and Sword: Arkansas, 1861–1874* by Thomas A. DeBlack (2003), *Arkansas and the New South, 1874–1929* by Carl H. Moneyhon (1997), and *Arkansas in the Modern Era, 1930–1999* by Ben F. Johnson III (2000). Another general history that many have enjoyed is Michael B. Dougan's *Arkansas Odyssey: The Saga of Arkansas from Prehistoric Times to the Present* (1994); a second edition of this is reportedly in the works.

Aside from UA Press, Butler Center Books, the publishing arm of the Butler Center for Arkansas Studies at the Central Arkansas Library System, also regularly publishes books on state history, including another EOA project, the *Encyclopedia of Arkansas Music*, edited by Ali Welky and Michael Keckhaver (2013). Arkansas is also home to a highly regarded journal of state history, the *Arkansas Historical Quarterly*, published by the Arkansas Historical Association since 1942. Most counties have a local historical association, and museums dedicated to state and local history exist throughout the state.

In short, if this book has piqued your interest, there are numerous avenues for further exploration. You won't believe what's out there. Enjoy!

Arkansas Loan and Thrift

THE ARKANSAS LOAN & THRIFT CORP. HAD ANOTHER NAME—

—ARKANSAS LOAN AND *THEFT!*

IT COLLAPSED.

Jokingly called "Arkansas Loan and Theft," Arkansas Loan and Thrift Corporation (AL&T) was a hybrid bank that operated for three years outside state banking laws with the help of political connections in the 1960s. AL&T became a symbol of the corruption and lethargy that were the products of Governor Orval Faubus's twelve-year control of the statehouse and, in the opinion of Governor Winthrop Rockefeller, the Democratic Party's unfettered reign since Reconstruction. The ensuing grand jury indictment said the AL&T's organizers ran the finance company illegally and dissipated depositors' money by making loans to themselves and their companies, friends, and confederates— loans that were never repaid—and by giving themselves and friends large stock dividends even though the company was broke. The chief operating officer and two other executives were convicted and sentenced to prison for fraud, as well as conspiracy and bribery. Bruce Bennett, who helped organize AL&T while he was attorney general, was indicted on twenty-eight counts, but a longtime friend from El Dorado (Union County), U.S. District Judge Oren Harris, delayed the trial when Bennett revealed

that he had throat cancer. Bennett died in 1979 without going to trial.

More than 2,000 people and churches lost money when AL&T collapsed. The receiver eventually recovered about a fourth of the $4.2 million placed in the company. Securities, bank, and savings-and-loan officials for Faubus backed off regulating the institution, heeding the official but secret advice of the attorney general and the intervention of powerful state legislators, two of whom, Representative Paul Van Dalsem of Perryville (Perry County) and Senator Joe Lee Anderson of Helena (Phillips County), would be listed in the indictment as co-conspirators, along with other state officials and politicians. Cartoons by George Fisher in the *Arkansas Gazette* popularized the scandal for some years.

The bank seemed to be the brainchild of Ernest A. Bartlett Jr., a twenty-five-year-old used-car dealer, and Bennett, a politician from El Dorado who was elected attorney general in 1956 by inveighing against racial integration. Bennett ran an unsuccessful race for governor against Faubus in 1960, accusing him of being soft on integration, and regained the attorney general's office in 1962. He made a final race for governor in 1968 while a grand jury was investigating his role in AL&T.

Bartlett, Bennett, and others set up AL&T in December 1964; the incorporation papers were prepared in the attorney general's office by an assistant attorney general, who received AL&T shares. Bartlett and Bennett found a defunct finance company, United Loan and Investment, which had a charter from 1937 as an industrial loan company. It was incorporated into AL&T and became the finance company's authority for taking deposits. Van Dalsem, a longtime leader of the House of Representatives and

Faubus's floor leader, arranged for Bennett to buy an inactive insurance company from the House speaker, J. H. Cottrell Jr. of Little Rock (Pulaski County). Bennett then sold it at a profit to AL&T, which renamed it Savings Guaranty Corporation, a shell company that would "insure" people's deposits in AL&T. It was given more than 1,000 shares of AL&T stock, the only assets it would ever own. AL&T wrote Savings Guaranty a check for $580,000, which allowed the state insurance examiner, who received AL&T stock, to certify that the insurance company had the capital to insure deposits. Then Savings Guaranty sent the money back to AL&T and took an IOU.

AL&T advertised that it would pay an interest rate of 5.75% for deposits, more than banks and savings-and-loan associations could offer, and that deposits were safer than if the Federal Deposit Insurance Corporation (FDIC) insured them. Actually, Savings Guaranty had no assets but the worthless AL&T stock, but in ads it used what looked like the official federal seal.

The company opened a headquarters at Van Buren (Crawford County) and offices around the state. It spent $150,000 on advertising and accumulated more than $4 million in deposits.

Bennett issued five official opinions to Van Dalsem and state regulators explaining that AL&T's operations were perfectly legal and that, because it operated under the auspices of an old industrial loan charter rather than a bank or savings-and-loan charter, the state securities commissioner, bank commissioner, and savings-and-loan commissioner could not regulate its activities. Bennett never released the opinions publicly; they were found in the files at AL&T when it went into receivership.

The state securities commissioner testified in Bartlett's criminal trial that when he moved to regulate AL&T and suspended Bartlett's broker's license, Bennett threatened to go to Faubus about his interference. Faubus insisted he never did anything to help the company and knew little about its operations. Bartlett maintained that Bennett's opinion giving legal sanction to AL&T was written by William J. Smith, Faubus's legal counsel, and that Smith advised Faubus on the company's formation. Smith denied this.

When Judge Joe Purcell defeated Bennett for the office of attorney general in 1966, he quickly moved to shutter AL&T. He filed a lawsuit in Pulaski County Chancery Court on January 23, 1967, ten days after taking office, contending that AL&T was selling securities illegally. The case was assigned to Chancellor Kay L. Matthews, a former Faubus aide. The next day, Bartlett visited Matthews's law and business partner, Claude Carpenter Jr., also a former Faubus aide, and paid him a substantial retainer for AL&T. Carpenter would be named a co-conspirator in the subsequent indictment. He testified at Bartlett's trial in 1969 that he never did anything for the fees except discuss football with Bartlett and accompany him on a private plane trip to Las Vegas.

Judge Matthews never brought Purcell's suit to trial. One of Carpenter's connections to AL&T was mentioned in a hearing more than two years later, and Matthews disqualified himself from the case. On March 13, 1968, acting on a motion by lawyers of the federal Securities and Exchange Commission, U.S. District Judge John E. Miller of Fort Smith (Sebastian County) closed AL&T and put it into receivership. At a hearing on the claims against the company, a minister said churches that had invested their building funds in AL&T should have first call on any recovered assets because such assets were "God's money." Judge Miller famously countered that God should have been wise enough not to put his money in AL&T.

A federal grand jury indicted Bennett, Bartlett, and two officers from Booneville (Logan County)—Afton Borum and Hoyt Borum—on twenty-eight counts. Judge Harris severed Bennett's case from the others and gave him a continuance when Bennett said he was ill. The government eventually gave up on trying Bennett. Bartlett was convicted and sentenced to five years and fined $5,000. The Borum brothers were convicted and received even shorter sentences.

Ernest Dumas
Little Rock, Arkansas

Arkansas Negro Democratic Association

The Arkansas Negro Democratic Association (ANDA) was founded in 1928 by Little Rock (Pulaski County) physician John Marshall Robinson, who served as president until 1952, and a number of other prominent black professionals. Between 1928 and 1952, ANDA was the leading voice of black Arkansas Democrats in the state. Although ANDA tackled a number of issues concerned with racial discrimination, its principal focus was on winning the right for black citizens to participate in the activities of the Arkansas Democratic Party, especially its primary elections.

In Arkansas, the payment of a one-dollar poll tax qualified a person to vote, irrespective of race. But exclusion from state Democratic Party primary elections significantly disfranchised black voters since that party dominated state politics. When white Democrats in Little Rock prevented African Americans from voting in the party's primary elections in 1928, Robinson petitioned the courts for redress. After a temporary restraining order was overturned, Robinson then sued for the right to vote in *Robinson v. Holman* (1930). The Arkansas Supreme Court upheld the use of all-white primaries, and the U.S. Supreme Court refused to hear the case on appeal.

Although Robinson's and ANDA's activism was muted by the Great Depression of the 1930s, it was revived again in the 1940s. A U.S. Supreme Court ruling in the Louisiana case of *United States v. Classic* (1941) declared that primary elections were subject to federal regulation. However, ANDA members were once more turned away from the polls on election day. It took another U.S. Supreme Court ruling in the Texas case of *Smith v. Allwright* (1944) to clarify the situation. In that case, the Court explicitly stated that the use of all-white primary elections to disfranchise black voters was unconstitutional.

Black Arkansans voted in the 1944 primary elections. In 1945, white Democrats sought to reverse this by amending party membership rules and initiating a complex double primary system. This provided for city and statewide primaries that excluded African Americans and for federal primaries at which blacks could vote but only at segregated ballot boxes. Arkansas Secretary of State C. G. Hall said that Robinson was not eligible to vote at all because of a conviction for manslaughter in 1911. Robinson believed that he had already been pardoned for the crime, but in exchange for his citizenship rights fully restored, he offered to resign as ANDA president. After the 1944 elections, Governor Homer Adkins pardoned him, apparently unconditionally.

Robinson found his authority increasingly challenged by younger black activists who sought to use the black vote more strategically to extract concessions from white politicians. In 1949, I. S. McClinton founded and became president of the Young Negro Democrats. In 1950, the Little Rock branch of the National Association for the Advancement of Colored People (NAACP) brought an end to the all-white primaries in Arkansas when it supported Little Rock minister J. H. Gatlin's lawsuit for a place on the Democratic Party primary ballot. The courts ruled in Gatlin's favor. Later that year, the State Democratic Convention changed party rules to admit African Americans.

When Robinson announced his retirement from politics in 1952, McClinton was elected ANDA president. McClinton and his

supporters then changed the name of the organization to the Arkansas Democratic Voters Association (ADVA) to assimilate into the integrated Arkansas Democratic Party. Both ANDA and ADVA were the forerunners of what is today known as the Arkansas Democratic Black Caucus. The common mission of all these organizations has been to give voice to the concerns of black Arkansas Democratic Party voters, members, and elected officials.

John A. Kirk
University of Arkansas at Little Rock

Arkansas Real Estate Bank and Arkansas State Bank

In 1836, the establishment of the Arkansas Real Estate Bank became the initial act to pass the first state legislature. Momentum for a state-sponsored bank began during the territorial phase when planters and other lowland agricultural interests sought ways to enhance the availability of capital. The Real Estate Bank's charter required the state to issue $2 million in five-percent bonds, the proceeds from which would serve as the bank's capital. But the state held no authority for immediate supervision of the bank's operations other than the appointment of a minority of the bank's directors. From 1836 to 1855, when the state took over control, the Real Estate Bank proved to be a source of political corruption, financial mismanagement, and intense sectional conflict among politicians.

The Arkansas State Bank, the sister institution to the Real Estate Bank, provided some funding for commercial projects, though most of its funds facilitated land sales. Its greatest legacy, however, was saddling the new state government with a burdensome debt and instigating several accounts of political corruption. In the end, the bank's failure jeopardized both public and private banking in Arkansas due to the public outcry against its operation.

Like the Arkansas State Bank (which operated from 1836 to 1843), the Real Estate Bank enjoyed bipartisan support. Anthony H. Davies and John Ringgold, both prominent Whigs, wrote the bank's charter, and the Democratic legislature approved it. Other than being a product of the surge of new banks established in the country at the time, the Real Estate Bank's stated purpose was to promote the interests of lowland planters. It had four locations: the headquarters in Little Rock (Pulaski County) and branches in the cotton belt areas of Columbia (Chicot County), Helena (Phillips County), and Washington (Hempstead County). The state appointed one-fourth of the board of directors, and

stockholders elected the rest. Each branch had a local board of directors based on a similar formula.

Subscribers to the bank's stock totaled 325 people, and most were leading men in the state, including Anthony H. Davies, Horace F. Walworth, and U.S. Senator Ambrose H. Sevier—all Chicot County planters. Most stockholders lived in counties bordering the Mississippi or Red rivers, with more than twenty-five percent of all stock owned by twenty-eight men in Chicot County. Subscribers typically bought stock by mortgaging land, which was appraised far above its market value. In turn, they borrowed up to half of the value of their stock, capped at $30,000.

Accusations of favoritism and spoilage in the Real Estate Bank dominated the 1837 legislative session. One critic, Joseph J. Anthony, a representative from Randolph County, wrote a resolution attacking the bank as a source of special privilege. House Speaker John Wilson, who was also president of the bank, defended its operation and vouched for its financial integrity. On December 4, during a debate on a bill to encourage the taking of wolf pelts, Anthony sarcastically alluded to Wilson's connections to the bank, after which Wilson killed Anthony with a bowie knife on the House floor. Wilson's friends secured a change of venue for his trial so that his acquittal was assured.

After that, Davies became bank president and authorized T. T. Williamson and Senator Sevier to float bank bonds in New York City to raise specie and paper issued by stable banks in other states. But most of the bonds were sold to the North American Banking and Trust Company and the U.S. Treasury. Sevier and his relatives (a.k.a. "The Family") continued to exercise great influence over the bank and benefit from its operation through the early 1850s.

With subscriptions, specie, and acceptable bank notes now available, the Real Estate Bank opened for business December 10, 1838, in Little Rock, and the other branches opened the next spring. By November 1839, all branches had suspended spe-

THE ARKANSAS STATE BANK RAISED SUCH A STINK—

ARKANSANS VOTED TO PROHIBIT *ALL* BANKS.

cie payments so that bank officials could issue far more credit than was held in reserve. Within a year, the bank's circulation increased from $153,910 to $759,000. Bank officials followed a fractional reserve policy whereby bank notes exceeded the amount of specie on deposit. When coupled with mismanagement, the bank's lending policy flooded the market with bank notes, whose value depreciated. By the end of the first year of operation, interest payments came due on the bank's bonds. To alleviate the crisis, bank officials skirted legality and took out a $121,000 loan from the North American Bank and Trust Company of New York.

Additional pressure on the bank came from small debtors, who believed bank officials discriminated against them in favor of large landowners and stockholders. One example, the Phillips

County uprising of May 1841, closed the circuit court of Judge Isaac Baker, who planned to auction seized land of small debtors who had defaulted.

In April 1842, the central board of directors passed a deed of assignment allocating the bank's assets to fifteen trustees, who replaced local branch boards and eliminated all state appointees. It was hoped the transfer would bring fiscal restraint to the bank, redeem depreciating paper, and pay interest for the state bonds used for capitalization. But the trustees, mostly Democrats, stifled outside surveillance of the bank's activities. Whigs as much as Democrats feared a full investigation of the bank's activities, but each side continued to blame the other for the bank's mismanagement. Outright repudiation failed to materialize, however, and the financial weakness of the Arkansas State Bank and the Real Estate Bank continued. The Arkansas State Bank ceased operation in 1843.

Almost immediately, politicians and voters led by Governor Archibald Yell blamed not only the bank's faulty and inflationary lending policy but the bank itself. Many blamed *all* banks. As a result, the first amendment to the state's constitution forbade banks from operating in Arkansas. It gained voter approval in 1846.

By the late 1840s, the Arkansas General Assembly followed many other states in imposing stiff constitutional regulations on the relationship between government officials and banking. The Real Estate Bank continued to function until April 1855, when the state assumed control of its assets and ordered a reckoning of its accounts.

The banking crisis in Arkansas reflected the end of an era both nationally and locally. But while a private banking system rapidly developed elsewhere, Arkansas long remained plagued by the lack of significant stores of capital. The impact of the banking prohibition remains unsolved by historians.

Carey M. Roberts
Arkansas Tech University

Big Lake Wars

THE **BIG LAKE WARS** SET POOR FISHERMEN AGAINST **BIG MONEY.**

Competition and contention over an abundant (and unregulated) storehouse of northeastern Arkansas wildlife from the mid-1870s until 1915 led to violence and controversy known as the Big Lake Wars. Big Lake refers to a section of western Mississippi County created by the massive New Madrid Earthquakes of 1811–1812. "War" may be a misleading description of the events because there were no formalities, declarations, truces, or settlements. However, the conflict had a lasting impact on the state and even on the nation. The Big Lake Wars pitted local residents, who were mostly poor, against affluent northerners, chiefly from St. Louis, Missouri.

Early Arkansas maps labeled the sparsely populated area between Crowley's Ridge and the Mississippi River as "the Great Swamp." After the Civil War, the railroad boom included the building of the St. Louis, Iron Mountain and Southern Railway from St. Louis to Texarkana (Miller County), as well as the construction of the St. Louis–San Francisco Railway (Frisco). Both railroads built branch lines in northeastern Arkansas to haul timber from the vast hardwood forests to meet the building needs of the nation.

The post–Civil War period also spawned hunting excursions as a pastime for the well-to-do. Groups, some that formed into hunting clubs, chartered railroad cars to travel to the Big Lake area for extended hunts in a time when there were no state or federal regulations on the taking of wild game.

The trains that took out timber also provided transportation for the products of the market hunters—mostly deer, ducks, and fish. Subsistence hunting, food for tables, became overshadowed by hunting that brought in money. Restaurants north of Arkansas often featured wild game from the Big Lake area, and iced barrels of venison, ducks, fish, and even frogs went aboard the trains in the area and headed north. The fish were usually largemouth bass and crappie, as catfish were disdained at that time.

Friction quickly arose between the local hunters and the visiting sportsmen, both using the same timberland lowland area. The St. Louis people began leasing land to keep out other hunters, and disputes flared into fights, shootings, and beatings. Some clubhouses and lodges, which were constructed with the readily available hardwood lumber, were burned.

Local residents regarded the watery Big Lake country as theirs to hunt. Clubs signed leases and bought land, and lumber companies bought the timber rights. Titles to the land, however, were sometimes questionable if not fraudulent. Numerous court actions resulted. An avalanche of local legislation came out of the Arkansas General Assembly but was largely ineffective. Some of the laws prohibited out-of-state residents from hunting in Arkansas, and the wealthy sportsmen often paid the fines and went on hunting.

At the beginning of the twentieth century, concerns over dwindling wildlife populations emerged on a national level as well as in Arkansas. The international Migratory Bird Treaty was passed by Congress in 1913, putting ducks and geese under federal control. New federal and state laws were passed to establish hunting seasons and, later, to set daily limits on the taking of wildlife.

Big Lake National Wildlife Refuge, the first such refuge in Arkansas, was established in 1915, and the Arkansas Game and Fish Commission (AGFC) was created, also in 1915. The prime mover behind the formation of the AGFC was state senator Junius Marion Futrell of Paragould (Greene County), which is near Big Lake; Futrell later became governor. Arkansas's governor in 1915, George Washington Hays, pitched his support behind Futrell's legislation to get it passed and signed into law. The new agency had a staff of nine part-time game wardens to patrol the entire state, and one was a Paragould resident. These agencies, refuges, and regulations helped bring the four decades of conflict to a close.

Not directly tied to the Big Lake situation was the arrival of rice farming in the Grand Prairie region of Arkansas. Migrating ducks made seasonal use of the farms' man-made reservoirs in addition to the nearby bottomland hardwood areas, and Stuttgart (Arkansas County) became a center of duck hunting. But the wintering ducks did not forsake Big Lake. To aid in their management, the AGFC in the early 1950s created Big Lake Wildlife Management Area on the eastern side of Big Lake National Wildlife Refuge, along with St. Francis Sunken Lands Wildlife Management area just to the west and southwest. A 1980s report by the federal refuge's manager estimated that one million ducks were on the refuge in an early December survey.

Joe Mosby
Conway, Arkansas

Brooks-Baxter War

The Brooks-Baxter War, which occurred during April and May 1874, was an armed conflict between the supporters of two rivals for the governorship—Joseph Brooks and Elisha Baxter. The violence spilled out of Little Rock (Pulaski County) into much of the state and was resolved only when the federal government intervened. The result of the war, recognition of Elisha Baxter as the governor, brought a practical end to Republican rule in the state and thus ended the era of Reconstruction.

Questions concerning the results of the state's 1872 gubernatorial election brought about the Brooks-Baxter War. In that election, Joseph Brooks—a carpetbagger with a radical reputation and the leader of the party faction known as the "Brindletails"—ran as a Reform Republican, supporting the national Liberal Republican movement, including Horace Greeley for president, and advancing a local plan to end the disfranchisement of former Confederates, reduce taxes, cut government expenses, and limit the power of the governor. His program attracted conservative Republicans and Democrats, who saw his programs as the best way for them to recapture power and backed him despite his radical past. Republican regulars, often called "Minstrels," backed Elisha Baxter, a scalawag who ran on a platform promising many of the same reforms proposed by Brooks. Central to the campaign was the issue of disfranchisement and the ability of the Minstrels to maintain control of the state government. Brooks may actually have won the subsequent election, but Baxter's supporters controlled the election machinery and declared Baxter and other regulars victors, despite evidence of widespread irregularities. Brooks and his supporters refused to accept the results. They appealed the seating of the regular party's candidates in Congress and secured one seat for a pro-Brooks candidate. Brooks also appealed the gubernatorial election to the legislature, but the legislature refused to hear his case.

The General Assembly's failure to act on Brooks's appeal did not settle the dispute, and he continued his efforts to displace Baxter, taking his dispute to the state courts. His legal appeals failed until changing political circumstances and shifting alliances created a court favorable to his position. The new condition was the regular Republican leaders' loss of faith in Baxter, who not only tried to get former Democratic leaders to support him but adopted a hostile attitude toward one of the Republican Party's major economic programs—state aid to railroads. Shortly after Baxter refused to sign bonds designated for the Arkansas Central Railroad and raised questions about the legality of all railroad bonds, Republican regulars, including U.S. senators Powell Clayton and Stephen Dorsey, met in Little Rock and determined to remove the governor. After that meeting, the Pulaski County Circuit Court of Judge John Whytock took up a request by Brooks for a writ giving him possession of the governor's office that had languished since June 1873. On April 15, 1874, Whytock ruled in favor of Brooks and issued the writ.

Brooks acted quickly and marched to the State House with a group of armed men and the Pulaski County sheriff. Confronting Baxter, the sheriff demanded that the governor leave his office. Alone except for his young son, the governor left under protest. Baxter immediately went to St. Johns' Military Academy, where he began to gather his supporters and telegraphed President Ulysses S. Grant, requesting support from U.S. forces at the Little Rock Arsenal in his efforts to retake his office. By the next morning, he had gathered 200 men, and they moved to the Anthony House, just east of the capitol, and began to prepare to recapture the State House by force. From the Anthony House, Baxter proclaimed martial law in Pulaski County, naming Thomas P. Dockery military governor of Little Rock, and called on the state militia for support.

Brooks, in turn, fortified the State House, using furniture to barricade windows and doors. Brooks's adjutant general, Robert F.

Catterson, broke into the state armory to obtain equipment and ammunition for his men. In addition, Catterson acquired two six-pounder artillery pieces that he placed on the capitol grounds, aimed at the Baxter men in the Anthony House. Brooks also called on militia companies for support.

The two governors had earlier stated their intention to hold on to their office even if it required the shedding of blood. The rapid gathering of large groups of armed men in Little Rock practically guaranteed that. After the call for support by the two parties, military companies loyal to one or the other began arriving. By April 20, Baxter's men numbered more than 1,000, and Brooks had mustered almost as many. By that day, Baxter's supporters crowed that they were ready to move against the State House. With orders from Washington DC to prevent a clash, Colonel Thomas E. Rose, commander at the arsenal, deployed U.S. regulars from the Sixteenth Infantry plus two pieces of artillery on Markham Street between the contending parties. Rose indicated his willingness to use force quickly. On the evening of April 21, after believing he had secured a twenty-four-hour truce, Rose confronted H. King White, who had arrived with Baxter supporters from Pine Bluff (Jefferson County) outside the Anthony House. Rose believed White was intent on inciting a riot. In the confrontation, someone fired a shot. In the resulting confusion, more shots were fired, producing several casualties. Rose returned to

Joseph Brooks
Courtesy of the Butler Center for Arkansas Studies, Central Arkansas Library System

his troops, cleared the street, and threatened to open fire on the crowd. The next day, federal troops began building a barricade between the two sides to prevent further bloodshed.

Baxter responded to the intervention of the army with a complaint to Grant that its presence prevented him from reclaiming his office. The federal force's actions also may have convinced him that violence would not regain him his office. On April 22, he informed Grant that he intended to call the legislature into session to settle the rival claims. The same day, Grant replied that he approved any peaceful solution. The war continued, but after April 22, the real struggle for the office shifted to Washington DC. The last week of April, Attorney General George H. Williams began meetings with representatives of the two factions in Washington. Prominent Little Rock attorney Uriah M. Rose, along with Albert Pike and former senator Robert W. Johnson, presented the case for Baxter. Senators Clayton and Dorsey represented Brooks.

In Arkansas, each contender kept his military force intact while events moved along in Washington, although their activities tended to center on preventing the other side from being reinforced. White was given command of Baxter's forces at Pine Bluff, and from that base, he repeatedly intercepted men trying to get to Little Rock to aid Brooks. On April 30, he intercepted a contingent of African-American troops near New Gascony in

Jefferson County. In the clash that followed, his men killed nine and wounded twenty of the troops. On May 1, White dispersed Brooks supporters in Lincoln County and Arkansas County, and two days later, they fought another battle near Arkansas Post (Arkansas County), killing five more men. Several other confrontations would take place, with skirmishes on May 8 at Lonoke (Lonoke County) and at the mouth of Palarm Creek, where Baxter's troops tried to stop delivery to Brooks of a shipment of weapons taken from Arkansas Industrial University—now the University of Arkansas (UA) in Fayetteville (Washington County). Later estimates put the number killed in all of these confrontations at more than 200.

In Little Rock, the situation also remained tense. Baxter's supporters dug up a buried Civil War sixty-four-pounder cannon, repaired it, named it "the Lady Baxter," and used it to threaten the opponent. One of Baxter's commanders, Thomas J. Churchill, kept the Brooks forces on edge with periodic orders for residents around the Lady Baxter to move out in preparation for a bombardment. As the Grant administration considered the problem, each side also maneuvered to improve its position. Serious skirmishing took place on May 12, when Baxter forces tried to secure a position north of the Arkansas River, only to be forced back by U.S. troops.

The beginning of the end came on May 9 in Washington DC, when representatives of Baxter and Brooks met with the attorney general. All agreed that a special legislative session should

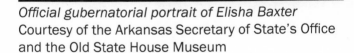

Official gubernatorial portrait of Elisha Baxter
Courtesy of the Arkansas Secretary of State's Office and the Old State House Museum

settle the issue. On May 10, Baxter and Brooks agreed, although Baxter replied that he saw no reason for a special session because he had already called the legislature into session. Attorney General Williams agreed, but Brooks objected and declared he would not abide by any decision of the legislature. Seeing that there could be no compromise, Grant now asked his attorney general for a decision on who should be governor. After having heard the cases of the contending parties, Williams issued his opinion May 15. He said Baxter was the legal governor. That day, the president issued a proclamation indicating that because the legitimate government of Arkansas, Baxter's, had asked for federal aid in suppressing insurrectionary forces, he would provide assistance and ordered all those opposed to the existing government to disperse.

With no hope of support from Washington, Brooks disbanded his forces. He and his men began moving out of the State House. Many, fearing retribution, fled the city or hid from their opponents. Indeed, for a time, Baxter considered prosecuting many of his opponents for treason. On May 19, Baxter returned to the State House, and his supporters staged a victory parade. Grant had ended the "war," and Arkansas once again had only one governor. The era of Reconstruction had come to an end.

Carl H. Moneyhon
University of Arkansas at Little Rock

Hattie Caraway (1878–1950)

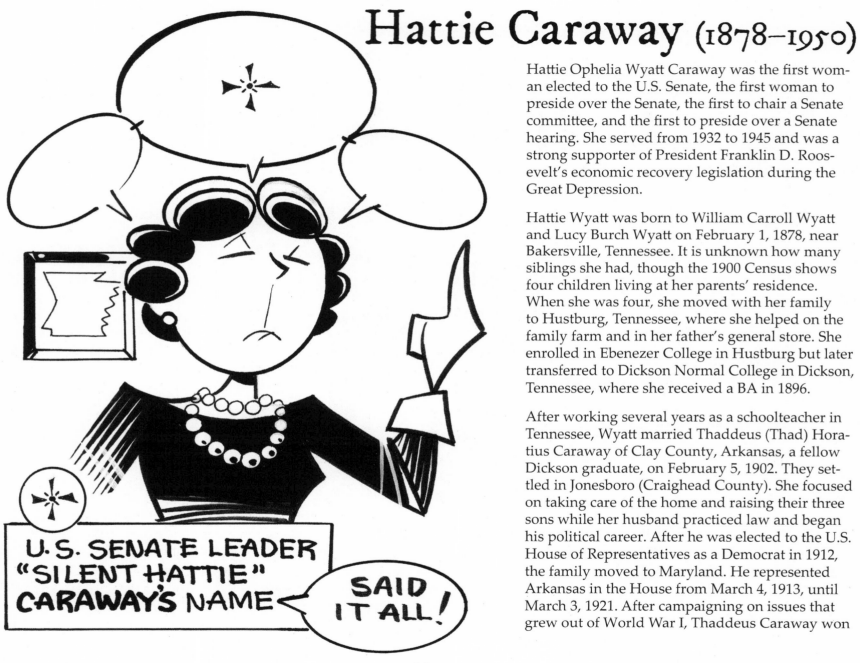

U.S. SENATE LEADER "SILENT HATTIE" CARAWAY'S NAME

SAID IT ALL!

Hattie Ophelia Wyatt Caraway was the first woman elected to the U.S. Senate, the first woman to preside over the Senate, the first to chair a Senate committee, and the first to preside over a Senate hearing. She served from 1932 to 1945 and was a strong supporter of President Franklin D. Roosevelt's economic recovery legislation during the Great Depression.

Hattie Wyatt was born to William Carroll Wyatt and Lucy Burch Wyatt on February 1, 1878, near Bakersville, Tennessee. It is unknown how many siblings she had, though the 1900 Census shows four children living at her parents' residence. When she was four, she moved with her family to Hustburg, Tennessee, where she helped on the family farm and in her father's general store. She enrolled in Ebenezer College in Hustburg but later transferred to Dickson Normal College in Dickson, Tennessee, where she received a BA in 1896.

After working several years as a schoolteacher in Tennessee, Wyatt married Thaddeus (Thad) Horatius Caraway of Clay County, Arkansas, a fellow Dickson graduate, on February 5, 1902. They settled in Jonesboro (Craighead County). She focused on taking care of the home and raising their three sons while her husband practiced law and began his political career. After he was elected to the U.S. House of Representatives as a Democrat in 1912, the family moved to Maryland. He represented Arkansas in the House from March 4, 1913, until March 3, 1921. After campaigning on issues that grew out of World War I, Thaddeus Caraway won a Senate seat in 1920 and served in the Senate from March 4, 1921, until his unexpected death on November 6, 1931.

On November 13, 1931, Arkansas governor Harvey Parnell appointed Caraway to fill the vacancy caused by her husband's death. She was sworn in on December 8, 1931, and was confirmed in a special election on January 12, 1932, thus becoming the first woman elected to the U.S. Senate. On May 9, 1932, she became the first woman to preside over the Senate (when the vice president, Charles Curtis, was resting), and she took that opportunity to announce her intention to run for reelection, to the surprise of many who had not expected her to run. Caraway was reelected in 1932 after a campaign tour with Huey P. Long, the populist senator from Louisiana. Long was motivated by sympathy for Caraway's being a widow as well as by his ambition to extend his influence into the home state of his rival, Senator Joseph Taylor Robinson. In 1938, Caraway ran for reelection against Congressman John L. McClellan, whose campaign slogan was "We need another man in the Senate," and she won with the support of veterans, women, and union members. Caraway's Senate career came to a close when she was defeated by J. William Fulbright in 1944. Her term ended on January 2, 1945.

Caraway spoke on the Senate floor so infrequently that she became known as Silent Hattie. She believed in speaking briefly with well-chosen words and stated that she did not want to waste the taxpayers' money on printing speeches in the *Congressional Record*. However, she often voiced her opinions in committee meetings. Caraway became the first woman to chair a Senate committee when she served as chair of the Senate Committee on Enrolled Bills from 1933 to 1944. She also requested and was assigned to the Agriculture Committee because of the importance of farming in her state. The committee governed flood control and the navigation of rivers, two issues also very relevant to Arkansas.

A strong supporter of Roosevelt's New Deal legislation, Caraway seconded his nomination for reelection at the 1936 Dem-
ocratic National Convention. In a rare speech to the Senate on relief and work-relief appropriations on May 25, 1938, Caraway stated, "My philosophy of legislation, and really on life, is to be broad-minded enough to consider human relationships and the well-being of all the people as worthy of consideration, to realize that all human beings are entitled to earn, so far as possible, their daily bread, and to try to prevent the exploitation of the underprivileged."

Occasionally Caraway did not support Roosevelt's policies. Although she voiced her opinions about equality of human beings when it came to New Deal legislation, Caraway was a woman from the South, where commonly held political views did not always coincide with those of Roosevelt. In 1938, Caraway joined many southern senators in voting against anti–poll tax and anti-lynching legislation, both of which Caraway viewed as unconstitutional. She also opposed the repeal of Prohibition.

Caraway was instrumental in securing Camp Robinson, Fort Chaffee, two Japanese relocation centers at Jerome (Drew and Chicot counties) and Rohwer (Desha County), five air bases, defense ordnance plants, and aluminum factories in Arkansas during World War II. Caraway also worked for the Equal Nationality Treaty of 1934, which extended to women numerous nationality rights previously limited to men. In 1943, she became the first woman in the Senate to cosponsor the proposed Equal Rights Amendment.

After leaving the Senate, Caraway remained in Washington in other civil service positions. She served on the United States Employees' Compensation Commission from 1945 to 1946 and on the Employees' Compensation Appeals Board from 1946 until her death. Hattie Caraway suffered a stroke in January 1950 and died in Falls Church, Virginia, on December 21, 1950. She is buried next to her husband at Oaklawn Cemetery in Jonesboro.

Julienne Crawford
Arkansas History Commission

Convict Lease System

Arkansas adopted the convict lease system to operate its state prisons in the mid-nineteenth century. The Arkansas system mirrored that of other southern states during this period and reflected the desire to reduce the cost and administrative problems of the state's prisons. While the system achieved its economic goals, it was typified by corruption and the abuse of prisoners, problems that ultimately brought about its abolition.

In Arkansas, the convict lease system originated during the Reconstruction era when, in 1867, the state contracted with the firm of Hodges, Peay, and Ayliff to provide work for prisoners in the penitentiary at Little Rock (Pulaski County). The state agreed to pay the company thirty-five cents a day for the convicts' support and also purchased the machinery to establish a factory within the prison. Managing the prison apparently was lucrative, and until 1873, several other individuals secured the management contract, including Asa Hodges, a Little Rock brick and wagon manufacturer and prominent Republican politician, who took over the prisons in 1869. Typically, the prison lessee not only provided work within the prison walls but also subcontracted prisoners to work throughout the area.

In 1873, as Reconstruction was coming to an end, the state legislature revised its program of prison leases and ended payments made to the lessee to support the prisoners. That year's contract with John M. Peck and his silent partner, Colonel Zebulon Ward, leased prisoners to Peck and required that the lessee furnish labor, food, clothing, and housing for them. The state was to have no expenses. In 1875, Ward bought out Peck and held the prison contract until 1883. Ward profited greatly from his contract, benefiting from the rapid increase in the state's prison population from 1876 to 1882 after the legislature's passage in 1875 of a law that made the theft of any property worth two dollars or more punishable by one to five years in prison. Ward also received the contract to expand the state prison, using convict labor.

Another major change in the nature of the convict lease system came in 1883. In the lease negotiated that year, Arkansas adopted the practice of other southern states by requiring the lessee to pay the state for convict labor. The lease became a major source of income for the state, making the system particularly difficult to eliminate. The 1883 lease was secured by J. P. Townshend and L. A. Fitzpatrick, Helena (Phillips County) planters, who later maintained the contract with Met L. Jones as a corporation, the Arkansas Industrial Company. The Arkansas Industrial Company continued to give work to some inmates at the prison, but hundreds were sent outside the walls to work for subcontractors. An 1890 prison report indicated that those working in camps around the state were laboring on plantations, building railroads, and mining coal in the Coal Hill (Johnson County) area of western Arkansas.

The convict lease system led to considerable corruption. In its early days, lessees took state payments and put little into the maintenance of prisoners. Later, contractors and subcontractors saw prison labor as a means of securing cheap workers who did not need to be provided proper care. Problems became so great that in 1888, a legislative committee investigated conditions at the Coal Hill camp; beginning in 1890, a prison inspector visited and reported on conditions in all of the camps. These examinations indicated that prisoners suffered from overcrowding, inadequate food and housing, and insufficient clothing. Health and hygiene facilities were non-existent. In addition, prisoners were subjected to violent physical punishment and abuse by the guards. Contractors also failed to provide security for the prison camps, and escapes became commonplace.

Concern with conditions in the camps became an issue in state politics after 1888, with farmer movements such as the Agricultural Wheel and the Farmers' Alliance, along with the Knights of Labor, calling for the end of the system. The legislature made an initial attempt to improve circumstances in 1893 when it did not renew the lease to the Arkansas Industrial Company. Unfortunately, state financial resources were inadequate to create a system that allowed the state to take over full maintenance of the prisoners. Instead, while the state assumed control over the inmates, it began its own subcontracting system by placing prisoners on farms as sharecroppers, at work on the railroads, and in other business enterprises around the state.

All the abuses seen in 1888 and 1890 continued as the state placed its prisoners under the control of private contractors, and in 1909, Governor George Donaghey, elected as a progressive Democrat, asked for the lease system to be abolished in his first message to the legislature. Legislators favored the reform but refused to appropriate the money necessary to create a prison farm big enough to employ all of the state's prisoners. In 1912, Donaghey resolved to end the system and determined how many prisoners could be placed on the existing state farm near Grady (Lincoln County); he then paroled enough prisoners to reduce the population to that number.

Donaghey had effectively ended the system, although the legislature's

purchase of land for a larger prison farm in Jefferson County, now known as the Tucker Unit, formally halted the leases the next year.

Carl H. Moneyhon
University of Arkansas at Little Rock

Crittenden County Expulsion of 1888

In July 1888, a group of influential white citizens in Crittenden County expelled from the county a number of prominent African-American citizens and county officials. Apparently weary of the fusion governments that had prevailed there for years, as well as fearful of the outcome of the upcoming September and November elections, they hoped their actions would intimidate black voters and ensure a victory for white Democrats.

Following the Civil War, land agents began to recruit black laborers from around the South to work in the cotton fields. By 1870, the black population in Crittenden County had reached sixty-seven percent, leading to the emergence of a black middle class tied to the Republican Party. After 1874, when the Democratic Party returned to power, Crittenden County, like several other black majority counties in the state, ran elections under a "fusion agreement," in which political parties met prior to the election and allotted certain offices to Democrats and others to Republicans, with concurrence that the candidates put up by each party would run unopposed. However, Democratic-led voter fraud, as well as racial tensions, were on the rise in the county. By 1880, the county population was eight percent African American.

Early in the summer of 1888, a group of approximately twenty-five of Crittenden County's white citizens met in Memphis, Tennessee, to formulate a plan to rid the county of its black officials. According to the *New York Times*, during the first week of July "a half dozen prominent planters" were reportedly "notified through their colored servants that their lives were in danger, as the negroes were determined to drive the white people out of the county or kill them." In response, the county's whites armed themselves with Winchester rifles procured in Memphis. Meanwhile, the county judge D. W. Lewis and the county clerk David Ferguson, both black, had been indicted for public drunkenness, and the trial was to be held on July 12. The trial, however, never took place.

Instead, on the morning of July 12, several prominent white citizens—among them Judge S. A. Martin, Sheriff W. F. Werner, Colonel J. F. Smith, Dr. W. M. Bingham, and L. P. Berry, all of whom had attended the Memphis meeting—reported that they had received anonymous letters asking them to leave the county. A group of armed whites came to the courthouse and ordered Lewis, Ferguson, and Ferguson's deputy, J. L. Flemming, to leave the building. The three were told about the letters and asked to leave the county. Ferguson replied that he knew nothing about the letters and asked that the circuit court investigate the accusations. According to the *Contested Election Case of Featherston[e] v. Cate*, a person in the infuriated crowd declared, "God damn you, you've got to leave this county, this is a white man's government and we are tired of negro dominance; we have been planning this for the past two years, and no more Negroes or Republicans shall hold office in this county."

A group of seventy-five to 100 armed whites also rounded up a number of the county's other prominent African Americans, forcing eleven of them at gunpoint to go to Memphis. After everyone had been expelled, white citizens searched homes, businesses, and lodge halls for weapons and ammunition. None were found. This first action was followed by a second wave of expulsions, focusing more on prominent citizens and black Republicans who owned property. Among these were York Byers, who owned 200 acres of land, and Jim Devers, a member of the Agricultural Wheel, a third-party organization. Black men began disappearing from the fields and going into hiding.

By July 15, the *Times* was reporting that the "race war" had ended. The situation was far from over, however. By July 16, Ferguson, county assessor J. R. Rooks, and O. W. Mitchum were in Little Rock to present Governor Simon Hughes with a petition, signed by seventeen other exiles, asking him for protection so they could return to the county. The governor took no action but

THE CRITTENDEN COUNTY EXPULSION LEFT A HOLE IN RACE RELATIONS.

instead filled all vacant county offices with white Democrats.

Within days, according to the *New York Times*, Judge J. E. Riddick had charged a grand jury "to discover and indict for conspiracy the persons who sent the threatening letters to white citizens of the county, which gave rise to the recent race troubles," adding, "There is no such punishment as expatriation known to the laws of this country, and even if there were, its

execution would not safely be intrusted [*sic*] either to a set of midnight conspirators or to a lot of armed and excited citizens." By July 24, the grand jury issued indictments against the nineteen African Americans they believed had conspired to produce the anonymous letters. No indictments were handed down against white citizens who had driven African Americans from the county. According to the *Times*, although there had been rumors about subsequent lynchings and trouble between blacks and whites in Marion: "The county has been quiet as a millpond since the drunken negro officials and their fellow conspirators were compelled to take 'French leave.'"

There were continued efforts on the part of whites to disrupt the upcoming September elections. Attempts were made to interfere with the county's Republican convention. The new Democratic county judge appointed all Democrats to be election judges. This, coupled with the fact that Democrats held all major county offices, made it possible for the Democrats to intimidate voters and effectively control the election process. Despite all this effort, however, the Union Labor Party still carried the county with fifty-four percent of the vote in the September gubernatorial election. The November elections were also marked by fraud. According to the official results, the Democratic candidate defeated Lewis Porter Featherstone in the race for the First Congressional District. Featherstone contested the results, and the U.S. House of Representatives found evidence of fraud and intimidation and awarded him the seat in February 1890.

In the long run, the Crittenden County expulsion failed to quash African-American participation in the electoral process. Black candidates, including state representative George W. Watson, continued to be elected until statewide disenfranchisement laws were enacted in the mid-1890s.

Nancy Snell Griffith
Clinton, South Carolina

TAKE A SPIN

LUCK HAS NOTHING TO DO WITH IT!

MACHINE COUNTIES PAID OFF ONLY FOR POLITICAL INSIDERS.

Election Fraud

Questionable balloting procedures and fraudulent vote counts began early in Arkansas's political history and were a regular component of the state's politics, especially in rural areas, until about 1970. The state's tradition of one-party rule in which consequential elections were decided in party primaries, the absence of unbiased political information in the form of independent newspapers, and a traditionalistic political culture in which the activities of the ruling elite were generally unquestioned by the masses all contributed to an environment in which fraud—fundamentally problematic for a representative democracy—could persist.

Such fraudulent behavior in Arkansas had its roots in the politics of "The Family," the Democratic regime that controlled the state's politics in the period following statehood. This Johnson-Conway-Sevier-Rector cousinhood accumulated 190 years of public office-holding, including two U.S. senators and three governors in antebellum Arkansas. Other offices went only to their partisans, and the Family's control of all aspects of the election machinery in the state made that control easier. For instance, U.S. senator Ambrose Sevier, about to be caught up in a public bank scandal in the early 1840s, was quickly reelected by the state legislature before an investigation of his impropriety could come to light. The fraud of this era created a norm that would follow even after the Family's political demise.

In the Reconstruction era, election fraud continued, most tellingly in the conflicted 1872 gubernatorial election between Elisha Baxter and Joseph Brooks that culminated in what came to be called the Brooks-Baxter War. Fraud intensified when the Redeemers, the Democrats who returned to political power in the state following the Reconstruction era, felt threatened elector-ally by a fusion of Republicans and Populists during the 1880s. The most consequential election in the state during this period was the governor's election of 1888 in which an allied group of political factions supported Charles M. Norwood, the gubernatorial candidate of the dissident Union Labor Party, against Democrat James P. Eagle. By the standards of states accustomed to closely competitive general elections, the attempt was an abject failure. Eagle received 99,229 votes to the 84,273 votes cast for Norwood. For those unaccustomed to genuine competition, however, this election was ominously close, especially because of the amount of fraud that had been necessary to secure even this "narrow" victory. A congressional election in the central portion of the state between Democrat Clifton R. Breckenridge and John Clayton, running as a Republican, resulted in an even more marginal (and even more dubious) Democratic victory. When Clayton attempted to provoke a federal investigation into the voting process, he was murdered in Plumerville (Conway County).

These events were followed by "electoral reform" in the form of an 1891 state law. Especially considering the fraud, thuggery, and violence that had come to characterize the election process, the Election Reform Act of 1891 had some genuinely laudable provisions for those with a normative preference for clean elections. One element of the law, for example, prohibited the last-minute transfer of polling places. However, the two most important provisions of the statute were obviously intended to ensure the future electoral fortunes of the Democratic establishment. One effectively turned over all the state's election machinery to the Democratic Party, with only token representation for minority parties. The other disfranchised illiterates (over one-fourth of the population at that time) by removing all political symbols from the ballot and providing that only the precinct judges (all Democrats) could assist illiterates in preparing their ballots.

During this period, the legislature also initiated a state constitutional amendment that placed a one-dollar poll tax on the "privilege" of voting, and in 1892 (by which time the 1891 reforms

were in effect), this amendment was ratified. While scholars debate the extent to which these changes reflected a genuinely reformist impulse in reaction to the flagrant election abuses that had become commonplace, there can be no dispute over the resulting dramatic decline in voting—from 191,448 participants in the 1890 election to 129,337 in 1900—nor about the growing importance of local political leaders with an ability to "deliver" the votes in their geographical enclaves.

According to V. O. Key, the foremost scholar on the politics of the South during this period, "These local potentates loom larger in Arkansas than in most southern states." In the absence of party competition to clarify issue differences and of mass technology for reaching the voters, a statewide contest depended largely upon lining up the support of local leaders, often housed in county courthouses or city halls, who could corral their area's vote. The foremost function of any statewide campaign manager was to line up these local bosses, and in many instances it was necessary to bargain on the basis of a quid pro quo. One gubernatorial campaign manager of the 1940s recalls, "Some wanted jobs, some wanted roads, some wanted both—but they all wanted something." Many also expected a cash payment, euphemistically called "walking-around money."

Virtually any statewide contest was tainted by the tactics necessary to ensure victory in certain counties, and despite numerous charges of fraud by the losers and occasional court challenges, the courts were generally as inclined as the citizenry to look the other way. Southern politics scholar Boyce Drummond, writing in 1957, concluded that "at least three gubernatorial races, two United States Senatorial races, and one Congressional race since 1930 were decided by corrupt practices." Key concluded that while "Tennessee has the most consistent and widespread habit of fraud," Arkansas was "a close second."

Despite a law requiring such, there were almost no voting booths in Arkansas until the late 1960s; thus, real or perceived intimidation of voters by poll workers appointed to their posts by the local leaders generally achieved the desired goal. Other, more entrepreneurial, voters asked for something in return for their votes. In Newton County, for example, it was traditional to wait outside the courthouse on election day until one got the "highest dollar" and then a congratulatory slug of whiskey afterward. However, should such practices prove insufficient, there remained the infinite possibilities of outright fraud: deliberate defacement and subsequent discarding of ballots as they were counted and wholesale destruction (through burning, trashing, and even, in one instance, eating) of ballots if necessary. Absentee ballots were particularly susceptible to such fraudulent acts. Perhaps most troubling was the role of poll tax receipts, the voters' ticket to the voting process, in electoral shenanigans. Savvy politicians learned to monitor the poll tax for citizens who failed to meet the deadline for payment and pay the tax (and receive the receipt) for the prospective voters. Unless challenged, anyone could vote who showed the poll tax receipt and signed the election register. It was not uncommon for a single person to cast multiple votes as proxies using such receipts, thus giving a local potentate immense electoral power.

Based on local mores and the perceived stakes of the outcomes of statewide elections, these kinds of practices were much more widespread and flagrant in some localities than in others. Perhaps the leader in electoral corruption was Garland County, where the sustainability of illegal gambling operations absolutely necessitated a compliant state political establishment and where Leo McLaughlin controlled Garland County politics from his seat as mayor of Hot Springs. Sidney McMath and other leaders of the so-called GI Revolt returned home after World War II and challenged McLaughlin's control. In the 1946 Democratic primary, McLaughlin used control of poll taxes to defeat the GI slate of candidates except McMath, who was elected prosecutor. In the fall general election, those who had been denied election in the primary all ran as independents. Included on the ticket was an independent candidate for Congress, important because it allowed a challenge of the poll tax issue in federal court. An investigation of the record showed that poll tax receipts had been issued in alphabetical order in every city ward. Handwrit-

ing experts provided evidence that the same hand had signed for all the receipts. Within months, McLaughlin was on his way to prison, and his electoral machine was broken. The GI Revolt, seen in other counties along with Garland, sensitized Arkansans to the shame of widespread, casual election fraud and the desirability of honestly conducted elections.

McMath rode his role as the leader of the movement to the governorship in 1948. Despite his success at the state level, electoral fraud in the state did not end. Indeed, in his six victories in gubernatorial races starting in 1954, Governor Orval Faubus developed an immensely powerful statewide machine. Thus, as Winthrop Rockefeller began to build a state Republican Party to challenge the Faubus-controlled Democratic Party, he saw electoral reform in the state as an essential element. After his loss to Faubus in the 1964 governor's race, Rockefeller funded the Election Research Council that worked with the League of Women Voters to gather the data that would justify major reform. The investigators found that a majority of absentee ballots cast in 1964 in the state were invalid, and they uncovered clear evidence of election-day fraud at polling places around the state.

When elected governor, Rockefeller fought for reforms such as private balloting. But, more than reformed laws, factors such as a change in public expectations about the sanctity of the vote, a vibrant two-party system, and an independent press that could uncover problematic electoral practices ultimately undermined fraud in the state. While the mechanics of voting continue to be dogged by problems in each election cycle in parts of the state and disputes still arise about the interpretation of state election laws, these clearly are not the purposeful shenanigans seen as recently as the early 1970s. Governor Mike Huckabee's statement on Don Imus's nationally syndicated radio program just before the 2000 election—that Arkansas was a "banana republic" rife with "ballot fraud"—was seen even by his own partisans as undeniably hyperbolic.

Jay Barth
Hendrix College

The Family

"The Family"—or "The Dynasty"—was the name given to a powerful group of Democrats who dominated Arkansas politics in the years between statehood and the Civil War. The roots of the Family stretched back into the territorial period, when it coalesced around territorial delegate Henry Conway, the scion of a wealthy Tennessee family. In 1827, Conway was mortally wounded in a duel with Territorial Secretary Robert Crittenden, his former patron and the most powerful political figure in Arkansas in the territorial era. The killing of Conway exacerbated the schism in Arkansas politics between Crittenden and his supporters, who made up the basis for the Whig Party in Arkansas, and the followers of the slain Conway, staunch Democrats and supporters of Andrew Jackson, who portrayed themselves as champions of the common man. Among the latter group were Conway's younger brother James; his cousins, Elias and Wharton Rector; and another cousin, Ambrose Sevier. Sevier was elected to the remainder of Henry Conway's term and served in that capacity until Arkansas became a state in 1836. On September 27, 1827, he married Juliette Johnson, the daughter of Benjamin Johnson, a Superior Court judge for the Arkansas Territory.

Since many members of the group were related by blood or by marriage, the political alliance of Conways, Rectors, Sevier, and Johnson soon came to be referred to as "The Family." The results of the first state elections in 1836 confirmed the Family's dominance in Arkansas politics. James Conway was elected the state's first governor, Ambrose Sevier was chosen by the state legislature to be one of the state's first U.S. senators, and Benjamin Johnson was appointed by President Andrew Jackson to be the state's first federal district judge. That same year, Benjamin Johnson's brother, Richard M. Johnson, was elected vice president of the United States on a ticket with Martin Van Buren.

"THE FAMILY" DOMINATED ARKANSAS POLITICS FOR DECADES.

In the late antebellum period, a second generation of Family politicians emerged. Foremost among them were Benjamin Johnson's son, Robert Ward Johnson, who served the state as a congressman and later as a U.S. senator, and Elias Conway, the youngest brother of Henry and James, who served two terms as governor between 1852 and 1860. Ironically, the end of the Family's domination of Arkansas politics came in 1860 at the hands of Henry Massie Rector, the son of Family member Elias Rector and blood relative of the Conways and Sevier. In the gubernatorial election of that year, Rector challenged Family candidate Richard H. Johnson. Following a bitter campaign in which the Family's long-time dominance of Arkansas politics was a central theme, Rector defeated Johnson by almost 3,000 votes. It was the first significant defeat for a Family politician since statehood. Robert Ward Johnson later served in the Confederate Senate, but Rector's victory and the coming of the Civil War effectively ended the Family's domination of Arkansas politics.

Thomas A. DeBlack
Arkansas Tech University

THE NEWSPAPER CLAIMED REP. LEWIS FEATHERSTONE WAS A *BIRDBRAIN*.

Featherstone v. Cate

In the Arkansas election of 1888, Agricultural Wheel members and other groups formed the Union Labor Party and allied with the Republicans to offer a serious challenge to the Democrats. In 1889, the *Featherstone v. Cate* congressional hearings resulted from allegations of election fraud in the race for U.S. representative from Arkansas's First Congressional District, a district comprising seventeen eastern counties including Craighead, Crittenden, Cross, Lee, Phillips, and St. Francis.

In 1888, the race for first district representative pitted Independent candidate Lewis P. Featherstone of Forrest City (St. Francis County) against Democratic judge William Henderson Cate of Jonesboro (Craighead County). Initially, the election results showed Cate the winner with 15,576 votes to Featherstone's 14,238. In late November 1888, Featherstone, alleging fraud in Crittenden, Cross, Lee, Phillips, and St. Francis counties, announced his contest of the election. Among those counties where Featherstone alleged fraud, only in Cross did Cate receive a majority of votes over him. Featherstone garnered a majority of votes over Cate in St. Francis County, as well as in the black-majority, heavily Republican counties of Crittenden, Lee, and Phillips. Featherstone apparently believed that his margin would have been larger had election fraud not occurred.

The Republican-controlled U.S. House of Representatives held the case hearings in 1889. A majority of the House Elections Committee ruled that there was "[sufficient] evidence…to establish a conspiracy to defraud in Crittenden County," citing a pre-election purge of the African-American Republican county officers. In July 1888, the white Democratic Crittenden County sheriff had led a group of armed whites who gained control of the county government by forcibly removing the black Republican county officers from office. State election law required the county court to appoint three election judges, representing different political parties, to preside over elections in each township. The House committee ruled that the July purge enabled the Crittenden County Democrats to appoint all Democratic election judges. In November 1888, the Democratic election judges in Crittenden County utilized fraudulent ballot boxes in the heavily Republican Scanlin, Cat Island, and Crawfordsville townships and held no elections in the Idlewild and Furgeson townships. The House committee also cited voting irregularities in Phillips County, which further reduced Cate's majority over Featherstone.

In his notice of contest, Featherstone, noting that he received only eighty-nine votes to Cate's 224 in Lee County's Independence Township, alleged that the Democratic election officers there had committed fraud. The House committee reported that, after giving testimony, a witness from Independence Township was "arrested for perjury and placed under $1,000 bond to answer to the state court." Cate's lawyer then claimed that he would have arrested anyone he believed to have testified falsely on Featherstone's behalf. Accusing Cate's lawyer of witness intimidation, the House committee ruled that Cate "must lose 224 votes returned for him, and [Featherstone] must be allowed 3 more votes than were returned for him."

In his home county of St. Francis, Featherstone alleged that the Democratic election officers in Franks Township had committed fraud. He also alleged fraud in St. Francis County's Blackfish Township, where no election was held in November 1888. In 1888, tension was high between Democrats and Union Laborites in the county. During the September 1888 election, three black Republicans and three white Union Laborites had won the county offices, and a shooting in the heavily black Franks Township had wounded a group of politically active Democrats.

Finally, the House determined that Featherstone was elected representative by a majority of eighty-six votes, and he was seated in Congress in March 1890. The outraged Democratic *Arkan-*

sas Gazette insisted that Featherstone "now sits in Judge Cate's seat…and is probably mentally the weakest man ever admitted to a seat in Congress." While in Congress, Featherstone earned even more enmity among Arkansas Democrats when he voted for the hated Lodge elections or "force" bill, which would have authorized federal supervision of southern elections to ensure that African Americans voted freely.

In 1890, Featherstone ran for reelection to Congress as a Union Laborite. He lost to Cate, although—as in 1888—he garnered a majority of votes in Crittenden, Lee, Phillips, and St. Francis counties. In November 1890, the *Arkansas Gazette* happily announced that "all Jonesboro is wild with enthusiasm tonight over [Cate's] great victory."

The *Featherstone v. Cate* hearings, by highlighting the extent of election fraud in Arkansas, testified to the seriousness of the interracial third-party challenge to Democratic dominance in the late nineteenth century.

Melanie Welch
Mayflower, Arkansas

THE **GI REVOLT** TARGETED **BUGS** IN THE SYSTEM.

GI Revolt

The political reform movement known as the GI Revolt emerged during the county political campaigns of 1946. Typically associated with World War II veterans eager to bring change to their hometowns and the state of Arkansas, the movement actually was broader than just military service veterans and had somewhat of a statewide impact.

The term "GI" was shorthand for "Government Improvement" (a play on the term GI—General Issue, i.e., enlisted men—because many involved in the movement were returning GIs and officers), and the movement had an identifiable organization in six counties: Cleveland, Crittenden, Garland, Montgomery, Pope, and Yell, as well as the city of Pine Bluff (Jefferson County).

Most attention on the GI Revolt has focused on Hot Springs and the rest of Garland County. There, hometown war hero Sidney Sanders (Sid) McMath organized fellow World War II veterans to challenge the political leadership of Mayor Leo P. McLaughlin and key city and county elected officials. McMath

graduated from high school in Hot Springs, a city in which he had observed firsthand how the McLaughlin organization controlled almost every aspect of the local government. After World War II, he took up a pledge to challenge the political leadership of the spa city. In 1946, McMath filed in the Democratic Party primary for prosecuting attorney of the Eighteenth Judicial District, which included Garland and Montgomery counties, and recruited fellow veteran Clyde Brown to file for district judge with jurisdiction over the same two counties. Before the filing period closed, the two GIs had succeeded in recruiting candidates for each of the elected offices. However, while the "reformers" shared a common interest in defeating the entrenched incumbents, they were not ideologically united. Some had been interested in seeking public office long before the GI Revolt was organized, and they used the new anti-establishment group as a means to advance their ambitions.

The call for reform in Hot Springs was based in part on two official reports. The first came from a 1942 federal grand jury report that found that Garland County election officials had ignored and/or violated most of the state's election laws in the elections of that year. Another grand jury report released while the 1946 primary campaign was in progress noted that graft and corruption had permeated the public school system, as well as the business, religious, and social activities in the city. Citing these abuses as evidence of a clear need for reform, the GIs used their military training to organize every voting precinct in Garland and Montgomery counties, working in pairs to reduce possible harassment from the opposition.

A number of other counties had earned a reputation as "machine counties," which meant the political offices were controlled by selected individuals who used a variety of tactics to gain and maintain office. Key among the "control" devices was the poll tax receipt. To be eligible to vote in a party primary, one had to show evidence of having paid a poll tax. For the general election in November, voters could pay the poll tax up to twenty days before the election. Savvy politicians had learned to monitor tax records and pay the poll tax for those citizens who failed to meet the deadline. Unless challenged, any individual could vote simply by showing the poll tax receipt and signing the election register. It was not uncommon in many counties for a single individual to cast multiple votes as proxies using poll tax receipts. To challenge a vote's legitimacy, the challenger was required to file a petition and present evidence of fraud with a state court—or federal court if the dispute involved a candidate for federal office.

In Garland County, McLaughlin and his allies used the poll tax as a way to defeat everyone on the GI ticket except McMath in the Democratic primary. Believing that their defeat had been engineered by fraudulent use of poll tax receipts, the GIs filed as independent candidates to run in the November general election. Included on the ticket was Pat Mullis—not a veteran but a friend and law school classmate of McMath—who filed for the Fourth Congressional District position. Mullis then filed a lawsuit in Arkansas Western District Court on behalf of his fellow "independents," claiming poll tax receipts had been illegally issued and used.

While collecting evidence for the trial, GI supporters found that in every city ward, poll tax receipts had been issued in alphabetical order, sometimes eighteen names to a block. Moreover, the signatures for each block of names appeared to be in the handwriting of a single individual. Judge John Miller ruled in favor of the GIs, noting in part that individuals organizing in alphabetical order and presenting themselves to the county clerk to pay their poll tax was a statistical improbability. Also, the testimony of an expert witness from the Kansas Bureau of Investigation saying that the signatures were in the same handwriting was sufficient proof to allow Judge Miller to issue an order setting aside almost twenty-four percent of the poll tax receipts issued for the primary election.

Motivated by their court victory, the GI independents mounted an aggressive campaign for the general election. Organizing a new "poll tax drive," they encouraged citizens to pay their own poll tax and be prepared to vote in November. Their efforts were rewarded in spectacular fashion. When the results were tabulated, the GI ticket had won every seat in Garland County.

Results from the GI tickets in the other five counties were not so clearly delineated. While a number of war veterans campaigning as reform candidates did get elected to public office in 1946, there was no definable pattern to their success, and as was the tradition in Arkansas politics, the personality of the candidate and local circumstances typically determined election outcomes. Moreover, in Garland County in particular, almost half of the candidates elected on the GI ticket in 1946 were themselves criticized for using public office for personal gain within a decade after their initial election. McMath tried, with some success, to extend his good government influence beyond Hot Springs by inviting fellow GIs to join the Young Democrats organization. He also used the publicity he gained from challenging the McLaughlin organization to launch a successful campaign for governor in 1948. As governor, McMath moved away from local government improvement issues and focused more on matters of statewide interest.

By 1950, the GI Revolt was in disarray. Organized initially to work for "honest government," the leadership failed to develop a broad-based agenda and was unable to negate the corruptive practices of the poll tax. Arkansas's more than 200,000 World War II veterans were never able to become a cohesive unit. While most had either witnessed first hand, or at least been informed of, the totalitarian practices of Germany, Italy, and Japan, few related those practices to their own counties and hometowns. Moreover, during the 1950s and 1960s, new "McLaughlin-like" organizations emerged in various parts of the state. It was not until the Twenty-fourth Amendment to the U.S. Constitution abolished the poll tax in federal elections that a measure of political reform was restored in the state. The GI Revolt lacked sufficient clarity on what constituted good government and was too localized to be considered a real revolt.

C. Fred Williams
University of Arkansas at Little Rock

Marlin Hawkins
(1913–1995)

Marlin Conover Hawkins served Conway County as an elected official for thirty-eight years. His ability to deliver votes to state-wide and national candidates gave Hawkins a profile in state politics that was rare for a county official. His political machine is an important part of Arkansas's political lore, and the effects of his political contacts are still evident in Conway County.

Marlin Hawkins was born on April 22, 1913, near Center Ridge (Conway County) to John Carl and Nettie Mae Hawkins; John Carl Hawkins, a sharecropper and part-time barber, died in 1929. As the second of seven children, part of the burden of supporting the family fell on Hawkins. He worked as a share-cropper and part-time janitor until Olen Fullerton, a family friend, encouraged him to enroll in a nine-month college course in bookkeeping at Harding College, then located in Morrilton (Conway County). In 1934, Hawkins landed his first government job as a bookkeeper with the Federal Emergency Relief Administration (FERA). In 1935, he became the Conway County Welfare Board's first case worker as part of the Works Progress Administration (WPA). He would stay in government service for the rest of his professional career. By the age of twenty-two, Hawkins knew the daily struggles that rural Arkansans faced in the Depression, as well as the importance of help from friends.

Hawkins combined his energy, his rural roots, and his new position on the Conway County Welfare Board to find jobs and government aid for the people in his district. He joked in his autobiography about turning his "blind eye" (he had lost it at the age of eight) to the livestock that belonged to some of the people he helped. The less he reported of a family's possessions, the more the family received in government assistance. Hawkins credits the gratitude of many of the people he helped for his 1940 victory to his first elected office, the Conway County circuit clerk and recorder. He held that office for six years, with

a two-and-a-half-year hiatus from March 1943 to September 1945 to serve in the U.S. Army at Camp Robinson in North Little Rock (Pulaski County). Hawkins had persuaded the local draft board to draft him in spite of his lost eye. He was then placed in a position of restricted service, where he performed a variety of clerical duties.

In 1946, and again in 1948, Hawkins won election as the county treasurer. His dominance of the absentee voting in those elections revealed an important tool that became part of Hawkins's machine. His supporters studied the electoral procedures to identify and use processes such as absentee voting to their advantage. Hawkins's supporters could identify the voters that would be sympathetic, aid them in receiving an absentee ballot, and then have the extra benefit of knowing the ballot had been mailed before election day. These tactics also first raised fraud accusations that followed Hawkins throughout his public life. In 1950, when Hawkins won the Democratic nomination for sheriff by 218 votes, his opponent, Sheriff Elmer Thomas, charged Hawkins with fraud in the applications for absentee ballots. Hawkins had dominated the absentee return, 253 to 49. When his petition to contest the election was overruled, Thomas ran against Hawkins as an independent candidate in the general election, only to lose again. Hawkins began the first of twenty-eight years as the Conway County sheriff and collector.

Hawkins had crafted a highly effective political machine that was built on his personal contacts with people throughout the county. His position on the welfare board had allowed him to direct government assistance, and as sheriff, he still had access to contacts that could provide direct aid, employment, or other forms of charitable aid. Before each election, people he knew received a letter in which Hawkins personally endorsed a slate of candidates and asked for political support. Hawkins also admitted to paying poll taxes for poor voters, which was a common practice at this time, but a violation of election law nonetheless. His continued success and remarkable power lay in his ability to deliver votes for state or national candidates. This ability garnered him notable enemies and gained equally notable favors for the county.

Hawkins, a life-long Democrat, shared Conway County with two-term governor Winthrop Rockefeller, a Republican. Rockefeller had moved to Petit Jean Mountain while Hawkins was sheriff and initially enjoyed the sheriff's cooperation on several matters, including security at his estate. As Rockefeller became more interested in running for governor, his relationship with Hawkins deteriorated. The battle for support in Conway County pitted Rockefeller's money against Hawkins's influence. In each of Rockefeller's two electoral victories as governor, he failed to carry Conway County.

Another of Hawkins's longest-running political feuds was with Gene Wirges, editor of the local newspaper, the *Morrilton Democrat*. Wirges wrote several scathing stories about Hawkins on topics ranging from election irregularities, comparatively high patrol car expenses, a speed trap on Highway 64, and mishandling of fines collected. As these stories ran in the early 1960s, Hawkins also enjoyed a contradictory set of headlines, some of which announced positive gains for Conway County.

Hawkins had achieved notoriety at the state level of a sort that is rare for a county official. He managed to use his political friend-

MARLIN HAWKINS'S MACHINE—DELIVERED ELECTIONS.

Votes
FOR
AGAINST
THEM
THOSE

ships with various legislators and especially Governor Orval Faubus to ensure the construction of Lake Overcup and the state's second vocational school, now the University of Arkansas Community College at Morrilton (Conway County). Hawkins personally donated twenty acres of land to guarantee the placement of the trade school in his county. Hawkins also claimed that contacts helped him land the construction of the Green Bay Packaging Paper Mill–Arkansas Kraft Division, which opened in 1966.

In 1978, Hawkins retired from public office. Hawkins's friend George Fisher, a popular political cartoonist, placed Hawkins with contemporaries such as Orval Faubus in a fictional rest home for Arkansas politicians, called the "Old Guard Rest Home." The popular cartoon series in the *Arkansas Gazette* was a fitting tribute to the impact of a generation of political personalities.

Hawkins lived in Morrilton until his death on September 16, 1995. He was survived by his wife, Marvine Treadwell Hawkins, daughter Kaye Anderson, and sons John Robert Hawkins and Donald Bruce Hawkins.

Traye D. McCool
University of Arkansas Community College at Morrilton

John Law's Concession

John Law's concession (also referred to as John Law's colony or the Mississippi Bubble) was established in August 1721 and was located at Little Prairie, just over twenty-six miles from the mouth of the Arkansas River, in present-day Arkansas County. The colony was located near the Quapaw city of Kappa. Its failure slowed the growth of Arkansas as a European colony, although settlers continued to live at Arkansas Post throughout the eighteenth century.

By the summer of 1686, Arkansas Post was already an important French trading post between New Orleans and Illinois, but no serious efforts were made to settle the land. The French government realized that, to compete with colonial Great Britain, it would need to establish profitable colonies.

John Law, a Scotsman, was an economist and banker who was also known for his gambling and dueling. Banned from more than one European nation, he ended up in France and received a government post with the hope that he could pull the French empire out of debt. Law created a private national bank and began issuing paper money based on the wealth the French government hoped to acquire from colonies in America. After the plan's initial success in 1717, Law's Compagnie d'Occident was given a twenty-five-year charter to manage and settle the Louisiana Territory for France in exchange for exclusive trading rights to the area. Law agreed to settle 6,000 colonists and

300 slaves in the territory and set aside a twelve-square-mile concession for himself near Henri de Tonti's abandoned trading post. Had Law's plan not failed, this settlement would have become the Duchy of Arkansas, with Law as duke.

Law was convinced that Louisiana would be rich with natural resources that would make the French government wealthy. To attract settlers, Law advertised gold and precious stones he said would be found in Arkansas soil, and his company spread rumors about the wealth of the Louisiana area. Stock in Law's company quickly increased, though few were eager to leave France to settle in Louisiana. Law recruited prisoners and bought slaves to send to the colony himself. To populate his own concession, Law personally paid the expenses of 200 German families, though they never reached the settlement, choosing instead to settle closer to New Orleans after later hearing of Law's bankruptcy.

Law's personal concession was established in August 1721 by a group of about eighty indentured servants, skilled workmen, and craftsmen, and it included a garrison established at the old trading post to protect the settlers. Jacques Levens was appointed by Law to manage the concession and prepare for future colonists. For the first year, the settlers were plagued by rains and flooding that made clearing and farming land difficult.

Law quickly became the most powerful man in France, but the national bank was issuing paper money on credit, and eventually the "Mississippi Bubble" burst, causing hundreds to lose their life savings, while Law fled France. Moving again from city to city (including Brussels, Rome, Copenhagen, and London), he eventually died in Venice in 1729. After the dissolution of the Compagnie d'Occident, plans to colonize Louisiana were put on hold, and the settlers already there either returned to their homeland or stayed to try and survive on their own.

When the expedition of Jean-Baptiste Bénard de La Harpe reached the Law concession on March 1, 1722, it found fewer than fifty settlers and only a handful of buildings. Only three acres of the concession had been cleared, and if not for relief boats sent from New Orleans, the colonists would have starved. La Harpe traded with the Indians for supplies for the settlers, forcing him to cut his expedition short and return to Illinois. In February 1723, company inspector Diron d'Artaguiette made an official visit to the colony and reported even fewer settlers, who were still struggling to raise their own crops.

After Law's bankruptcy, his personal concession was returned to the crown, and Bertrand Dufresne du Demaine became director of the Arkansas colony. Some of the indentured servants from the colony stayed behind to become hunters and traders, settling in the Lake Dumond area. In 1725, the military post was abandoned, and Governor Jean-Baptiste Le Moyne de Bienville of the Louisiana Territory ordered the evacuation of all but eight men, who stayed behind to maintain the French alliance with the Quapaw.

Caty Henderson
Ward, Arkansas

Virginia Johnson (1928–2007)

Virginia Lillian Morris Johnson was the first woman to run for the office of governor in Arkansas. Running as a conservative Democrat, Johnson campaigned against six other Democrats, all male, vying to be the candidate to run against the Republican incumbent, Winthrop Rockefeller, in the gubernatorial race of 1968.

Virginia Lillian Morris was born on January 21, 1928, in Conway (Faulkner County) to Jesse Lyman Morris Sr. and Frances Morgan Morris. Her family later moved to El Paso (White County). Upon the death of her mother when she was fourteen, Morris moved to Bee Branch (Van Buren County) to live with relatives while her father served in the U.S. Marine Corps. Following her graduation from Southside High School in Bee Branch, Morris received a scholarship to study at Draughon's School of Business in Little Rock (Pulaski County). After graduation, she was employed as a secretary at the law firm of Carter, Pickthorne, and Jones. Later, she worked as an under-insurance secretary for William E. Terry of Little Rock.

On December 21, 1947, Johnson married James (Jim) Johnson, a lawyer practicing in Crossett (Ashley County). They had three sons and later settled permanently near Beaverfork Lake, outside of Conway. Following Jim Johnson's election to the Arkansas Senate, she served on the Senate staff during the 1951 and 1953 legislative sessions. She was chairman of her husband's petition drive in 1956 to put a proposed state constitutional amendment on the ballot calling for the legislature "to pass laws opposing in every constitutional manner" the U.S. Supreme Court's decisions for school desegregation. It remained in place until officially repealed in 1990, though Johnson never wavered in her support of it, writing in a March 2005 letter to the *Arkansas Democrat-Gazette*, "The people of Arkansas have solid convictions and, if offered the opportunity, they will demonstrate once again that they prefer their own." She helped her husband

campaign for various offices, including his 1956 failed campaign for governor and his successful 1958 campaign for a spot on the Arkansas Supreme Court.

On April 30, 1968, Johnson filed for the office of governor. Her husband, who lost in the gubernatorial race to Winthrop Rockefeller in 1966, reportedly urged her to run. A self-proclaimed "true conservative," Johnson often called herself the "people's candidate," and a popular theme throughout her campaign was her promise that she was free of machine politics. She promised to run the state with "housewife efficiency." Her platform included promises to oppose gambling and any measure legalizing mixed drinks—two issues that were heatedly debated at that time. She also supported raising teachers' salaries "as much and as rapidly as possible," as well as increasing per capita income in the state, which she called the state's most important issue. She also promised to restore a "moral tone" to the office of the governor.

Johnson was often asked why a woman would make a good governor, and time and time again, Johnson replied, "Why not?" One local reporter noted that she was "the only novelty in a rather dull campaign."

On July 31, 1968, Johnson came in second in the Democratic primary, defeating Ted Boswell of Bryant (Saline County) by only 409 votes. She faced Marion Crank in the Democratic runoff on August 13. In her first television appearance following the initial primary, Johnson made the unusual step of calling on young voters to participate, promising to include them if she were to succeed in obtaining the gubernatorial office. She also bought advertisements in the *Southern Mediator Journal*, an African-American publication in Little Rock, even though she strongly supported maintaining the status quo for most of the state, where schools remained segregated.

In the weeks before the runoff, Johnson increased her claims that her opponent was tied to political bosses around the state and vowed that she remained untied to this political machine. She also called Governor Winthrop Rockefeller's two years in office "futile follies" and "a comedy of errors." She often criticized the governor for bringing "outsiders" to run many of the state's offices.

Johnson lost the Democratic nomination to Crank, who captured sixty-four percent of the vote, with turnout reported as light. Johnson vowed to help Crank unseat the governor but later renounced her support. Rockefeller was reelected.

On September 17, 1968, Johnson turned down an offer to serve on the state Democratic Committee on Revision of Party Rules because of the committee's intention to force local Democrats to give support to national Democratic candidates. She was a supporter of Alabama governor George Wallace, who was a stalwart segregationist and an independent candidate for the president in 1968. When the committee passed the rule, Johnson renounced her support of all state Democrats.

Though Johnson never ran for additional offices, she and her husband remained in the political spotlight while her husband served as a state

Ginny's No-Gin Gin Mill

UNHAPPY HOUR ALL DAY!

VIRGINIA JOHNSON WAS THE FIRST WOMAN TO RUN FOR THE GOVERNOR'S OFFICE — PROMISING NO! MIXED DRINKS.

Supreme Court justice. She died at her home in Conway on June 27, 2007, and is buried in Oak Grove Cemetery in Conway. Her husband died in 2010.

Sarah E. Blair
Fayetteville, Arkansas

Guy Hamilton "Mutt" Jones (1911–1986)

Guy Hamilton "Mutt" Jones was a lawyer and politician who became one of the most influential state lawmakers of the post–World War II era. Jones served nearly twenty-four years in the state Senate representing Faulkner County and, at various times, five other counties in north-central Arkansas.

"Mutt" Jones was born on June 29, 1911, in Conway (Faulkner County), the youngest of nine children of Charles C. Jones and Cora Henry Jones. His father was a country schoolteacher and later operated a motel in Conway. Jones was short, barely exceeding five feet as an adult. His stature made him feel inferior until a teacher told him that he spoke exceedingly well and should try debating. He became a champion debater, finishing second in the state debate contest in 1928, and his inferiority complex vanished, though his stature earned him the lifelong sobriquet of "Mutt."

In the depths of the Great Depression, Jones managed to go to Hendrix College in Conway, graduating in 1932. He taught at Joe T. Robinson High School west of Little Rock (Pulaski County) for two years and briefly at the state vocational training school at Clinton (Van Buren County). He became a co-owner of a service station and, at night, attended law classes at what is now the University of Arkansas at Little Rock William H. Bowen School of Law. He passed the bar in 1935, understudied with a Conway lawyer, and started his own practice in 1937. In 1941, he married Elizabeth Relya of Almyra (Arkansas County). They had two sons.

Drafted into the army in 1942, Jones served four years, starting as a private and completing his service as a captain. He fought in the European theater during World War II with the Seventy-first Infantry Division. In 1946, he was elected to the state Senate.

Jones was the legislature's most compelling orator and also its most partisan, craftiest, and—some said—most vengeful member. The *Arkansas Gazette* called him "the noisiest, newsiest, most ferocious, entertaining and controversial man in the legislature." In the Senate, Jones would exhibit many idiosyncrasies, such as relaxing with his red cowboy boots propped on his desk. Each day, he bought a dozen red boutonnieres and ceremoniously pinned them on people he decided to favor: senators, Senate employees, the chaplain, or reporters. At adjournment, he sometimes whipped a harmonica from his desk and played "Dixie."

While he was feared and often resented in Faulkner County for his political intrigues, Jones changed the physical landscape of the community. His conniving and connections brought huge state investments to the county and elsewhere in his district.

His clout grew after he ran for governor in 1954. Jones finished third in the preferential primary behind Governor Francis Cherry, who received forty-eight percent of the votes, and Orval Faubus. Faubus wanted Jones to endorse him in the runoff, which Jones agreed to do only if Faubus would pay for him to make six television talks around the state. Faubus agreed and, with Jones's endorsement, won the election. For the next twelve years, Faubus obliged Jones's whims, which consisted of placing many government facilities in Faulkner County, where they operated under Jones's monitoring. These facilities included a state institution for the mentally disabled (now the Conway Human Development Center), the headquarters of the State Civil Defense Agency (now the Arkansas Department of Emergency Management), and the studios of Arkansas Educational Television Network (AETN). The state also built a park at Woolly Hollow sixteen miles north of Conway.

One product of Jones's craftiness was the construction of a bridge across the Arkansas River at Toad Suck, linking Perry County and Conway. The state highway director had refused to buy a privately operated ferry at Toad Suck. At the end of the legislative session in March 1957, Jones checked out the Arkansas Highway Department's appropriation bill for the next two years and took it home. The legislature adjourned without appropriating any money for the agency. The highway director relented, and Faubus called a special session to enact a highway appropriation. Jones amended the bill in the Senate to set aside $25,000 to buy the ferry. The federal Bureau of Public Roads (now the Federal Highway Administration) then built a bridge on the lock and dam at Toad Suck to relieve the state of operating the outmoded ferry.

When Winthrop Rockefeller, the first Republican governor of Arkansas since Reconstruction, was elected in 1966, he inherited a ferocious enemy in Jones, who fought him at every turn. The feud became personal for both men.

In 1972, Jones was indicted by a federal grand jury on charges of income-tax evasion. His first trial ended in a mistrial because someone had tampered with the jury, but he was convicted in 1973. He was fined $5,000, but the presiding judge remarked that he suspected that Jones's prosecution had been politically motivated.

Jones's colleagues in the Senate at first refused to expel him, but after a public outcry, the Senate reassembled on August 1, 1974, and voted twenty-five to six to remove him. The Arkansas Supreme Court revoked his license to practice law for a year, but, by 1982, he had regained the right to practice in both Arkansas and federal courts.

Jones died on August 10, 1986, and is buried at Oak Grove Cemetery in Conway.

Ernest Dumas
Little Rock, Arkansas

Little Rock Censor Board

THE LITTLE ROCK CENSOR BOARD BANNED THE 1916 EYEFUL, *PURITY*.

The Little Rock Censor Board operated in Arkansas's capital city for nearly seventy years trying to regulate forms of entertainment—from literature to movies—to protect citizens from influences perceived to be immoral. As social mores changed and the legality of the board was challenged, it saw its influence diminish, until it quietly disbanded.

In the early twentieth century, officials around the country attempted to censor salacious or obscene materials. For example, Memphis's Board of Censors, created in 1911, was notorious for its harsh rulings, and Maryland established its censor board in 1916, which remained influential until its demise in 1981.

The Little Rock Censor Board was created in 1911 by

Mayor John S. Odom and the city council in response to the announcement that the city's Dixie Theater would show a film of the prize fight between Jack Johnson and James J. Jeffries. Racial disturbances had occurred around the South after Johnson, an African American, had defeated the white defending champion Jeffries, and Little Rock (Pulaski County) city leaders feared that screening the fight would reignite the troubles. The mayor, city attorney, and chief of police served as censor board members, and the stated mission was to protect the morals of the citizens of Little Rock. To accomplish this, they reviewed any public entertainment event or movie before it was exhibited and issued a decision on its moral appropriateness. One example of the board's censoring powers was its 1916 banning of the art film *Purity*, which featured its female star completely nude.

The board operated sporadically until 1926, when Mayor Charles Moyer reconstructed it at the urging of the city's Parent Teacher Association (PTA). Leaders in the PTA approached Moyer because they were distressed by the increasing number of films they believed to be inappropriate for children. The city council re-created the board, which was composed of nineteen members this time, with the PTA having one representative while the rest were appointed by the city aldermen. The board exercised its police power over not only films—as it had in the earlier incarnation—but also print media. The brutal killing of a black man named John Carter in Little Rock in 1927 and the following racial tension prompted the board to ban two black national newspapers that covered the incident. Despite its involvement in such high-profile events, the censor board operated only sporadically through the mid-twentieth century.

Citing an increase in immorality, Mayor Sam Wassell called upon the city council to reorganize the Little Rock Censor Board at the end of World War II in 1945. Although the board had the power to ban any form of entertainment—such as carnival shows, artwork, magazines, and books—it focused mainly on theatrical films. The mission of this third group was similar to those professed by the earlier boards, but in addition, it banned the irreverent use of the name of Jesus Christ, nudity, and interracial love scenes, among other things, in films. The number of members on the board increased to twenty-four and included representatives of the mayor, the city council, and PTA, but also the Men of the Churches of Little Rock. In 1959, board membership was reduced to fifteen, with the mayor and the religious group losing their representatives.

One notable decision concerning something other than films involved the board banning the novel *Return to Peyton Place* and ordering the Little Rock Public Library to remove it from its shelves. The library refused to acknowledge the board's authority and kept the book on the shelves, resulting in a stalemate.

As the social climate changed in the 1960s and '70s, so did the tone and graphic nature of films, and the mainstream popularity of sexually explicit adult movies distressed the censor board. Despite its waning influence, lack of support from city leaders, and legal challenges, the board clung to a semblance of authority, resulting in the banning of the X-rated movie *Deep Throat* (1972). Its showing at the Adult Cinema in Little Rock in 1973 immediately resulted in the arrest of the theater's employees. The resulting trial ended with guilty verdicts for the violation of Arkansas's obscenity statute. Although the censor board was concerned by these movies, its involvement in the trials was non-existent, and the large numbers of people attending the movie's showings provided evidence that the board's authority was tenuous. After the U.S. Supreme Court's landmark *Miller v. California* (1973) decision, which established stricter criteria for state regulation of obscene material, city officials refused to clarify the censor board's authority. As a result, Chair William Apple Jr. stopped calling meetings, and new members were not appointed. In 1975, Apple requested that the board be revived, but the city attorney refused, thus ending the Little Rock Censor Board.

Timothy G. Nutt
University of Arkansas Libraries

McLean v. Arkansas Board of Education

The 1981–82 federal court case *McLean v. Arkansas Board of Education* constituted a challenge to the state's Act 590, which mandated the equal treatment of creation science in classrooms where evolution was taught. On January 5, 1982, U.S. District Court Judge William R. Overton ruled Act 590 unconstitutional in light of the establishment clause of the First Amendment. His determination that creationism constituted a religious doctrine rather than a scientific theory had a profound impact on the nation, the ramifications of which are still being felt today.

The draft of the model act which eventually became Act 590 originated in an Anderson, South Carolina, organization called Citizens for Fairness in Education. Its founder, Paul Ellwanger, working from a model prepared by Wendell Bird of San Diego's Institute for Creation Research, wrote a draft for a state act mandating the teaching of creationism alongside evolutionary theory and distributed it to various people across the country. One recipient was state senator James L. Holsted of North Little Rock (Pulaski County), who introduced the act into the Arkansas Senate, where it passed without hearings on

FORTY-FIRST GOVERNOR FRANK WHITE ORDERED TEACHING CREATION SCIENCE.

March 13, 1981. The House of Representatives held no hearings either, debating the bill for only fifteen minutes before passing it by a vote of 69–18. Governor Frank White signed it into law on March 19, 1981.

The bill's passage resulted in a great deal of public outrage, with many state newspapers, universities, and the Arkansas Academy of Sciences arguing against it. A few legislators, embarrassed at letting such a bill pass, talked of repealing the law, but that would have required the cooperation of Governor White, who refused to consider it. Therefore, the challenge to the law moved to the courts, with the trial contesting its constitutionality beginning in December 1981.

The American Civil Liberties Union (ACLU) lined up twenty-three plaintiffs to challenge the law, twelve of whom were themselves clergy representing Methodist, Episcopal, African Methodist Episcopal, Catholic, Southern Baptist, Reform Jewish, and Presbyterian groups. The inclusion of such individuals as plaintiffs was to counter the rhetoric of the Moral Majority and other fundamentalist groups who saw *McLean* as representative of a larger, national struggle between atheism and Christianity. In addition, a number of teachers' associations signed on as organizational plaintiffs.

For the trial billed as "Scopes II" by the media, the ACLU divided its ten expert witnesses into two teams. The "religious team" argued that "historically, philosophically, and sociologically, creationism is a religious movement of fundamentalists who base their beliefs on the inerrancy of the Bible and that creation science is no more than religious apologetics," according to witness and Cornell University sociologist Dorothy Nelkin. The "scientific team," which included such luminaries as Stephen Jay Gould, presented arguments undercutting the supposed scientific basis for creationism. Thus, the plaintiffs sought to demonstrate that creationism was in fact a religious doctrine, the teaching of which violated the establishment clause.

By all accounts, witnesses for the defense performed rather poorly in contrast. The state's goal was two-fold: a) to argue that the theory of evolution was itself religious in nature and that to teach it violated the establishment clause, and b) to present scientific evidence proving the theoretical validity of creationism. Judge Overton confronted the logic of the former, writing in his opinion: "Assuming for the purposes of argument, however, that evolution is a religion or religious tenet, the remedy is to stop the teaching of evolution, not to establish another religion in opposition to it."

Many of the state's witnesses also seemed to undermine the supposed scientific proofs of creationism. Norman Geisler rather embarrassed the state when he admitted under cross-examination his belief in UFOs as a satanic manifestation, while Harold Coffin noted that only with scripture as an aid could scientists understand the young age of the earth.

When Judge Overton ruled against the constitutionality of Act 590, he took particular issue with Section 4(a) of the act, which defined creation science as positing the "creation of the universe, energy, and life from nothing," as well as explaining the earth's geology "by occurrence of a worldwide flood." Such a definition, he argued, violated the establishment clause due to its naked references to events in the Book of Genesis. The state did not appeal the case. However, many creationist groups today, recalling this ruling, work to press their ideas into the classroom under the guise of Intelligent Design Theory, which posits an anonymous, supernatural creator now stripped of confessional markers. Thus does *McLean v. Arkansas Board of Education* continue to affect public policy today.

Guy Lancaster
Encyclopedia of Arkansas History & Culture

Martha Mitchell (1918–1976)

Martha Elizabeth Beall Mitchell gained worldwide recognition for her outspokenness during the Watergate scandal—a scandal that forced President Richard Nixon to resign from office on August 9, 1974. She was a renowned character in Washington DC. During President Nixon's first term, her husband, John Mitchell, was attorney general. Nixon once said, "If it hadn't been for Martha Mitchell, there'd have been no Watergate."

Martha Beall was born on September 2, 1918, in Pine Bluff (Jefferson County). Her father, George V. Beall, was a cotton broker, and her mother, Arie Elizabeth Ferguson Beall, was a speech and drama teacher for fifty years in the Pine Bluff School District. Beall graduated in May 1937 from Pine Bluff High School, where she was known as friendly, outgoing, and extremely talkative. She attended Stephens College in Columbia, Missouri, and the University of Arkansas (UA) in Fayetteville (Washington County) before receiving a BA in history from the University of Miami. She was a school teacher for a year in Mobile, Alabama, but decided teaching was not for her and moved back home to Pine Bluff. In 1945, she was hired as a secretary at the Pine Bluff Arsenal and, after six weeks, was transferred to Washington DC with her boss, Brigadier General A. M. Prentiss.

Beall met Clyde Jennings Jr., a young U.S. Army officer from Lynchburg, Virginia, and went on a date with him. Soon after he was honorably discharged, they were married in Pine Bluff on October 5, 1946. They moved to Rye, New York, and had a son named Clyde Jay Jennings. The couple separated in 1956 and divorced on August 1, 1957. On December 30, 1957, she married John N. Mitchell, an attorney in New York City. They had one daughter, Martha (Marty) Elizabeth Mitchell Jr.

Her husband managed Richard Nixon's successful presidential campaign in 1968 and was appointed attorney general after Nixon took office in 1969. Martha Mitchell became so well known as the outspoken wife of a cabinet member that, whenever her first name was mentioned, everyone knew who she was. She shared her views on everything: the Vietnam War, school busing, nominations to the U.S. Supreme Court, and more. She was known to call reporters at all hours of the day to comment on particular issues, including relaying information about the Nixon administration's corrupt activities. Mitchell claimed that, as a result, she was drugged and imprisoned in a California hotel room in an effort to keep her quiet.

In 1972, John Mitchell resigned his position to manage Nixon's second campaign and became entangled in the Watergate scandal. He left his wife in September 1973 without giving her any financial support. She got a job as a TV show host to try to support herself. Martha Mitchell was a special guest host for Washington's WTTG television program *Panorama* during the first week of April 1974. On April 27, the station aired the best of the week's interviews as "Panorama Presents: The Best of Martha Mitchell." This job lasted one week. The following year, on January 1, 1975, John Mitchell was convicted of conspiracy, obstruction of justice, and perjury for his role in the Watergate break-in and cover-up; he served nineteen months in federal prison.

Martha Mitchell died in New York City on May 31, 1976, two years after her diagnosis of multiple myeloma, a rare bone cancer. The funeral was held at First Presbyterian Church in Pine Bluff. Her children, Jay and Marty, entered in the side door with Mitchell's estranged husband John after the funeral started. One floral tribute at the service spelled "Martha was right" with white chrysanthemums. It was never known who sent them. She is buried at Bellwood Cemetery in Pine Bluff.

The psychological term "the Martha Mitchell effect" arose as a result of Mitchell's experiences with mental health professionals who originally believed her to be delusional when she discussed matters related to the Watergate scandal—matters that turned out to be true.

The former Pine Bluff home of Mitchell's maternal grandparents, Sallie Culp and Calvin Mc Fadden Ferguson, is now the Martha Beall Mitchell Home and Museum. It was placed on the National Register of Historic Places in January 1978. On May 31, 1978, the second anniversary of her death, the section of U.S. Highway 65 that ran through northern Pine Bluff was renamed the Martha Mitchell Expressway. On May 31, 1981, the fifth anniversary of her death, a bust was dedicated to Martha Beall Mitchell on the Civic Center grounds between East 10th and 11th streets. On the plaque were the words, "Ye shall know the truth and the truth will make you free." Martha Mitchell's life has been dramatized in the plays *Dirty Tricks* and *This is Martha Speaking*.

Brenda J. Hall
White Hall, Arkansas

Carrie Nation
(1846–1911)

Carrie Amelia Moore Nation was a temperance advocate famous for being so vehemently against alcohol that she would use hatchets to smash any place that sold it. She spent most of her life in Kansas, Kentucky, and Missouri, but she lived in Arkansas for several years near the end of her life; her last speech was in Eureka Springs (Carroll County). The house she lived in, which is in Eureka Springs, was made into a museum called Hatchet Hall.

Carrie Moore, whose first name is sometimes spelled Carry, was born on November 25, 1846, in Garrard County, Kentucky, to George and Mary Moore. George Moore was of Irish descent, and he owned a plantation with slaves. Mary Moore had a mental illness that caused her to be under the delusion that she was a lady-in-waiting to the queen of England, and later she imagined that she actually was the queen. Despite this, she was the mother of six children, including Carrie.

Moore grew up under the care of her father's slaves. She was close to one of the slaves, named Aunt Eliza. It was not until Moore was older that she was allowed to eat at the same table as her parents because her mother believed that being with the slaves was the best way for children to be brought up.

When the Civil War began, the family moved to Texas, and on the way, they stopped near the Pea Ridge battlefield in Benton County. Moore was sickly at the time.

She married a doctor named Charles Gloyd on November 21, 1867. Her parents did not approve of the marriage because they knew that Gloyd was an alcoholic, though she did not know about his drinking problem

until after they were married. Their marriage was unhappy, especially since their only child, a girl they named Charlien, had a mental disability. Carrie Gloyd believed it was caused by her husband's drinking. She left him, and he died only months later.

Her second husband was David Nation, an editor of a newspaper and a part-time preacher and lawyer. Their marriage was not happy either,

48

because they argued about religion. She believed in helping needy people by taking them in, even when it inconvenienced her husband and stepchildren. David Nation was asked to resign as preacher of his church because his wife stirred up trouble. In 1877, the Nation family moved to Texas, although Carrie Nation did not want to go. The couple divorced in 1901, not having had any children.

During this time, Nation had already been speaking against tobacco and alcohol. She especially disliked alcohol, most likely because of her experience with her first husband. She referred to alcohol as evil spirits. On one occasion, at a store owned by a man known as O. L. Day, she rolled a keg of whiskey onto the street, opened it with a hatchet, and set it on fire. She would go into any place that sold any kind of alcohol, even for medical purposes, and get rid of it. She broke windows and mirrors as well as destroyed kegs of beer or whiskey with her hatchets. At times, she attacked the people who sold the alcohol.

Nation was arrested many times in several states, including Oklahoma, Kansas, and Missouri. She spent time in the Little Rock (Pulaski County) jail, and she was arrested in Hot Springs (Garland County) in the winter of 1907. She was released when she made a deal with the mayor to speak at the opening of a new subdivision, for which he paid her fifty dollars. She made an additional sixty dollars selling souvenir hatchets. In Little Rock in 1906, she took a tour of twenty-six saloons and bars. She made speeches, and many people admired her. Some followed her on her travels and helped her smash saloons and bars, but she also made a lot of enemies, some of whom threw eggs at her.

Nation's daughter, Charlien, was committed to the Texas State Lunatic Asylum in 1905. Nation tried to move her to Austin, Texas, and then to Oklahoma, but she finally brought her to Hot Springs, where Charlien stayed for only a few years.

When Nation wrote her autobiography, *The Use and Need of the Life of Carry A. Nation*, at the age of sixty, she was living in Oklahoma, and she wrote that she planned to stay there. However, not long after that, she bought her home in Eureka Springs. She wanted a quiet place to live, and she said that Arkansas reminded her of Scotland, where she had recently traveled. In the time she lived there, the house was both a boarding house and a school. She did most of the cooking herself and provided religious instruction for her boarders. The school was founded in 1910 and was called "National College" although it did not offer classes at a college level. Although she continued to travel, she owned the house until her death.

Her final speech was in Eureka Springs on January 13, 1911. She had recently had health problems, but the speech had been going well. Suddenly she stopped and gasped out, "I have done what I could." Then she lapsed into a coma. She was taken to Evergreen Place Hospital in Leavenworth, Kansas, where she remained in poor health until her death on June 2, 1911. The cause of death was listed as paresis.

She is buried in Belton, Missouri. Her grave was unmarked for many years until the Woman's Christian Temperance Union (WCTU), of which she had been a member, erected a gravestone with her name and the quote: "Faithful to the Cause, She Hath Done What She Could."

A fountain was built in her honor in Wichita, Kansas, not far from the place of one of her first acts against alcohol. The fountain was destroyed only a few years later when the driver of a beer truck lost control and ran into it.

If Nation had lived just a few years longer, she could have seen Prohibition become the law of the land. She was not the only temperance advocate, but she was probably one of the most influential. Hatchet Hall still stands and can be seen in Eureka Springs. Nearby is a spring named after Nation.

Anastasia Teske
North Little Rock, Arkansas

Plumerville Conflict of 1886–1892

During the late 1880s, electoral politics in Conway County turned violent, resulting in serious injuries and several deaths. In the Plumerville (Conway County) community, actions such as voter intimidation and the theft of ballot boxes were flagrant and seemingly condoned by public officials. The violence became widely known and was the subject of a federal investigation after the assassination of a congressional candidate, John Clayton.

While the political conflict renewed itself after the 1884 election, the underlying causes date back to the pre–Civil War days. Conway County was a microcosm of Arkansas in terms of geographic culture and economics. The northern part of the county was composed of highlands and held small subsistence farms, while the Arkansas River bottomland supported a cotton-based slave-holding economy, leading to different opinions on secession within the county. During the war, several Confederate and two Union companies were raised within the county. There were a number of skirmishes in Conway County, and the area was contested by guerrilla actions throughout the war. The Union occupation of Lewisburg (Conway County) and the burning of the county courthouse in Springfield (Conway County) by Union forces hardened the attitudes of many for years to come. Associated with both of these events were the actions of Captain Thomas Jefferson Williams, who commanded an independent Union company of scouts and spies, sometimes known as Williams's Raiders, which created havoc for Southern sympathizers and helped enforce strong occupation rules in Lewisburg.

During the Reconstruction period, Conway County again became embroiled in its own civil conflicts. In December 1868, martial law was declared in Lewisburg after residents—both white and black—were lynched by warring factions. The reconstituted Williams militia from Center Ridge (Conway County) once again was in the center of the conflict, along with an organized African-American militia. Earlier that year, in August,

Governor Powell Clayton, himself having authorized the armed locals, had been required to travel to Lewisburg to intercede and quell the violence.

Once the Democrats regained power in the 1872 election, the county seat was moved from Springfield back to Lewisburg. Additionally, the Republicans of the northern areas and the former slaves of the bottomland plantations were relegated to isolated minorities. Over the next twelve years, changes began and the balance of power shifted once more. Of particular importance was the influx of large numbers of migrants from east of the Mississippi River. The percentage of African Americans in the county had grown from less than seven percent before the war to over thirty-nine percent by 1890, being drawn largely by cheap railroad land and agricultural work. The African-American men could vote, and they became a vital voting bloc for the Republicans. Most of the "colored vote" came from black citizens of Howard Township, composed of Plumerville and Menifee (Conway County), who worked in the cotton fields. Five other minority communities were established, some in the northern hill country.

Also during this period, two significant agrarian movements, the Agricultural Wheel, founded at Des Arc (Prairie County), and the Brothers of Freedom, organized in west-central Arkansas, served to gather the isolated hill farmers into functional political organizations. The two organizations held a statewide merger meeting in Springfield in December 1884. Reactionaries on both sides of the merger question sought to use these groups to rekindle old cultural and economic divisions, given that these groups somewhat aligned themselves with local Republicans (and later formed a fusion ticket in 1888).

The federal election of 1888 was heavily contested, and accusations of voter fraud and the theft of a ballot box led to the murder of John Clayton, the Republican candidate for Congress

STEALING
BALLOT BOXES
LED TO THE PLUMERVILLE CONFLICT.

and brother of the former governor, while he was in Plumerville investigating allegations of election fraud in 1889. Cover-ups, intimidation, beatings, and the attempted murder of federal officials resulted. A prominent black legislator, the Reverend G. E. Trower, was forced at gunpoint from a train in 1887 as it arrived in Plumerville and was never seen again in Conway County. Local braggarts were reported to say that "he is feeding the catfish at the bottom of the Arkansas River," but Trower was later found to have relocated to Independence County.

More closely associated with the Clayton assassination, George Earl Bentley of Morrilton (Conway County) was seen in the company of a Pinkerton private detective, Albert Wood, and was feared to be "turning" with regard to the stolen ballot box. The next day, November 27, 1888, Oliver T. Bentley, a deputy sheriff (and chief suspect in the ballot box theft), killed his brother George by "accidentally shooting him five times." Federal, state, and local authorities investigated many murders like this one, but no charges were brought.

The Pinkerton Agency, employed by the Clayton family, expanded its investigation, and one of their local hires, a black man named Joseph W. Smith, was, on March 30, 1889, accosted by three men and shot and killed one mile north of Plumerville. With that incident, the Pinkerton investigation was brought to an end, and the agency left the area. The violence continued as an official of the state Republican Party was mauled and caned at the railroad depot when he arrived in Morrilton. He boarded the next train and never returned. Almost comically, a federal election official, Charles Wahl, had moved his family to Plumerville to follow leads and to "set the investigation on the right path." During a December 16, 1889, poker game in the office of Plumerville dentist Dr. Benjamin White, an attempt to kill Wahl failed by less than an inch as the bullet tore through his ear. He quickly left the area, and the only charges brought were brought against him for gambling. He paid a nominal fine by mail, sent for his family, and never returned to Conway County.

In 1890, the federal election drew national attention, and mounted riflemen from the old Williams militia in Center Ridge came to Plumerville to ensure a fair election. More than 100 Winchester rifles had been delivered to Plumerville reportedly for the use of the African-American population. Armed militiamen marched "two by two" into town as the voting ended. Ballot boxes were protected, and the Republican candidate, I. P. Langley, carried Conway County. Statewide totals, however, went to the Democrats, and their full control of statewide politics was firmly established for decades to come.

The racial oppression and the dire circumstances faced by many black families prompted much interest in the "Back-to-Africa" movement, which involved emigration to the Republic of Liberia in western Africa. More than 1,500 people from southern Conway County made application to the American Colonization Society for relocation. It is thought that almost one in five black families in Conway County made the application. From 1890 to 1892, more applications for Liberia were made in Arkansas than in any other state, and more from Conway County than from any other county in Arkansas.

Larry Taylor
Springfield, Arkansas

V. V. Smith

VOLNEY VOLTAIRE SMITH CLAIMED HE KNEW HOW TO FIX THE NATION'S MONEY PROBLEMS—

IT'S EASY!

HE DIED IN THE STATE INSANE ASYLUM.

The last Reconstruction Republican lieutenant governor, known for attempting a coup d'état aimed at displacing a sitting governor, Volney Voltaire Smith was also the most distinguished nineteenth-century figure to have died in the state insane asylum.

V. V. Smith was born in 1842, reportedly in Rochester, New York. His father was Delazon Smith, a noted Democratic news-paperman and politician. V. V. Smith's father attended Oberlin College and then wrote an exposé on it for its support of ab-olition, became lost for eleven months while on a diplomatic assignment in Ecuador (thus becoming known as "Tyler's Lost Commission"), and served less than three weeks as one of Ore-gon's first U.S. senators. V. V. Smith's mother, Eliza Volk, died in 1846. Two years later, his father married Mary Shepherd, with whom he had five additional children. In November 1860, his father died under mysterious circumstances.

Smith apparently had a troubled youth, at one point being seen playing billiards and a lower-class card game called Seven-up while supposedly in college. Despite his father's sudden death in 1860, he maintained a correspondence with his stepmother. At the onset of the Civil War, he enlisted in Rochester, most like-ly in the First Regiment New York Mounted Rifles. In 1864, he was shot through both legs. After he was able to walk again, he retrieved his wife, Mary Jane, from Philadelphia, Pennsylvania, and then served as provost marshal at Camp Nelson in Ken-tucky, where he seems to have joined the 114th U.S. Colored In-fantry and accompanied it to Ringgold Barracks in Texas in 1865.

When and why the Smiths came to Arkansas is not known, but he was associated with newspaperman James Torrans of the *Washington Post* in Hempstead County, a Republican newspaper established in 1868. The *Post* later moved to Lewisville (Lafay-ette County), where, as the *Red River Post*, it expired in 1870. Smith found work with the Freedmen's Bureau, being the third agent in the southwest region. Despite his military background, he was classified as a civilian. He served as Lafayette County clerk from 1868 to 1872. His house was opposite the courthouse, and, in 1870, he owned real estate valued at $1,600 and personal property valued at $3,000.

Smith was a prominent figure in Republican politics during Reconstruction. Determined to follow his father's example, he sought election to Congress. However, in 1870, Oliver P. Snyder won the Republican nomination. Smith was closely associat-ed with the "Minstrels," the pro–Powell Clayton faction of the

Republican Party and, in 1872, became that faction's nominee for lieutenant governor on a ticket headed by Elisha Baxter. In a heavily disputed election, complete with allegations of fraud, Baxter and Smith were the declared winners over the "Brindletail" candidate, Joseph Brooks. However, Baxter's policies provoked a sharp reaction in Clayton, who shifted his support for Brooks in 1874, thus prompting the onset of the Brooks-Baxter War.

Smith figured in the early plans to restructure the government. If Baxter alone were removed, Smith would have become governor. However, Clayton mended his fences with Brooks and sought the ousting of both Baxter and Smith from power. The resultant Brooks-Baxter War ended in Baxter's victory but also marked the end of Reconstruction. Smith attended the constitutional convention of 1874 but, along with other Republicans, refused to sign the document. In the election that followed, Augustus Hill Garland was elected governor even though two years remained in Baxter's and Smith's terms.

Smith then insisted he was governor, based on an opinion from former Arkansas Supreme Court chief justice Thomas D. W. Yonley that Baxter had abdicated and that Garland's election was unconstitutional. Smith then appointed Edward Wheeler as secretary of state and issued a proclamation setting forth his claims, reportedly selling copies for five cents each.

Garland responded by calling out the militia under Thomas J. Churchill to defend the State House and securing from Judge John Joseph Clendenin of the Sixth Circuit Court arrest warrants for Edward Wheeler, Smith, and John G. Price, who as editor of the *Republican* had printed the proclamation. Clendenin discharged Price from the warrant, but Garland got the legislature to increase the reward to $1,000 for the still-missing Smith. Smith apparently expected intervention from President Ulysses S. Grant but, failing to receive that or local popular support, fled first to Daniel P. Upham's home and then to Pine Bluff (Jefferson County), where Sam Mallory spirited him out of the state.

By December, he was in Washington DC, pushing his claims. The *New York Tribune* described him as "dirty, footsore, with cotton seed in his tangled beard," while a more sympathetic paper found him "strutting around the capital with as much pomposity as a full-fledged peacock." During this time, he was variously nicknamed "Vice Versa Smith," a reference to his conflicting roles in the Brooks-Baxter War; "Vae Victis Smith" (from the Latin for "Woe to the vanquished"), after his attempted coup was aborted; and most commonly "Wee Wee," the nickname the national press adopted.

Meanwhile, the congressional committee headed by Luke P. Poland of Vermont was investigating affairs in Arkansas. Although it reached its conclusion in early 1875 that federal intervention was not warranted, President Grant took a different view but lacked any viable option.

Grant appointed Smith to the St. Thomas Island consulate, where he remained until the election of Grover Cleveland. Back in Lewisville by 1888, Smith reentered politics, running unsuccessfully for his old county clerk office, serving as an elector for William McKinley, and practicing law. In January 1897, he was brought to the state insane asylum, suffering from what was described as "acute mania." He insisted that he could solve the nation's monetary problems if given twenty minutes to speak to Congress. His mania increased, and his death on April 17, 1897, was due to "exhaustion." He is buried in the Wilson Cemetery near Lewisville. His wife, who immediately received a post office appointment, reportedly remarried.

Smith's return to Arkansas is another example of so-called "carpetbaggers" who made a life-long commitment to Arkansas. He had friends among the white community in Lafayette County and was remembered for assisting a Democrat to gain a post office position. He was long active in the Masons, who supplied his tombstone.

Michael B. Dougan
Jonesboro, Arkansas

Union Labor Party

The Union Labor Party (ULP) participated in only two election years in Arkansas (1888 and 1890), yet during that brief span, it mounted the most serious challenge that the state's Democratic Party faced between the end of Reconstruction and the rebirth of the Republican Party in the mid-1960s. The ULP appealed to farmers and industrial workers and drew significant support from white and black voters alike. The party's failure to topple the Democrats from power underscored the failure of democracy itself in Arkansas while shedding light on some of the ugliest episodes in the history of American politics.

Origins

The national Union Labor Party was formed in Cincinnati, Ohio, in February 1887 by some 300 to 600 delegates at a convention called the Industrial Labor Conference. The party's founders included members of the Knights of Labor, the Agricultural Wheel, the Farmers' Alliance, the declining Grange, and the defunct Greenback Party. Each of these organizations was or had been active in Arkansas, and, along with the earlier farmers' organization the Brothers of Freedom, they helped lay the groundwork for farmer-labor third-party political activity during the late 1870s and 1880s. In 1886, the Agricultural Wheel nominated Charles Cunningham, a former Arkansas Grange leader and Greenback congressional candidate, for governor. (He received a scant twelve percent of the vote.) The Agricultural Wheel and the Knights of Labor, many of whose members were galvanized by a failed railroad strike against Jay Gould's Southwestern system that spring, both put forth or openly supported third-party or independent candidates in local or congressional races that year, despite their claims to be nonpartisan organizations. In some instances, the two organizations engaged in unofficial cooperation in these endeavors. The ULP became the vehicle for both organizations to enter politics more fully without further undermining the nonpartisanship called for in their constitutions.

ULP Campaigns and Accomplishments

In Little Rock (Pulaski County) on April 30, 1888, the Arkansas ULP held its first state convention—which drew representatives (including some African Americans) from the Knights of Labor, the Agricultural Wheel, and the Farmers' Alliance—and endorsed the platforms of each of these organizations. The convention nominated Charles M. Norwood, a one-legged Confederate veteran, for governor. Norwood condemned Democratic Party corruption and what he characterized as that party's orientation toward the interests of banks and businessmen at the expense of farmers and laborers. The Republican Party supported Norwood rather than nominating its own candidate. When Norwood lost to Democrat James P. Eagle by 15,000 votes out of more than 180,000 ballots counted, Union Laborite Reuben Carl Lee wrote a letter, subsequently published in the *Arkansas Gazette*, in which he made detailed allegations of Democratic intimidation, murder, and fraud, denouncing "the fraudulent state government of Arkansas." ULP (and Republican) congressional candidates faced similar challenges later that fall. ULP candidate Lewis P. Featherstone won a seat as the congressional representative from the First Congressional District of eastern Arkansas—but only after filing charges of election fraud with the U.S. House of Representatives. Republican John Clayton also filed charges of fraud in the case of his narrow defeat in the Second Congressional District, but he was assassinated in Conway County while gathering evidence for his case. Arkansas elections followed the same deplorable pattern in 1890, with ULP candidates losing again by narrow and suspect margins, but none of them attempted to challenge the official results this time.

During his brief term in Congress, Featherstone introduced several bills on behalf of the Arkansas Farmers' Alliance and Agricultural Wheel, primarily intended to provide economic relief to beleaguered farmers and protection for the prices of the goods they produced. In the Arkansas General Assembly, ULP representatives fought for election reform, railroad regulation, antitrust legislation, and credit reform, but with only fourteen seats (by the highest count), they lacked the strength of numbers to accomplish these goals. Republican representatives did not always support the ULP agenda, despite the GOP's support for ULP gubernatorial and (in some instances) congressional candidates.

Demise
After the formation of the national People's (or Populist) Party during 1891–1892, the Arkansas ULP ceased to exist as it submerged itself into the new party, with many of the same leaders and essentially the same platform. But the state's "election reform" law of 1891 disfranchised many black and poor white voters who had been essential to the ULP's strength at the polls. A state poll tax approved by voters in 1892 further decimated any prospect of third-party success, as did the decision of GOP leaders to resume the nomination of Republican

THE UNION LABOR PARTY'S ANGRY FARMERS ALMOST BEAT THE DEMOCRATS.

gubernatorial candidates. Therefore, the Arkansas Populist Party never achieved the same level of electoral support that the ULP had, and the party disintegrated by the end of the decade. With it vanished the hopes of a biracial (though white-led) coalition of poor-to-middle-class farmers and laborers that, in a more democratic setting, might well have brought a measure of economic and social justice to the residents of Arkansas who needed it most.

Matthew Hild
Georgia Institute of Technology

Paul Van Dalsem (1907–1983)

CIGAR-PUFFING LAWMAKER PAUL VAN DELSEM SAID THE WAY TO SILENCE A WOMAN—

— WAS TO GET HER A *COW!*

in the Arkansas House of Representatives.

Paul Van Dalsem was born in Aplin (Perry County) in 1907 to Pyke Van Dalsem and May Thompson Van Dalsem. He had one sister. He attended public school in Perryville (Perry County) and began college at what is now Arkansas Tech University before transferring to Louisiana Tech University in Ruston, Louisiana, where he earned his degree. He later attended the University of Arkansas (UA) in Fayetteville (Washington County), earning a degree that allowed him to join the university's Cooperative Extension Service. He worked as a county agricultural agent and a farmer, as well as acquiring a number of businesses over the years, including the *Perry County News*, which was edited by his wife, Royce Irene Haydon Van Dalsem, whom he married in 1941. The couple had one son and two daughters.

Representative Paul Van Dalsem—with his cigars, his aggressive style, and his fiscal conservatism— came to represent the classic southern politician. He was a master of the legislative process and parliamentary procedure. This mastery served him well, allowing him to serve on and off for thirty years

First elected to the state House of Representatives in 1936 as a Democrat to represent Perry County and part of Pulaski County, Van Dalsem was known for his fiscal conservatism, his close alliance with Orval Faubus, and his ability to change his political tactics to fit any situation. He made three political comebacks: he was defeated in 1938, reelected in 1940, defeated once again in 1947, reelected in 1948 by a nearly two-to-one margin, defeated in 1966, and reelected in 1972.

Van Dalsem rose to become one of the most powerful members of the Arkansas General Assembly, holding a place on the powerful Arkansas Legislative Council during the 1950s and 1960s. A master legislator, he was known for filing multiple bills and allowing most to die in order to achieve his ultimate goals, a tactic he used to create the law school in Little Rock (Pulaski County). During the desegregation of Central High School, as the chair of the education subcommittee of the Legislative Council, he led a McCarthy-style investigation, even predicting the involvement of communists, which led to even greater harassment of proponents of integration. This investigation resulted in the "teacher purge" by the Little Rock School Board in 1959.

Comments concerning women's participation in government and women's rights are what Van Dalsem remains best known for. The Arkansas division of the American Association of University Women (AAUW) lobbied the legislature to enact a series of electoral reforms in the 1950s and 1960s, legislation directed at preventing election tampering and voter fraud. During a speech to the Optimist Club of Little Rock on August 27, 1963, Van Dalsem stated: "We don't have any of these university women in Perry County, but I'll tell you what we do up there when one of our women starts poking around in something she doesn't know anything about. We get her an extra milk cow. If that don't work, we give her a little more garden to tend to. And then if that's not enough, we get her pregnant and keep her barefoot." When the *Arkansas Gazette* reported his remarks on August 28, it created a firestorm.

Arkansas, like many states, did not have proportional representation for the legislature. At the time, each county elected a state representative with twenty-five seats apportioned among counties with higher populations; this practice gave a small county like Perry County—and its representative—disproportionate power. Beginning in 1962, the U.S. Supreme Court handed down two rulings, *Baker v. Carr* and *Reynolds v. Sims*, challenging such forms of apportionment. In 1965, federal courts ruled specifically on Arkansas's apportionment in *Yancey v. Faubus*. The state was given until June 15, 1965, to develop a constitutional plan. The reapportionment board developed a plan with multimember districts. This plan paired Perry County with the more populous Pulaski County. Van Dalsem was subsequently defeated in the 1966 Democratic primary by Herb Rule, had emphasized Van Dalsem's remarks about women and who went on to defeat Marion Burton in the general election. Van Dalsem also had a rocky relationship with Governor Winthrop Rockefeller during his time in office.

In the 1967 legislative session, Van Dalsem acted as though he had not been defeated. He took advantage of a House rule allowing former members on the floor during the session and continued to run bills he supported and oppose others; the House eventually amended the chamber's rules to stop such actions. Elected once again in 1972, Van Dalsem entered a far different legislature than the bodies he had previously served in. In this session, he supported women's groups and the Equal Rights Amendment. However, in 1976, he was defeated by Larry Mahan of Faulkner County.

Van Dalsem died on April 29, 1983, in Perryville after several months of poor health. He is buried near where he was born in Aplin.

Rodney Harris
Fayetteville, Arkansas

Waldron War

The Waldron War was a decade-long period of violence that began during the Reconstruction era and was characterized by arson, general lawlessness, personal and political feuds, electoral misconduct, and violence—including murder—throughout Scott County. The civil strife resulted in Governors Augustus Garland and William Read Miller dispatching the state militia to the county on at least three occasions to restore order.

With much of Waldron (Scott County) burned by departing Union troops during the Civil War in 1864, the citizens faced the reestablishment of the infrastructure of the town. While hostile feelings remained between those sympathetic to the Union cause and the Confederate cause, much of the strife was attributed to personality conflicts within the local Republican Party. Although there was the occasional outburst of lawlessness—such as arson and election fraud, in the period immediately following the Civil War—for the most part, the town progressed with rebuilding and economic growth.

The cycle of contentious elections began in 1870 with the naming of the Scott County Board of Registrars by Governor Powell Clayton. J. M. Bethel, a member of the board, was later declared to have defeated the father of fellow board member W. J. Ellington in a race for the legislature, resulting in rumors and accusations about the election. The gossip and intrigue were compounded by Bethel's failure to arrive in Little Rock (Pulaski County) to begin his term. He was soon found dead on an area mountain, and published reports attributed Bethel's death to causes varying from natural to weather-related to murder.

The election of 1872 saw a pattern not unlike the election of 1870. Reports of voter registration books missing from the clerk's office circulated, as did rumors, accusations, and innuendos about the election process. Local "correspondents" composed reports to the editors of several newspapers establishing a pattern of unreliable, biased, and sometimes inflammatory views of events.

Lorenzo D. Gilbreath, who had resigned the office of county clerk and was state representative-elect, and James C. Gilbreath, a deputy clerk and the county clerk-elect, were arrested for "resisting process" and "refusal to produce papers." The substance of the charges was that the men had declined to turn over the books and papers of the office to L. L. Hyman, who had been appointed to serve the remainder of Lorenzo Gilbreath's term. Gilbreath supporters countered that the arrests were designed only to prevent Gilbreath from being in Little Rock. While the charges were not sustained, rhetoric ran high, and feelings were reinforced.

Pursuant to an order from Governor Elisha Baxter, Scott County saw new voter registration in 1873. Increasing political pressure and personality conflicts ushered in a new intensity and violent fervor to the already unsettled political climate in 1874. The year was marked by a violent cycle, though with few apprehensions and convictions of rumored perpetrators. A longtime feud within the Republican Party was highlighted with the shooting of prominent citizen Cerop Malone. Former sheriff Nathan Floyd was charged with the shooting but was later acquitted. In 1875, Floyd sustained a gunshot wound and chose to leave the state.

Arson during an outburst of violence in 1876 left Waldron's business district in ashes, and there were several murders. As public opinion rose to demand restoration of law and order, the sheriff, F. C. "Buck" Gaines, appealed to Governor Garland, who dispatched Adjutant General Carroll D. Wood to the county. Order was briefly restored until about June 1876, when Judge Frank Fuller was wounded by shots fired into his home. With that event, the factions were feuding again, with murders and general lawlessness frequent. Peter Beam, a prominent citizen who had notified former sheriff Floyd that he had been offered a large sum of money to kill Floyd, was shot and killed by hidden assailants as his young daughter watched. Several shootings, some fatal, took place in public locations such as the town square. The sheriff again appealed to the governor, who dispatched General Robert Newton. Newton organized a militia, and a strained period of order prevailed.

In the summer of 1877, panic again reigned, and Judge John Rodgers was warned not to hold circuit court. The August term of the court was held but resulted in the formation of local militias of unknown missions and motives. With this turn of events, Adjutant General James Pomeroy took up residence at Waldron, directing the militias and ensuring an orderly term of the court in the spring of 1878.

The apparent climax of the "war" took place in Waldron in February 1878 with the murder of John L. "Shabe" Davenport, a well-known citizen of the area. A mob of citizens from the northern part of the county formed, supposedly to restore order in the county. The citizens of Waldron, alerted to the mob, prepared for engagement, but high water levels on the Poteau River made crossing impossible for the mob. This likely prevented significant bloodshed. A concerned Governor William Miller staged an encampment of militia from Franklin County nearby to wait for the sheriff's call. With two militias composed of local citizens aligned with factions, Governor Miller felt that objective leadership poised as an alternative was needed. The presence of the state militia helped bring about a gradual restoration of order, and Miller later remarked, "Their presence rendered their employment unnecessary." An investigation into the disorder at Waldron brought a trial and acquittal of several prominent citizens, but the return to normality did not ameliorate the animosity toward Governor Miller and the adjutant general for the perceived indignity imposed upon Scott County. State senator R. T. Kerr, who represented Scott and Sebastian counties, sought revenge by securing passage of Act 49 of 1879, which abolished the Office of Adjutant General and required that those duties be performed by the governor's private secretary. A last

LEGISLATOR J.M. BETHEL MET A BAD END ON THAT MOUNTAIN.

SOME BLAMED THE WEATHER, SOME CALLED IT MURDER—

SOME CALLED IT THE START OF THE *WALDRON WAR!*

attempt at revenge came in 1882 with an attempt to sue the auditor of state for recompense for the unpleasantness stemming from what had become known as the Waldron War.

Wes Goodner
Little Rock, Arkansas

Wilson-Anthony Duel

The only recorded violent death on the floor of the Arkansas General Assembly occurred on December 4, 1837, in a knife brawl leaving state representative Major Joseph J. Anthony of Randolph County dead at the hands of Speaker of the House Colonel John Wilson of Clark County, who was subsequently expelled and tried for murder. The *Arkansas Gazette* cited it as "another example of the barbarity of life in Arkansas," lamenting how it "stained the history of the state."

The events have long been obscured by variants of the narrative. Speaker Wilson, who was presiding over an extraordinary session of the Arkansas General Assembly called by Governor James Conway to deal with a predicted tax surplus, was debating a wolf-scalp bill, sent over from the state Senate, authorizing paying a bounty on wolf pelts presented to a county justice of the peace. Faced with wrangling over how to verify where a pelt was derived, Representative Anthony, an outspoken opponent of the notoriously corrupt Arkansas Real Estate Bank, offered a tongue-in-cheek amendment asking that "the signature of the President of the Real Estate Bank be attached to the certificate of the wolf scalp," angering Speaker Wilson, who was president of the bank. After exchanging words, Wilson set upon Anthony with a large knife, killing him even as Representative Grandison D. Royston of Hempstead County tried to stop the fight by throwing a chair between the two.

The legislature expelled Wilson, but authorities took three days before acting against him—and then only after a relative of Anthony's (possibly James C. Anthony) made a complaint. Wilson reportedly presented himself to the court by arriving in a horse-drawn carriage accompanied by many friends, whereupon a three-judge panel released Wilson on bail.

On the day of trial, Wilson's lawyer, Chester Ashley, successfully argued that Wilson could not get a fair trial in Pulaski County. The venue was changed, making this the first murder trial ever to be held in Saline County.

In the May 1838 Saline County court term, multiple prosecutors—including John J. Clendenin, Albert Pike, John Taylor, and Bennett H. Martin—directed the state's case against Wilson. Taylor lodged in the home of the grandfather of future Confederate "boy martyr" David O. Dodd while Wilson lodged at the same place as the judge, paying for the judge's meals over the course of the trial.

The state called six witnesses and the defense two, taking four or five days to examine them. Ashley's defense was based on Wilson protecting his honor. Some claim Wilson hired "a mob to demonstrate in his favor outside the courtroom during the prosecuting attorney's address." However, an anonymous letter writer known only as "Saline" wrote to the *Arkansas Gazette* following the trial claiming that Bennett Martin, a prosecuting attorney assisting Taylor, "felt Taylor was doing their case more harm than good. Martin himself created the diversion in the yard, in a desperate attempt to shut Taylor up." The jury returned a verdict of "guilty of excusable homicide," the same as not guilty or a pronouncement of justifiable killing.

Wilson celebrated his acquittal by directing the sheriff "to take the jury to a dram-shop, and he would pay for all that was drunk by the jury and everybody else." A crowd of well wishers paraded through the streets of Benton (Saline County) all night, hollering and dancing, even gathering around the lodging place of Anthony's relatives in a show of open contempt as symbolically barbaric as the crime. Pike's poetry seems to have summed up the situation best: "And a jury set right with a Dollar, or two; / And though justice is blind, / Yet a way you may find; / To open her eyes with a Dollar, or two."

This was not the last the state would hear of John Wilson, who moved to Pike County, where, in 1840, he was again elected to the Arkansas House. During an 1842 debate on the Real Estate Bank, Wilson became enraged with Dr. Lorenzo Gibson, a Pulaski County Whig. However, multiple House members came between both men, and no blood was shed this time. Wilson eventually left Arkansas and moved to Texas, where his efforts to get elected to the Texas legislature failed. He died in Texas in 1865.

John Spurgeon
Bella Vista, Arkansas

Women of the Ku Klux Klan

Headquartered in Little Rock (Pulaski County), the national Women of the Ku Klux Klan (WKKK) was formed on June 10, 1923, as a result of the exclusively male Klan's desire to create a like-minded women's auxiliary that would bring together the existing informal pro-Klan women's groups, including the Grand League of Protestant Women, the White American Protestants (WAP), and the Ladies of the Invisible Empire (LOTIE). However, the group was ultimately short lived, waning in influence with its male counterpart.

Lulu Markwell, a civically active Little Rock resident and former president of Arkansas's chapter of the Woman's Christian Temperance Union (WCTU) for twenty years, was the national organization's first Imperial Commander, establishing its national office in Little Rock's Ancient Order of United Workmen hall. According to historian Kathleen Blee, by November 1923, the WKKK had chapters in all forty-eight states and boasted a membership of 250,000. After Markwell's resignation in June 1924, Robbie Gill, the WKKK's Imperial Kligrapp, or secretary, replaced her as the group's leader. A year later, Gill married the Arkansas Klan's Grand Dragon, lawyer James A. Comer, who had been instrumental in convincing the Klan to ratify the WKKK's charter. Comer continued his involvement with the WKKK, serving as its Imperial Klonsel, or attorney—involvement that soon caused problems for the organization.

From 1923 to 1931, the Little Rock–based national WKKK wrote, published, and disseminated numerous documents in which the Imperial Officers set forth the tenets to which all members were to adhere. To qualify for membership, one had to be a native-born, white, Protestant woman; membership in turn signaled a Klanswoman's belief in Christianity "as practiced by enlightened Protestant churches," the separation of church and state, the home as society's foundation, free public schooling, the "supremacy of the Constitution of the United States," free-dom of speech and worship, impartial justice, no racial mixing, and immigration restriction. The WKKK viewed racial mixing as an offense parallel to treason, stating that "intermingling" was "opposed to the laws of God and man." Promoting a nativist ideology of "America First," the WKKK denounced immigrants and Catholics as "un-American," claiming Protestantism as the birthright of Americans and that the United States was a country founded "not for the refuse population of other lands." Klanswomen understood themselves as emancipated women whose role as voters—a right obtained only three years prior to the WKKK's founding—was essential for the protection and purification of the country's political, social, and moral fabric.

The WKKK consisted of local chapters, provinces (county units), realms (regional/state units), and the Invisible Empire (national unit), with each group governed by officers exercising various executive, legislative, and judicial powers. Ritualized meetings, initiation ceremonies, and secret funeral services—interspersed with both Christian hymns and patriotic songs—blended the secular and the sacred. While the WKKK's internal documents reveal a great deal about its tenets and ideology, records concerning the exact nature of Klanswomen's activities in Arkansas and across the nation are sparse.

It is clear that only two years into its existence, the WKKK began to encounter some difficulties. In August 1925, Alice B. Cloud of Dallas, Texas—who had been Vice Commander at the time of Markwell's resignation—filed a lawsuit with two other Klanswomen against WKKK head Robbie Gill Comer and her husband, claiming that the Comers had put WKKK funds toward their personal use and that Cloud had been the rightful successor to Markwell's position. Two more lawsuits followed, and a judge eventually allowed Cloud and her fellow plaintiffs to look at the WKKK's financial records. Those records revealed the Comers as greatly profiting from sales of WKKK garb and as having "squandered $70,000 of WKKK funds, equipping WKKK headquarters with goldfish, song-birds, police dogs, flowers, and a piano and purchasing for their own use a $5,000 sedan."

A few weeks later, members of the Little Rock KKK broke away to form a separate organization due to their unhappiness with Judge Comer's ineffective leadership; Lit-tle Rock's Klanswomen also broke away from the national WKKK, according to historian Charles Alexander. In general, the WKKK's membership waned with that of the male Klan. According to historian Kathleen Blee, by 1930, membership had dropped to fewer than 50,000 men and women due to internal problems of competing leadership and financial corruption, as well as the increased visibility of the male Klan's violence. Publication of the WKKK's documents appears to have continued into the early 1930s, but the extent to which the organi-zation's chapters remained active is unknown.

Margaret T. McGehee
Emory University

THE KU KLUX KLAN HAD A LADIES' AUXILIARY—

BAKE SALE

- THE WOMEN OF THE KKK.

Arkansas State Police

The Arkansas State Police is the state's primary statewide law enforcement agency. Although it has had many duties since its inception, the primary functions of the agency remain criminal investigation, traffic safety, and highway patrol. As a state agency, the State Police is overseen by a director bearing the rank of colonel who serves at the pleasure of the governor. The State Police's main headquarters are located in Little Rock (Pulaski County), with the highway patrol organized into twelve regional troops, each commanded by a captain, and the criminal investigation division organized into six regional companies, each commanded by a lieutenant.

The creation of a centralized, statewide law enforcement agency in Arkansas proved to be a difficult process, as many state legislators worried that such a force would infringe upon the authority of local officers. Still, the rise in popularity of automobiles in the 1920s resulted in a corresponding increase in the number of fatal traffic accidents, which provided enough incentive for the establishment in 1929 of a precursor to the State Police, known as the Road Patrol.

By 1935, the continued rise in traffic fatalities combined with the need for enforcement of newly enacted liquor laws after the legislature voted to end Prohibition in Arkansas had made a new agency necessary. This new law enforcement body was designated the Department of Arkansas State Police and consisted of thirteen officers of which seven were known as rangers. In an effort to appease the new agency's opponents, state police officers could be called to investigate a crime only if specifically requested by local authorities.

By 1948, the force had expanded to more than sixty-five officers and included separate divisions for highway patrol and criminal investigation. That same year, the State Police began referring to its highway patrol officers as troopers for the first time. By 1957, the State Police had doubled in size after Governor Orval Faubus's push to have "a trooper in every county."

The period from 1965 to 1975 saw the greatest changes within the State Police. Marion Taylor became the first African-American state police officer in 1967. Later that same year, Winthrop Rockefeller won election as the state's first Republican governor since Reconstruction and vowed to reduce the influence of politics on the agency. The clearest example of Governor Rockefeller's intent occurred in Hot Springs (Garland County), where a multitude of casinos openly flouted the state's gambling laws. During Rockefeller's four years as governor, the State Police repeatedly and consistently cracked down on the casinos in Hot Springs. This effectively ended illegal gambling despite strong political pressure from powerful state legislators, including Garland County's Q. Bynum Hurst and Conway County's "Mutt" Jones, to end the raids.

This heightened level of activity continued throughout the late 1960s and mid-1970s as troopers and investigators deployed throughout the state in an attempt to head off violence resulting from civil rights demonstrations. Incidents in Hazen (Prairie County), Little Rock (Pulaski County), Forrest City (St. Francis County), Pine Bluff (Jefferson County), Marianna (Lee County), and Arkadelphia (Clark County) kept the department focused on keeping the peace instead of its traditional role patrolling the highways and investigating crimes. In 1968, following the assassination of Martin Luther King Jr., State Police officers were requested by the City of Memphis, Tennessee, and deputized as sheriff's deputies to assist in bringing order back to the city when civil unrest erupted.

Also during this period, the State Police installed the first computerized automobile registration database and linked up with the national crime information center database. It hired its first female officer, Barbara Cart, in 1975.

In the 1980s and 1990s, the State Police expanded its efforts in drug enforcement by starting an annual marijuana eradication program and establishing drug interdiction and canine units that worked throughout the state's interstate highway system. The department also benefited from the federal government's Community Oriented Policing (COP) program started in 1994, which provided millions of dollars in federal grants that allowed the department to hire nearly 100 additional officers.

By the start of the twenty-first century, the State Police had grown to almost 1,000 officers and civilian workers. Concurrently, the traffic fatality rate fell from twenty-four deaths per 100 million miles traveled in 1934 to two deaths per 100 million miles traveled in 2001.

Michael Lindsey
Fayetteville, Arkansas

Arkansas State Police headquarters, adjoining the old state prison on Roosevelt Road in Little Rock. The red brick building was the prison, and the white building belonged to the State Police. This was the second home to the State Police after its legislative creation, the first being in the east annex of the Old State House in Little Rock.
Courtesy of the Arkansas State Police

Barker-Karpis Gang

The Barker-Karpis Gang, later known as the "Ma Barker Gang," was a famous criminal group of the Depression era. Led by Alvin "Creepy" Karpis (1907–1979) and Fred Barker (1903–1935) during most of its criminal tenure, the lethal gang had many different members over the course of its exploits. Some of the core members besides Karpis and Barker were Arthur "Doc" Barker (brother of Fred), Lawrence DeVol, Harvey Bailey, Frank "Jelly" Nash, Bernard Phillips, Harry Sawyer, Volney Davis, Harry Campbell, and Verne Miller. Although it was most well known for committing crimes throughout the Midwest, the gang's first murder was of a town marshal in Pocahontas (Randolph County), and members later holed up in Hot Springs (Garland County).

Fred Barker and Alvin Karpis became acquainted while they were both incarcerated at the Kansas State Penitentiary in Lansing, Kansas. Shortly after their release, they were arrested again in June 1931 in Tulsa, Oklahoma, for the theft of some jewelry. Barker escaped from jail after he was transferred to Claremore, Oklahoma, shortly after his arrest. On September 10, 1931, Karpis pleaded guilty to the burglary but received a four-year suspended jail sentence. After his release, Karpis joined Barker in Thayer, Missouri. It was here that the Barkers' mother, Kate "Ma" Barker, lived with Arthur W. Dunlop on a rented farm.

Before daylight on November 8, 1931, Fred Barker, William Weaver, and quite possibly Alvin Karpis were driving around the town of Pocahontas looking for places to rob. Their vehicle stopped to allow Weaver to answer a call of nature while the night marshal of

MA BARKER'S GANG HOLED UP IN HOT SPRINGS.

the town, Manley Jackson, began jotting down the car's license plate number. Jackson, who had been on patrol most of the night, was summoned into the car at gunpoint by Fred Barker. The officer was driven several miles outside of Pocahontas, and Barker shot him numerous times in the back with a .45 caliber pistol. His body was found later in the day, at about

11:00 a.m., by local residents Charles Johnson and his wife.

Soon after the murder of Jackson, two local men—Lige Dame and Earl Decker—were accused and convicted of the crime. Dame eventually confessed to the murder, but he repudiated his statements several times in the months and years afterward. In his confession, he accused the Pocahontas chief of police, John G. Slayton, of hiring him to commit the murder. It was not until the 1971 publishing of Alvin Karpis's autobiography that the murder of the night marshal was attributed in detail to Fred Barker.

The murder of the night marshal marked the beginning of the evolution of the Barker-Karpis Gang. The month after the murder, Barker, Karpis, and Weaver were involved with the murder of Sheriff C. Roy Kelly of West Plains, Missouri, after they burglarized stores in that town. After leaving a trail in Missouri, they went to a criminal safe haven of the gangster era—St. Paul, Minnesota—where the gang began to take shape. One of the seasoned criminals they met during this time was Frank "Jelly" Nash, a former Arkansas resident and experienced bank robber. Nash would accompany the gang on several bank heists.

Between 1932 and 1935, the Barker-Karpis Gang robbed dozens of banks and committed two kidnappings. Some of their most successful bank robberies amounted to $250,000 and up. On June 15, 1933, the gang kidnapped William A. Hamm Jr., a wealthy St. Paul beer brewer, and held him for a $100,000 ransom. On January 17, 1934, they kidnapped the president of the Commercial State Bank of St. Paul, Edward George Bremer. They were able to ransom $200,000, but the fingerprints of Doc Barker were found on a gas can left at the scene of the ransom exchange. The Federal Bureau of Investigation (FBI) was soon on the gang's trail.

The members of the gang scattered and hid out in areas across the country after the Bremer kidnapping. In 1934, the FBI had already taken down such criminals as John Dillinger, Bonnie and Clyde, Pretty Boy Floyd, and Baby Face Nelson. This left the Barker-Karpis Gang at the forefront of its attention. On January 16, 1935, federal agents fired about 1,500 rounds of ammunition into a house located on Lake Weir in Ocklawaha, Florida, killing Fred Barker and Ma Barker.

At this time, Alvin Karpis was still on the run, and in June 1935, he was in the resort town of Hot Springs. He used the town for his hideout off and on for the next several months. Hot Springs had one of the most corrupt police departments in the United States at the time and was a safe haven for many criminals of the era. In the later part of 1935 and early 1936, Karpis and his accomplice Fred Hunter stayed at two different cottages on Lake Catherine and Lake Hamilton. Karpis and Hunter moved frequently in the Hot Springs area, as they knew the FBI and U.S. postal investigators were in the area looking for clues to their whereabouts.

In March 1936, Karpis rented a house on Malvern Road between Malvern (Hot Spring County) and Hot Springs. On March 30, 1936, the FBI raided the house only to find that Karpis had already fled to New Orleans, Louisiana. He continued to evade the FBI for another month until, on May 1, 1936, Karpis and Hunter were apprehended by FBI agents and Director J. Edgar Hoover. On July 27, Karpis pleaded guilty to charges from the Hamm kidnapping and was sentenced to life imprisonment, entering his incarceration at Alcatraz (where most of his prison time was spent). Karpis served nearly thirty-three years of his life sentence and was released from prison in December 1968. Karpis died on August 26, 1979, from an overdose of sleeping pills while living in Spain.

The 1970 movie *Bloody Mama* was loosely based on the exploits of the Barker-Karpis Gang. Directed by Roger Corman and starring Shelley Winters and Robert De Niro, it was filmed in the Arkansas Ozarks and Little Rock (Pulaski County).

Will Walker
Pocahontas, Arkansas

WEST BOGAN WAS GUILTY OF AN AXE MURDER—

ABRAHAM LINCOLN SAVED HIM FROM HANGING.

West Bogan
(Trial of)

Bound in slavery on a cotton farm near Helena (Phillips County), West Bogan fought and killed his subjugator, Monroe Bogan, with an axe the morning of December 15, 1863. After many months in jail and a court sentence to hang, Bogan's case was presented by Judge Advocate General Joseph Holt to President Abraham Lincoln on the fresh legal grounds of the Emancipation Proclamation. Bogan was ultimately seen as having acted in self defense and freed, but the rest of his life remains a mystery.

Two weeks after the murder, West Bogan was discovered by plantation neighbors hiding among the thousands of former slaves in the contraband camps around Helena. They handed him over to Union troops. Bogan was held at a Helena jail, where he awaited his trial for over a month under the watch of Union troops. His three-day murder trial was heard before a military commission beginning on February 1, 1864. Few records remain, but a sketch of the scene on file at the National Archives and Records Administration shows where Monroe Bogan's body lay, just southwest of the ten slave houses near "the main road." According to the 1860 census, Monroe Bogan's plantation was in Planters Township between Barton (Phillips County) and Oneida (Phillips County) along Lick Creek.

The military commission found West Bogan guilty and sentenced him to hang. General Napoleon Bonaparte Buford approved the findings but recommended Bogan's sentence be commuted to hard labor at a northern penitentiary before execution. Due to mitigating circumstances, General Frederick Steele, commander of the Union troops in Arkansas and based in Helena at the time, suspended the sentence three months after the verdict and forwarded the case to the president through Holt.

In a May 30, 1864, letter to Lincoln, Holt notes the mitigating circumstances for suspension. The killing took place near the slave quarters during broad daylight when West Bogan was "on his way to his day's task." Monroe Bogan, Holt wrote from testimonials, was a "cruel and exacting master" who "forced his slaves to labor night and day, and frequently on Sundays, giving them no holiday or resting time." One witness also testified that Monroe was prone to "whipping someone every day."

A field hand named Tom went on record for the prosecution as having heard West Bogan declare his intention to kill Monroe Bogan "because his master was going to kill him for running about and going away from home." It was also offered into evidence that Monroe Bogan had expressed, "only the night before, his intention to whip the prisoner on the following day."

Maria Bogan, possibly the sister of West, testified that she was sitting in her cabin at the time of the homicide and heard her children say that "master was trying to whip Uncle West." She then saw West Bogan strike two blows with the axe to Monroe Bogan's neck.

In the letter to Lincoln, Holt noted: "The administration of the Government must and does recognize the colored population of the rebellious States, as occupying the *status* of freedmen….It is, therefore, held that Munroe [*sic*] Bogan, when he met his death, was in violation of law and right holding the prisoner in absolute slavery—not only holding him in slavery but also imposing upon him ceaseless toil and cruel punishments." Lincoln replied with the decision "sentence disapproved" on July 8, 1864.

Recitation of the entire case can be found in the 1865 book *The Political History of the United States of America during the Great Rebellion* by Edward McPherson. Mark Neely Jr. writes about the case in his 1992 book *Fate of Liberty: Lincoln and Civil Liberties*.

Elizabeth Leonard also discusses it in her 2011 book *Lincoln's Forgotten Ally: Judge Advocate General Joseph Holt of Kentucky*. Amy Murrell Taylor describes the case in the spring 2013 issue of *The Civil War Monitor*'s "Casualties of War" section.

West Bogan largely disappears from the historical record after these events. No trace of him is found in the Freedmen's Bureau records, and neither is he listed in Union pension records. However, three of Bogan's fellow slaves were found by Taylor as having joined the First Arkansas Infantry–African Descent, which later became the Forty-sixth U.S. Colored Infantry.

John Lovett
Hot Springs, Arkansas

Bullfrog Valley Gang

The Bullfrog Valley Gang was a notorious counterfeiting ring that operated in the wilderness of Pope County during the depression of the 1890s. The gang's origin and methods were mysterious, but the *New York Times* reported its demise on its front page on June 28, 1897. The article said deputy U.S. marshals attached to the federal district court at Fort Smith (Sebastian County) had captured three men, effectively breaking up "the once-famous band of counterfeiters known to secret service operators all over the United States as the Bullfrog Valley Gang." Previous arrests were reported in Arkansas earlier in the year. In all, some fifteen men were arrested and convicted in federal courts at Fort Smith and Little Rock (Pulaski County). Others, in Arkansas and other states, were convicted of passing the bogus money. A young doctor and his friend in the remote mountain town of Timbo (Stone County) were convicted of smuggling and passing the gang's bills.

Counterfeiting was an endemic problem in the South after the Civil War, particularly during the steep depression that followed the Panic of 1893. The

South did not enjoy the benefits of the national banking system, and currency was in short supply. The wilds of Arkansas were home to a number of counterfeiting operations, some in caves in the Ouachita Mountains and in the wilderness of southwest

Arkansas. None, however, received the notoriety of the Bullfrog Valley Gang.

If the Secret Service's accounts are to be believed, the head of the Bullfrog Valley Gang was George Rozelle, who moved from Nebraska to Pope County in 1893 and, within a couple of years, had printing equipment shipped by rail from Chicago, Illinois. He took the machine into Bullfrog Valley, a remote and inhospitable glen north of Russellville (Pope County) that was famous as a hideout for highwaymen, bandits, and moonshiners. The remote valley, which follows Big Piney Creek from Long Pool to Booger Hollow, was named for Chief Bullfrog, a Cherokee who, according to legend, settled there after his tribe's forced removal from Georgia (on the Trail of Tears) by the Indian Removal Act of 1830. There, Rozelle set up a mint where he and his associates made bogus five- and ten-dollar bank notes.

The June 28, 1897, article in the *New York Times*, along with similar ones that week in the *Arkansas Gazette* and a number of other newspapers around the state and country, reported that the Bullfrog Valley ring had agents in many large cities around the country and in Toronto, Canada, and Mexico City, Mexico. The spurious money had baffled the government until the Secret Service bureau in Chicago followed a lead on a shipment of supplies to Pope County and tracked the fake money's source to the infamous Bullfrog Valley. (Four years earlier, the *New York Times* had carried a story about the ambush by moonshiners of six deputy U.S. marshals in Bullfrog Valley. Two marshals were killed, two were wounded, and two were missing and presumed to have been kidnapped.)

The *Mountain Wave*, a newspaper at Marshall (Searcy County), commented on the counterfeiting arrests this way: "Everyone knows where the Bull Frog Valley is. The name of Pope County cannot be spoken without recalling to memory this famous valley. That is where the genuine wild-catter [moonshiner] blooms and flourishes as prolific as morning glories on the back porch of a farm house." Three weeks after the Bullfrog Valley arrests,

national newspapers ran stories about a marshal's arrest of "the noted and desperate female outlaw Rhoda Fuller" at Batesville (Independence County) for passing counterfeit currency, although the stories did not link her with the Bullfrog gang but with another in the mountains of Independence County.

An article in the *Gazette* said the Bullfrog counterfeiters had dodged federal agents operating out of the federal courts at Fort Smith and Little Rock by ducking back and forth across the Pope-Johnson county line and evading jurisdiction, but some fifteen men had been arrested by August 1897. Rozelle, who was never mentioned in articles at the time, managed to escape with his printing press.

A later lengthy article in the *New York Times* on May 12, 1901, which recounted the tireless work of the Secret Service in tracking down thugs, finally explained what happened to Rozelle, although the bureau may have embellished the truth in praising the steadfastness and cunning of its men. It reported that the Secret Service learned that Rozelle (it spelled his name Roselle) had fled Bullfrog Valley and had buried the equipment. An agent found three men who had provided Rozelle with money and assistance. He discovered the general area where the machine was buried, and he moved there and waited for two years. One of the three men weakened under the pressure and was about to turn in the other two when he was slain by a load of buckshot fired through his front window, according to the Secret Service. Feeling safe then, one of the men dug up the equipment one night, and the agent arrested him.

The man gave the agent a tip on Rozelle's location in southern Missouri, but Rozelle had by then moved to Goff Cove in Cleburne County, Arkansas, and had started to farm under another name. Several weeks before the agent arrived at Goff Cove, Rozelle got sick and died. The agent found only his grave.

Ernest Dumas
Little Rock, Arkansas

Edward Coy (Lynching of)

On February 20, 1892, Edward Coy, a thirty-two-year-old African-American man, was burned at the stake in Texarkana (Miller County) before a crowd of approximately 1,000 people. Ida B. Wells, a journalist and prominent anti-lynching crusader from Memphis, Tennessee, described Coy's murder as one of the most shocking and repulsive in the history of lynching. Coy, described in press accounts as "mulatto," was charged with a crime "from which the laws provide adequate punishment. Ed Coy was charged with assaulting Mrs. Henry [Julia] Jewell, a white woman. A mob pronounced him guilty, strapped him to a tree, chipped the flesh from his body, poured coal oil over him, and the woman in the case set fire to him."

According to the *New York Times*, Jewell was attacked and raped by a "negro" who visited her house to sell hogs to her husband. The man attacked her when she told him her husband had gone to town. Following the attack, her husband returned and gave the alarm.

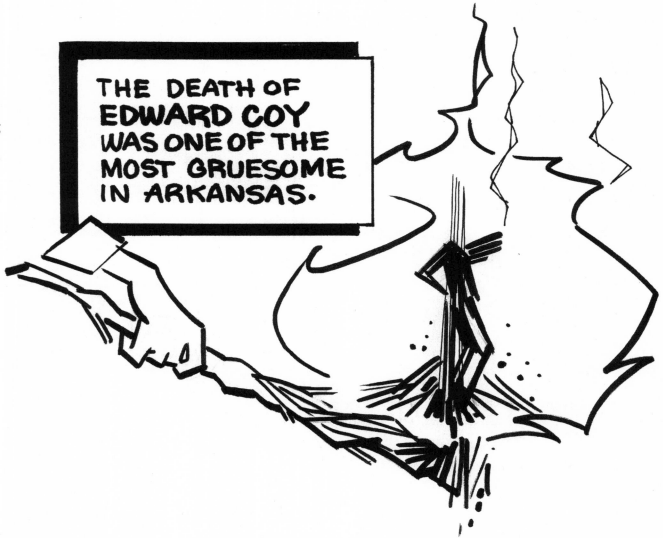

THE DEATH OF EDWARD COY WAS ONE OF THE MOST GRUESOME IN ARKANSAS.

Men scoured the country around Texarkana in all directions. Two suspects were apprehended, but Julia Jewell pronounced them innocent.

During the search, it was learned that the suspect being sought was named Ed Coy. It was believed that Coy had fled "northwards towards Little River County, Arkansas." Another suspect was arrested and brought before Jewell, who "pronounced him not the man, although the hat and clothes he wore looked exactly like those of her assailant." The prisoner explained the clothing by saying that "he and Coy had been together on Sunday and Monday and at the latter's request they had swapped clothes. Coy said that they were after him for some minor offense."

The next morning, farmer W. B. Scott, who lived just five miles outside of Texarkana, found Ed Coy and held him until a posse headed by Noah Sanderson arrived and took possession of Coy. The posse, consisting of about fifty mounted guards, "attended the prisoner to town, arriving...about 9 o'clock." Jewell identified Coy as the man who attacked her.

By 2:00 p.m., a decision had been made to hang Coy. A crowd of 1,000 marched Coy to the Iron Mountain roundhouse. A large stake was found here, "and in a twinkling he was securely bound to it. One from the mob advanced with a can of coal oil, and the crowd then knew what fate was in store for the negro." The crowd cried, "BURN HIM! BURN HIM!" Julia Jewell, the alleged rape victim, was given a torch. She looked at Coy, looked at the torch, and seemed to falter until, as one, the entire crowd yelled, "Burn him!" She applied the torch, and the crowd watched Coy burn alive.

It was reported in a "Special" to the *Republic* newspaper of Texarkana that "Mrs. Henry Jewell was a respectable farmer's wife, with a five-months-old child at the breast." However, an investigation by Judge Albion Winegar Tourgée, a pioneer civil rights activist, published in the *Chicago Inter Ocean* on October 1, 1892, stated, "The woman who was paraded as a victim of violence was of bad character; her husband was a drunkard and a gambler. She was publicly reported and generally known to have been criminally intimate with Coy for more than a year previous. She was compelled by threats, if not by violence, to make the charge against the victim." (It is unclear if Tourgée traveled to Arkansas for his investigation.) Indeed, Coy contended right up until his death that he and Jewell were lovers by mutual desire and consent. As she applied the torch to his oil-soaked body, he turned to her and asked how she could burn him after they had "been sweethearting" so long.

Coy's murder attracted national attention, and the *New York Times* supported Wells's accusation that sheriffs and police simply looked on when it wrote, "Marshal Crenshaw, accompanied by a small posse, took the negro in charge." The *Times* continued with, "a crowd of 1,000 people secured Coy from his captors as they were bringing him to the city." The *Arkansas Gazette* added a sad commentary on the South when it wrote, "People witnessed his burning, thus endorsing it with their presence." The murder of Coy typifies a trend in lynching toward greater public spectacle, the acts being carried out by people who felt no need to hide their identities. By contrast, lynching in the early decades following the Civil War was often done in secret, usually at night.

The lynching of Edward Coy remained a part of public consciousness throughout the United States for many years. On June 4, 1899, the Reverend D. A. Graham delivered a sermon at Bethel AME Church in Indianapolis, Indiana, on the subject of lynching. In part, Graham said, "The greatest affliction we have to suffer is the lack of trial by jury when accused of crime. Lynching of Negroes is growing to be a Southern pastime." When speaking of Coy, Graham said, "The relatives and husband of the woman who made the charge were fully cognizant of the fact that she was equally guilty with Coy. They compelled her to make the charge and then to set fire to her paramour."

Larry LeMasters
LeMasters' Antique News Service

Maud Crawford
(Disappearance of)

Maud Robinson Crawford, a lawyer with the Gaughan, McClellan and Laney law firm in Camden (Ouachita County), mysteriously disappeared from her stately Colonial home on Saturday night, March 2, 1957, at age sixty-five. U.S. Senator John L. McClellan, a former partner in the law firm, was at the time of her disappearance the chairman of a high-profile Senate investigation into alleged mob ties to organized labor. The disappearance of Sen. McClellan's former associate was international news, a first assumption being that she had been kidnapped by the Mafia to intimidate the senator. When no ransom note appeared, however, the theory was rejected by law enforcement. No body was ever found, and the case was never solved.

Maud Robinson was born on June 22, 1891, at Greenville, Texas, the oldest of four children of John W. "Jack" Robinson and Ida Louise Faucett Robinson. In 1911, Robinson graduated from Warren High School as valedictorian of her class. She attended the University of Arkansas (UA) in Fayetteville (Washington County) for the 1911–12 school year. Crawford began her career in 1916 as a stenographer at the Gaughan law firm in Camden. In 1927, only ten years after women were first allowed to practice law in Arkansas, she took the bar exam and passed. She excelled in abstract examination and title work during the southern Arkansas oil boom of the 1920s through the 1950s.

The night she disappeared, her husband, Clyde, had gone to a movie. When he returned home at about 11:00 p.m., all the lights were on inside and outside the house, his wife's car was in the driveway where she always left it, the television was on in the living room, her purse was on a chair with $142 cash in it, and her guard dog was undisturbed. At 2:00 a.m., after checking nearby cafes and friends' homes, he drove to the police station and reported her missing. The next day, the police and concerned citizens began an extensive search for her. Two weeks

after her disappearance, the local newspaper, the *Camden News*, reported that, according to Police Chief G. B. Cole, the investigation was "stalemated" and quoted Ouachita County sheriff Grover Linebarier as saying, "We have not turned up a single clue." In 1969, the Probate Court of Ouachita County legally established Crawford's death, stating in part: "It is the finding of the Court that Maud R. Crawford is deceased and has been dead since March 2, 1957, as a result of foul play perpetrated by person or persons unknown."

LAWYER MAUD CRAWFORD DISAPPEARED IN 1957—

THE CASE REMAINS A *MYSTERY*.

In 1986, twenty-nine years after Maud Crawford's disappearance, an eighteen-article investigative series by Beth Brickell was published on the front page of the *Arkansas Gazette*. The series implicated a deceased Arkansas State Police commissioner, Henry Myar "Mike" Berg, in the case. Berg, a Camden multimillionaire businessman, was appointed to the Arkansas State Police Commission in 1955 by Governor Orval E. Faubus. Berg served as a commissioner for twenty-one years until his death in 1975.

The series revealed sensational new information from Odis A. Henley, the original State Police detective on the case. Henley was quoted as saying that he was assigned to the case the day after Crawford disappeared. According to Henley, he reported to the captain of the State Police Criminal Investigation Division, Alan R. Templeton, that all of his findings pointed to State Police Commissioner Mike Berg having had Crawford murdered. However, Henley was told, "There's too much money involved," and he was taken off the case and told to leave his reports at the headquarters. The next time Henley went to Little Rock, all of his files had disappeared.

The *Gazette* series also revealed for the first time a motive for the murder of Crawford. The motive involved two fraudulent deeds that the reporter located in the Hempstead County Courthouse. The first deed transferred extensive timber assets belonging to Berg's aunt—Rose Newman Berg, an elderly woman declared incompetent in 1955 by the Ouachita County Court—to a timberman, Hugh Moseley, who worked for Berg. On the same day, a second deed transferred the same assets from Moseley to Berg. The newspaper series quoted former state attorney general Jim Guy Tucker as saying, "If I wanted to prove that Mike Berg defrauded Rose Berg, these deeds would be powerful evidence."

According to Henley, one or two months before Crawford disappeared, she went to Berg's office and angrily accused him of stealing timber from Rose Berg's estate. Crawford was Rose Berg's attorney and had been appointed her personal guardian by the court when Rose was declared incompetent. At an earlier time, Crawford had drawn up a will for Rose leaving her estate, valued in excess of $20 million, to three out-of-state nieces on Rose's side of the family: Jeannette Newman Simpson, Marian Newman Peltason, and Lucille Newman Glazer. Mike Berg was not named in the will.

According to the nieces, shortly before Crawford disappeared, she told them she "had the goods" on Mike Berg and that, upon her retirement, she intended to bring a lawsuit against him that would expose a pattern of fraudulent deeds designed to thwart Rose Berg's will. In addition to the timber deeds, earlier deeds had been discovered at the Ouachita County Courthouse transferring assets over a period of years from Rose Berg to Mike Berg. One deed, eight pages in length with a shaky Rose Berg signature, conveyed to Mike Berg 21,211 acres of timberland in fifteen counties, as well as sixty-two city properties and an estimated 150 producing oil royalties.

When Crawford disappeared, Rose Berg's will disappeared. Mike Berg succeeded in getting all of Rose Berg's estate. In a settlement one year after the disappearance, Berg granted $187,000 to each of Rose Berg's three nieces in exchange for a relinquishment of all claims to their aunt's estate.

As a result of allegations in the investigative series, the twenty-nine-year-old case was reopened by the southern Arkansas prosecuting attorney, Bill McLean, based in El Dorado. McLean obtained a subpoena to interview Mike Berg's bodyguard, Jack Dorris, whom Henley believed was involved with Berg in Crawford's demise. Dorris was dying of cancer at the time. When McLean arrived at the Dorris home for the interview, Dorris was surrounded by family members and the current Ouachita County sheriff, Jack Dews, a cousin of another Mike Berg employee who was angry that McLean was operating in his county without his cooperation. According to McLean, Dorris was "groggy and couldn't talk." Dorris died seven hours later.

Beth Brickell
Luminous Films Inc.

Bill Doolin
(1858–1896)

William (Bill) Doolin was an Arkansas-born outlaw who rode with the infamous Dalton outlaws in the Oklahoma Territory and formed his own outlaw bunch, which operated in the Oklahoma Territory from October 1892 until Doolin died on August 25, 1896.

Though his exact date of birth is unknown, Bill Doolin's tombstone states that he was born in 1858. He was born on a homestead near Big Piney River approximately thirty-five miles northeast of Clarksville (Johnson County). He was the son of sharecroppers Artemina and Michael Doolin and worked on his family's farm until his twenty-third birthday.

In 1881, Doolin left Arkansas for the Indian Territory (which became the Oklahoma Territory in 1890) and found employment as a cowboy on the ranch of Oscar D. Halsell in what was then called Logan, Oklahoma. After some restless drifting and trouble with the law, Doolin joined the infamous Dalton gang in 1891. Led by Robert (Bob) Dalton, with his brothers Gratton (Grat) and Emmett, the Daltons were labeled the "most cold-blooded robbers in the West." The Daltons came from a family of fifteen children, though only Bob, Grat, and Emmett Dalton turned to a life of crime.

Bill Doolin was reported to be riding with the Dalton gang when they robbed several trains and depots in the Oklahoma Territory from May 1891 through July 14, 1892. Doolin decided to forego the gang's ill-fated and final double bank robbery at Coffeyville, Kansas, on October 5, 1892, where only Emmett Dalton survived the legendary shootout in the streets.

ARKANSAN **BILL DOOLIN** RODE WITH THE DALTON GANG.

MARSHAL **HECK THOMAS'S** POSSE SHOT HIM FULL OF HOLES.

After the Coffeyville fiasco, Doolin organized his own gang and, with an assortment of misfits, commenced to terrorize southern Kansas and the Oklahoma Territory, robbing banks, trains, and stagecoaches over a four-year period. Nearly all these men met violent deaths, but not before the gang amassed a purported $165,000.

On July 1, 1893, Evett Dumas Nix, a Guthrie, Oklahoma, businessman, was appointed U. S. marshal under the jurisdiction of Judge Isaac Parker, the "Hanging Judge." Nix quickly assembled an impressive group of over 100 field deputies, including Heck Thomas, Chris Madsen, and Bill Tilghman, known collectively as the "Three Guardsmen."

Late in August, Nix was informed that the Doolin gang was in Ingalls, Oklahoma, and he dispatched Deputy Marshal John Hixson and a posse of thirteen to the town. It was in Ingalls that Doolin met and married Edith Ellsworth, the daughter of a part-time minister and purported town official. The Ingalls raid has been considered by many western historians as the most deadly gun battle between outlaws and U.S. marshals in the history of the Southwest. Six men in the posse were wounded or killed on the streets during the raid, but Doolin and several others escaped.

Elevated due to his intelligence and successes, Bill Tilghman was assigned as a U. S. marshal. He learned that Doolin had fled to Eureka Springs (Carroll County) to nurse his wounds and take the healing powers of the baths. On January 15, 1896, Tilghman arrested Doolin in the Eureka Springs Bathhouse. Doolin was indicted in Stillwater, Oklahoma, for murder in connection with the Ingalls shootout. The U.S. District Attorney offered the outlaw fifty years in prison in exchange for a plea of guilty, but Doolin entered a plea of "not guilty," telling a surprised Tilghman later that fifty years was too long to stay in prison.

On the night of July 5, 1896, before his trial, Doolin and a number of fellow inmates escaped from the Guthrie Federal Prison. Within an hour of the massive jail escape, Marshal Heck Thomas formed a posse and rode after the escapees but found none. Doolin made his way over the Cimarron Brakes toward Lawson, Oklahoma (now called Quay in Payne County), where his wife and son were staying with her father on his farm nearby.

Thomas received information from a local blacksmith that Doolin was at his father-in-law's homestead. On the night of August 25, 1896, Thomas and nine deputies went to the farm and hid near the house. When Doolin emerged from the barn, Thomas shouted for the outlaw to halt, but Doolin shot at the marshal instead. The posse, in turn, shot and killed Doolin. He is buried in Guthrie, Oklahoma.

Russell E. Bearden
White Hall, Arkansas

This entry, originally published in *Arkansas Biography: A Collection of Notable Lives*, appears here in an altered form. *Arkansas Biography* is available from the University of Arkansas Press.

Connie Franklin
(Alleged Murder of)

The alleged murder of Connie Franklin in 1929 scandalized the state and served to reinforce negative stereotypes about Arkansas in the national mass media. The uproar surrounding the apparent murder only increased with the reappearance of the "victim," alive and well, shortly before the trial of his accused murderers.

In January 1929, Connie Franklin wandered into the community of St. James (Stone County), where he found work cutting timber and as a farm hand. He claimed to be twenty-two years old, rather than his actual age of thirty-two. He reportedly courted the town's girls, particularly sixteen-year-old Tillar (or Tiller) Ruminer. According to later testimony by Ruminer, on March 9, 1929, she and Franklin were going to Justice of the Peace Finis Ford's office to obtain a marriage license. The two were attacked by a gang of men, identified by Ruminer as Hubert Hester, Herman Greenway, Joe White, and Bill C. "Straight Eye" Younger. Hester and Greenway were alleged to have taken Ruminer into the woods and raped her, while Franklin was reportedly tortured, mutilated, and murdered.

A spring 1929 grand jury did not grant an indictment due to the fact that there was no body and no evidence that a crime had occurred other than hearsay from Bertha Burns, who, according to her own account, found the bloody hat belonging to Franklin and subsequently went to Ruminer, demanding to know what had happened and

78

convincing her to report the attack to the authorities. Burns had recently secured a guilty verdict in May 1929 against Alex Fulks, Baxter Canard, and Ross Younger for the flogging she and her husband, Haywood, had suffered at the hands of the three men the previous year.

The sheriff thought he had evidence to continue the investigation into the attack, probing neighbors around the areas of Dry Creek and Cajun Creek over the next several months. Ten days prior to the convening of the fall grand jury, in November 1929, Burns led the sheriff and some deputies to a place in the woods where they found an assortment of charred bones in a pile of ashes. The bones were sent to the state crime lab, and the grand jury, with this new evidence, issued five indictments, adding Alex Fulks to the list, as he was widely considered the ringleader of the group. The five men were soon arrested and held in separate jails for their own protection.

Brothers Hugh Williamson, the prosecuting attorney, and Ben Williamson, the defense attorney, were pitted against each other in front of Judge Marcus Bone, with the trial set for December 16, 1929. (Complicating matters, the Williamson brothers both worked in the firm of their father, president of the Arkansas Bar Association.) As the attorneys prepared their cases, the accused men held to their stories that they had not seen Franklin on said date and that Franklin had wandered away from the community just as he had wandered in. Deputy O. L. Massey from Morrilton (Conway County) was provided information on December 3, 1929, from Elmer Wingo that Franklin had spent the night at the Wingo home after the alleged murder. Many newspapers—including the *Arkansas Gazette*, the *Arkansas Democrat*, and the *Commercial Appeal* of Memphis—ran this information along with a photo of Franklin. On December 7, 1929, Franklin was found by F. K. Marks, a cotton buyer, working on the farm of Murray Bryant near Humphrey (Arkansas County), who convinced Franklin to come to Mountain View (Stone County).

Prosecutor Hugh Williamson warned that "somebody had lied and somebody was going to jail," stating that there would be a sweeping inquiry into the matter once Franklin's identity was confirmed. It became known that the man claiming to be Franklin had been drafted into the military in 1926, serving five days before entering the Arkansas State Hospital, from which he escaped in February 1927. He was married and had at least three children, whom he had abandoned.

Judge Bone went ahead with the trial while the November grand jury heard evidence to establish the true identify of the man who claimed to be Franklin. During the trial, Ruminer admitted that she had not seen anyone killed or burned, only beaten unconscious. The identify of Franklin was established by a number of people who knew him before and after the alleged date of the murder and by a comparison of handwriting, fingerprints, and dental and medical records from the Arkansas State Hospital. However, Ruminer continued to deny that the man in the courtroom was the same man she had known before March 9. The jury deadlocked and the defendants were found not guilty.

Some sources explain the alleged murder case as a revenge plot by Bertha Burns against Fulks and the others, who were the self-appointed moral enforcers of the rural area. *Time* magazine covered the trial, as did newspapers throughout the nation. The little town of Mountain View was inundated with reporters, spectators, and gawkers by the thousands, creating a circus-like atmosphere during the week leading up to the trial and during the trial itself. Heavy rains made the roads almost impassable. On December 11, 1929, Governor Harvey Parnell issued a public denouncement of the "yellow" journalism being practiced that branded the people of northern Arkansas as peons and idiots. The cost of the trial was more than $8,000, breaking the already financially burdened county. It was rumored that Judge Bone, upon the not-guilty finding of the jury, ordered that all records of the trial, other than those required by the court, be destroyed so as to end the chain of gossip. However, the story lives on in local folklore.

Freda Cruse Phillips
Mountain View, Arkansas

Hot Springs Shootout

The Hot Springs Shootout, also known as the Hot Springs Gunfight or the Gunfight at Hot Springs, occurred on March 16, 1899. Sparked by a dispute over which agency would control gambling in Hot Springs (Garland County), this shootout between the Hot Springs Police Department and the Garland County Sheriff's Office left five men dead.

The shootout represented a continuation in the battle for control of gambling in Hot Springs and was preceded by the Flynn-Doran blood feud that lasted from 1884 until 1888. Frank Flynn controlled gambling in Hot Springs until former Confederate major Alexander Doran began opening gambling houses there in 1884. The first blood was drawn when Flynn challenged Doran to a duel. Flynn was shot once in the chest but survived. Subsequently, the Flynn and Doran factions clashed, with murders and injuries on both sides. Finally, Doran was killed in 1888, ending the feud. Flynn remained in business and continued using the Hot Springs Police Department to collect debts owed to him, or to force competition to leave town.

By the mid-1890s, Mayor William L. Gordon had reappointed Thomas C. Toler, who had been chief of police for the city of Hot Springs during the Flynn-Doran feud. Hot Springs police chief Toler and Garland County sheriff Bob Williams openly clashed over which law enforcement agency would control illegal gambling activities in Hot Springs and the illegal profits, in the form of graft and kickbacks, associated with the gambling. When Mayor Gordon announced a crackdown on illegal gambling, Chief Toler openly defied the mayor, while Sheriff Williams publicly supported the crackdown even as he plotted to continue the kickbacks and illegal gambling.

On the morning of March 16, 1899, mayoral candidate C. W. Fry, Toler, and other members of Toler's faction held a meeting. Following the meeting, a list of all those present was given to Williams, who was enraged by the secret meeting.

At approximately 1:30 p.m., Sheriff Williams and part-time deputy Dave Young encountered Hot Springs police sergeant Tom Goslee on Central Avenue in downtown Hot Springs. Williams began to abuse Sergeant Goslee verbally, and Goslee pulled a derringer on Williams, threatening to shoot him. Williams lifted his coattails to show Goslee that he was not armed. During this time, Johnny Williams (Sheriff Williams's son and part-time sheriff's deputy) strolled up and handed his father one of two .44 caliber revolvers he had with him. Both Sheriff Williams and his son opened fire on Goslee, who returned fire with his derringer as he fled the scene. No one was injured.

Around 5:00 p.m. on the same day, the two factions held a meeting at Lemp's Beer Depot. Captain Haley and Sergeant Goslee of the Hot Springs Police Department met with Johnny Williams, Coffee Williams (Sheriff Williams's brother), and Deputy Sheriff Ed Spear. Captain Haley's brother-in-law, Louis Hinkle, was tending bar.

When Hinkle grabbed Spear around the neck and sliced his throat with a knife, Spear wrestled free and pulled his service revolver, shooting Hinkle in the throat. Coffee Williams then pulled a pistol and shot Hinkle one time in the chest. Johnny Williams quickly joined the deadly encounter, pulling his gun and shooting Goslee twice. Goslee returned fire, shooting Johnny Williams in the head. Coffee Williams then shot Goslee a third time, killing him.

Police Chief Toler, having arrived at the meeting at about the same time that Captain Haley fled the scene, was instantly fired upon by Coffee Williams and Spear. Toler returned fire, wounding Spear. As Toler tried to get behind cover, Coffee Williams shot Toler once in the head as Spear shot Toler once in the chest. He died instantly.

Sheriff Williams arrived at the scene just prior to Hot Springs

THE **HOT SPRINGS** SHOOTOUT WASN'T COPS AND ROBBERS.

IT WAS POLICE VS. THE SHERIFF'S OFFICE.

police detective Jim Hart's arrival. Sheriff Williams, finding his son Johnny dying, walked over to Hart and said, "Here's another of those sons of bitches," and then shot Hart point blank in the face. Deputy Will Watt (nephew to Sheriff Williams), having also arrived on the scene, then leaned over the sheriff and fired two more bullets into Hart's dead body.

With the shootout finally at an end, Toler, Goslee, Hart, and Hinkle lay dead, and Johnny Williams died around 9:00 p.m. Bystander Alan Carter had been wounded by a stray bullet, and Spear was badly hurt but would survive.

The following day, Bob Williams, Ed Spear, Will Watt, and Coffee Williams were charged with murder. All four were arrested but were released on bail. Eventually, Spear and Coffee Williams were found not guilty by reason of self defense. The trials of Bob Williams and Will Watt ended in hung juries due to conflicting testimonies from witnesses.

Although gambling kingpin Frank Flynn was run out of Hot Springs by a citizens' commission formed by Mayor Gordon, illegal gambling in Hot Springs continued well into the twentieth century, as did corruption in both the Garland County Sheriff's Office and the Hot Springs Police Department.

Larry LeMasters
LeMasters' Antique News Service

Island 37

Island 37 is a stretch of land that is in the legal possession of the State of Tennessee but is physically joined to Arkansas. Because competing claims of jurisdiction left it in something of a legal void, Island 37 became, in the early twentieth century, an outpost for bootleggers and other criminals. Police action taken against those criminals resulted in one of the many U.S. Supreme Court cases regarding ongoing boundary disputes between Arkansas and Tennessee.

The Mississippi River is a dynamic waterway, often cutting new channels and thus either forming islands or causing former islands to merge with the eastern or western banks. The legal principle of avulsion holds that land cut off by the river from one state and joined to another due to the changing flow of the river does not become the property of the new state to which it is joined. On March 7, 1876, the river cut a path through a section of Tennessee land known as Devil's Elbow; subsequently, the channel that previously went around the land partially dried up, leaving the land, for all practical purposes, a part of Arkansas. Decades of boundary disputes between the two states followed with regard to Devil's Elbow, designated Island 37 by the U.S. government.

The nebulous legal status of the "island" made it the perfect refuge for criminals. After all, they could claim to be occupying Tennessee land and thus not under Arkansas jurisdiction. For lawmen from Tipton County, Tennessee, to mount an expedition across the river was expensive, and those on the island were frequently tipped off in advance about raids from that quarter. In 1911, "blind tigers," places that sold bootleg whiskey, appeared on the island. The outlaws were reportedly led by Andy Crum, who owned more than 400 acres of land on the island.

Believing that he had jurisdiction over the area, Sheriff Sam Mauldin of Arkansas's Mississippi County led a raid on Island 37 on the morning of July 31, 1915, taking with him a detachment of the state militia. The sheriff was killed leading a charge against an establishment owned by Crum, who was captured later that day while hiding in a cotton field. Outraged Arkansas citizens reportedly burned down all criminal establishments upon hearing of Mauldin's death.

The following day, Tipton County, Tennessee, authorities demanded that Mississippi County turn over its prisoners to Tennessee, but they were refused. Crum and others swiftly hired lawyers who planned to argue that the prisoners should rightly be tried for their crimes in Tennessee. However, this did Crum little good, as on August 12, a group of armed men broke into the jail in Osceola (Mississippi County) and shot him to death;

an inquest the next day failed to hold anyone responsible for the murder, and no one was ever arrested. Soon, rumors spread that Tennesseans were intent upon crossing the river and liberating the remaining prisoners by force, and Governor George Washington Hays called out the Arkansas National Guard to prevent that from happening. No such force from Tennessee appeared, and the prisoners were tried and convicted in an Arkansas court.

However, the swift dispatching of these bootleggers and other criminals did not halt the legal efforts between Arkansas and Tennessee over their boundary. The battle between the two states went all the way to the U.S. Supreme Court, which, on March 4, 1918, ruled that the boundary "should now be located according to the middle of that channel as it was at the time the current ceased to flow therein as a result of the avulsion of 1876," leaving Island 37 in the hands of the State of Tennessee. Island 37 is today covered in cotton and soybean fields, with only a handful of small farm houses upon the land, though a few roads leading into Arkansas service the area.

Guy Lancaster
Encyclopedia of Arkansas History & Culture

Maxine Jones (1915–1997)

Maxine Temple Jones was a Hot Springs (Garland County) businesswoman during the period from 1945 to the early 1970s. A well-known madam with numerous political connections, she managed a lucrative brothel operation that catered to politicians, businessmen, and mobsters. She documented her life in an autobiography published in 1983 titled *Maxine "Call Me Madam": The Life and Times of a Hot Springs Madam*.

Dora Maxine Temple was born on June 15, 1915, in Johnsville (Bradley County) to David F. Temple and Maude Orr Temple. She had five brothers and one sister. Her father was a farmer and logging contractor. When referring to her early youth, Temple described herself as a tomboy who preferred spending time with her father in the fields, dressing in overalls, and learning how to shoot a rifle and hunt. However, by the time she turned fifteen, she had developed a taste for "fancy, beautiful things" and had begun to yearn for independence.

Upon graduation from high school, Temple moved to Paris, Texas. It was there, while working in a department store, that a co-worker introduced her to prostitution as a way to expand her meager earnings. During this period, Temple became acquainted with Nell Raborn, madam of a large brothel in Texarkana, Texas. The two women developed an immediate rapport, with Temple eventually relocating to Texarkana to work for Raborn.

During her association with Raborn's business, Temple showed an aptitude for managing all aspects of the operation and gained a reputation for strong nerves and solid business sense. However, after the United States' entry into World War II, the government closed the red-light district of Texarkana. Caught up in the fever of war and patriotism, Temple quickly married a young soldier named Eugene Harris, who was soon sent overseas. In 1943, Temple decided to join the Women's Army Auxiliary Corps, hoping to be sent overseas as well. Instead, she was stationed for two years at Andrews Air Force Base in Washington DC. When her enlistment period ended, she returned to Arkansas, where she was employed as a security guard at the Camden (Ouachita County) arsenal. After the war ended, she eventually returned to her former employment at Raborn's. When her husband returned, she confessed that she was a "rackets" woman and had no desire for marriage or children. Although he hoped that she would change her mind, the couple eventually divorced.

Temple continued working at Raborn's until 1948, when a short visit to Hot Springs changed the direction of her life once again. Attracted to the city, she quickly found a job in a local house of prostitution on Prospect Street. By 1950, she had amassed enough money to buy out the proprietress and establish the business as her own.

According to her autobiography, Temple established political connections in Hot Springs that would best serve her interests, thus allowing her operation to flourish. She was able to expand her business, most notably with the purchase of a large home on Palm Street, which became known as "The Mansion." She entertained her "high-classed" clientele, including local businessmen, doctors, top state officials, congressmen, and prominent mobsters who were expanding an illegal gambling empire in the city. However, Temple soon clashed with the mob over its attempts to control her operation. She married Worth Gregory, a drug addict with a criminal background, who drained her finances and forced her to defend herself against narcotics charges (for which she was acquitted). As a result, she was eventually forced out of business, with Gregory returning to prison, where he died in 1963.

Temple reestablished her operations and was soon back in business, but she continued to be harassed by the mob and a coalition of law enforcement agents under its influence. In 1963, she was arrested and sentenced to two years in Cummins Prison, which housed female prisoners from 1951 to 1976.

After her release in 1965, Temple returned to Hot Springs. (She later received a full pardon from Governor Winthrop Rockefeller after disclosing information concerning illegal gambling operations in Hot Springs.) With a loan from a friend, she purchased the Central Avenue Hotel and began operations. Feeling that she needed protection, she partnered with Edward Jones, a career criminal whom she married in 1968. Jones's criminal lifestyle proved an emotional and financial drain. Shortly after Jones's death in 1971, she closed her remaining businesses and relocated to Little Rock (Pulaski County) for a few years before retiring in Hot Springs.

Seeking "peace of mind" and to "set the record straight" concerning corruption and politics in Hot Springs, she published her autobiography, under the name Maxine Jones, in 1983, documenting her life as well as the political system she encountered as a businesswoman in Hot Springs.

Jones died at Wagnon Place Nursing Home in Warren (Bradley County) on April 15, 1997, and is buried in

Palestine Cemetery. One of her former business locations, the Central Avenue Hotel, was renovated in 1989 and reopened in 1991 as Maxine's Coffee House and Puzzle Bar.

Toney Butler Schlesinger
Granite Bay, California

Owney Madden
(1891–1965)

Owen Vincent "Owney" Madden was a gangster and underworld boss in New York City in the 1920s who retired to Hot Springs (Garland County) in the 1930s. Though his role in Arkansas politics and history will forever remain enigmatic, he was a powerful figure (from about 1935 until his death) during the heyday of illegal gambling in Hot Springs and an emblem of the bad old days of machine politics.

Owney Madden was born on December 18, 1891, in Leeds, England, to Irish parents, Francis and Mary Madden. He spent his early childhood in Wigan and Liverpool, where Francis worked in textile mill sweatshops until his death in 1902. Mary then took her family, including Madden and perhaps two siblings, to New York. They settled in a crime-ridden Manhattan district along Tenth Avenue known as Hell's Kitchen. She worked as a scrubwoman, while Madden sporadically attended St. Michael's Parochial School on West 33rd Street.

According to his own account, Madden committed his first crime at age fourteen, clubbing a man and stealing $500. He rose to lead the area's most violent gang, the Gophers. In 1911, Madden married and briefly lived with Dorothy Rogers, with whom he had a daughter named Margaret, his only known child. A professional killer and gunman, he was wounded many times. In 1915, he was sentenced to Sing-Sing Prison in Ossining, New York, for manslaughter, and he was paroled in early 1923. By then, the Eighteenth Amendment, which marked the beginning of the Prohibition Era, had made the manufacture, transportation, and sale of intoxicating liquor illegal. During Prohibition, numerous underground bars and saloons appeared, and the market for bootleg alcohol boomed.

Now in his element, Madden made fast profits in bootlegging, nightclubs, and show business. Among other enterprises, he

turned a failing Harlem night spot at Lenox Avenue and 142nd Street into the Cotton Club, the fabled showcase for black musical talent performing for white patrons in the Jazz Age. Madden also bankrolled the Hollywood careers of George Raft and Mae West, both of whom had lived in Hell's Kitchen. He was Mae

West's boyfriend and protector: "Sweet, but oh so vicious" was how she described him in later years.

By the late 1920s, Madden was a millionaire, chief of an underworld empire that included real estate, boxing, gambling, bootlegging, breweries, and entertainment. With Frank Costello, Charles "Lucky" Luciano, and other mob figures, he organized a "crime commission," or syndicate, whose objective was high profits, a businesslike operating style, and a minimum of bad publicity.

By 1930, New York governor Franklin D. Roosevelt was seeking a presidential nomination; a crackdown on the blatant corruption of New York City was essential to his plan. On July 7, 1932, Madden was sent back to Sing-Sing for parole violations. In 1933, he was released, and Prohibition was repealed late that year.

In his forties and in chronic ill health because of his old bullet wounds, Madden was persona non grata in the New York underworld. Looking for a new life, he began visiting Hot Springs, which had for years been a haven for gambling, prostitution, and bootlegging. The city was also a peaceful little spa, known for its beauty and its health-giving hot spring waters. Perhaps contemplating a settled life as an exiled but still active mobster, Madden began romancing a Hot Springs gift-shop clerk, Agnes Demby, the daughter of the local postmaster. On November 26, 1935, when she was thirty-four and he was in his mid-forties, they married and moved into a modest house on West Grand Avenue. Contrary to myth, Agnes was not a small-town ingénue but was well acquainted with her husband's racketeer friends, his prison record, and his way of life.

Under what terms Madden left New York will never be known; high-placed New York politicians and criminals may have struck the deal, possibly with Frank Costello as broker or Lucky Luciano, who may have commissioned Madden to oversee mob operations in Hot Springs. Confined to Arkansas, Madden played a public role as a small-town gentleman, but it is reasonable to think that he played an active part in illegal activities in the city. Hot Springs mayor Leo P. McLaughlin and Municipal Judge Vern Ledgerwood ran their own syndicate to manage gambling and prostitution, and while they stoutly denied that Madden had any hand in things or took any rake-offs, it was common knowledge that Madden furnished the wire service that brought racing results to bookmakers. It seems unlikely that he and his mob associates provided this valuable service for free. Madden stayed underground until around 1940 but eventually came to own a controlling interest in the Southern Club, a lucrative gaming establishment on Central Avenue, as well as other gambling operations. A who's who of gangland chiefs—Costello, Luciano, Meyer Lansky, and Joe Adonis—visited Madden regularly and openly.

In 1946, the McLaughlin machine was voted out, but local rackets, after a few setbacks, continued to flourish, and Madden grew more visible and more powerful. Under constant FBI surveillance, Madden continued as godfather to local charities and became a familiar figure in his trademark cap and scarf. In 1961, after a federal investigation concluded that Hot Springs was the site of the largest illegal gambling operation in the United States, Madden was summoned before the senate Committee on Organized Crime under Arkansas senator John McClellan ("the rackets committee"), where he repeatedly invoked the Fifth Amendment.

In 1964, the state government took its first decisive steps to shut down illegal operations in Hot Springs. A year later, on April 24, 1965, Madden died of emphysema and was buried in Greenwood Cemetery.

Shirley Tomkievicz
New York City, New York

This entry, originally published in *Arkansas Biography: A Collection of Notable Lives*, appears here in an altered form. *Arkansas Biography* is available from the University of Arkansas Press.

Olyphant Train Robbery

THE OLYPHANT TRAIN ROBBERY
WAS THE LAST IN ARKANSAS.

During the nineteenth century, travelers on steam locomotives were at risk for train robberies. In Arkansas, one particularly high-profile train robbery happened in the small town of Olyphant (Jackson County) in 1893. What followed was a sensationalized manhunt and the execution of three bandits involved in the incident.

On November 3, 1893, the seven-car Train No. 51 of the St. Louis, Iron Mountain and Southern Railway pulled off to a side track so that the Cannonball Express, a much faster train, could pass. It was about 10:00 p.m. on a cold and rainy night; the train had left Poplar Bluff, Missouri, at noon that day and was headed to Little Rock (Pulaski County). Many of the 300 passengers were wealthy tourists who were coming back from the World's Columbian Exposition in Chicago, Illinois, which had closed on October 30. Its stop was made in the small town of Olyphant, about seven miles south of Newport (Jackson County). The Irish-born conductor, William P. McNally, had been making the Poplar Bluff to Little Rock trip since the early 1880s, and his outgoing personality made him very popular on the route. At the time of the robbery, he was planning to be retired by the end of the month.

While No. 51 was stalled, a group of bandits took the opportunity to rob it. Gunshots rang out, and the baggage attendant rushed to McNally, warning of a holdup. McNally immediately went through the passenger cars, advising everyone to hide their valuables. He also borrowed a gun from a passenger named Charles Lamb and retreated to the front of the train. The bandits eventually made their way to the front of the train, stopping to rob the passengers; the net value of what they stole reached $6,000. When they got to the front of the train, McNally fired at them, and one of the men shot him with a rifle. After a twenty-minute hold-up, the bandits made their getaway, and, once they were gone, the train made it to Little Rock. By that time, however, McNally was dead from his gunshot wounds.

In the following days, sheriffs from ten counties pulled together posses to search for the bandits, for whom a large reward was offered. The St. Louis, Iron Mountain and Southern Railway had published an offer of a $300 reward, and both the Pacific Express company and Governor William Fishback had also promised rewards, though the amount was not specified. Because McNally was such a beloved character in the railroad business, thousands attended his funeral, and a statewide fervor to find the perpetrators took hold. The ensuing manhunt created a media sensation; many "suspicious" characters were arrested and harassed all over Arkansas, and the *Arkansas Gazette*'s coverage of the incident filled the entire front page. There were frequent reports of near-captures and exciting gunfights with suspects as the sheriffs and their posses combed the hills for the robber gang.

By December 1893, four major suspects had been rounded up: Tom Brady, Jim Wyrick, Albert Mansker, and George Padgett. Rather than leave the state or adopt aliases, all of them had remained within a fairly close range of the scene of the crime. The first three were tried in January 1894; all were convicted of first-degree murder for the death of McNally and were sentenced to execution by hanging. Because of his service as a witness, Padgett was not given the death penalty.

During the trial, the robbers' plan was exposed by Padgett, who was the main witness against the other men. The four had met in Indian Territory (present-day Oklahoma) while peddling whiskey, and it was Padgett and Brady's idea to rob a train. Rendezvousing at a railway station near Searcy (White County), they made plans to rob the Cannonball Express, which had cash and gold from the Federal Reserve Bank, in what they convinced each other was a get-rich-quick scheme. Only Mansker had a history of train robbing. Padgett took a ride on No. 51 and learned that it stopped in Olyphant, both to drop off mail and to allow another scheduled train to pass. Hearing that "a bunch of rich folks from Chicago" would be riding on it, the prospective thieves changed their plans, and No. 51 became the target. For a few days before the robbery, they had ridden their horses up and down the track, reconnoitering, until the night of the robbery finally came. Beforehand, they all had drunk heavily to calm their nerves.

Brady, Wyrick, and Mansker were hanged on April 6, 1894, outside of the city jail in Newport. Before the hanging took place, they were allowed to address the crowd, and all three claimed innocence for the murder. The incident in Olyphant proved to be the final train robbery to take place in Arkansas.

Bernard Reed
Little Rock, Arkansas

Officials check nooses prior to hanging the men who perpetrated the Olyphant Train Robbery. Courtesy of Jacksonport State Park

Isaac Parker
(1838–1896)

Isaac Charles Parker served as federal judge for the Federal Court of the Western District of Arkansas in Fort Smith (Sebastian County). He tried 13,490 cases, with 9,454 of them resulting in guilty pleas or convictions. His court was unique in the fact that he had jurisdiction over all of Indian Territory, covering over 74,000 square miles. He sentenced 160 people to death, including four women. Of those sentenced to death under Parker, seventy-nine men were executed on the gallows.

Born on October 15, 1838, in Barnesville, Ohio, Isaac Parker was the youngest son of Joseph and Jane Parker. Joseph was a farmer. Parker attended Breeze Hill Primary School when he was not needed on the farm. Once he completed his primary education, he attended Barnesville Classical Institute, a private school. Parker taught in a country primary school to pay for his higher education.

At seventeen, Parker decided to study law. He became an apprentice, working under a Barnesville lawyer, and studied on his own, passing the bar in 1859. He began his legal career with his uncle, D. E. Shannon, in St. Joseph, Missouri, at the Shannon and Branch law firm, and by 1861, he was operating on his own. It was during this time that he met Mary O'Toole, whom he married on December 12, 1861. He won election as the city attorney on the Democratic ticket in April 1861, but he had been in office only a few days when the Civil War broke out, causing him to re-evaluate his political beliefs. He then enlisted in the Sixty-first Missouri Emergency Regiment, a home guard unit for the Union forces.

Parker ran for county prosecutor of the Ninth Missouri Judicial District on the Republican ticket, making his break from the Democratic Party official. He also served as a member of the Electoral College (he cast his vote for Abraham Lincoln) in the

election of 1864. He served two terms in the U.S. Congress, being elected in 1870 and 1872. While in Congress, he assisted veterans of his district in securing pensions, lobbied for construction of a new federal building in St. Joseph, sponsored legislation that would have allowed women the right to vote and hold public office in U.S. territories, and also sponsored legislation that would have organized the Indian Territory under a formal territorial government. During his second term, his speeches supporting the Bureau of Indian Affairs received national attention, and he put most of his effort into Indian policy and the fair treatment of the tribes that were living in the Indian Territory. After his second term in Congress, he began to seek a presidential appointment as judge of the Western District of Arkansas in Fort Smith.

On March 18, 1875, President Ulysses S. Grant appointed him to the position.

Parker arrived in Fort Smith on May 4, 1875, and held court for the first time on May 10, 1875. During his first term, he found eight men guilty of murder. Six of them were hanged on September 3, 1875, on the gallows at Fort Smith. Parker's court was supposed to hold four terms each year—in February, May, August, and November—but the caseload for the court was so large that the four terms ran together. Parker held court six days a week, each day often lasting up to ten hours, in order to try as many cases as possible.

In 1883, Congress made cuts to jurisdiction areas. Jurisdiction over some portions of the Indian Territory was given to federal courts in Texas and Kansas, providing some relief to Parker's court. There was, however, a continuous stream of settlers into the Indian Territory, over which he still had jurisdiction, and the crime rate increased.

Over the years, Parker became very involved in the community of Fort Smith. At his urging, the government gave the majority of the 300-acre military reservation to the city in 1884 to fund the public school system. He also held many positions besides judge in the community, including serving as the first board president of St. John's Hospital (now known as Sparks Regional Medical Center), and he was active on the school board. His wife was also involved in many different social activities, and their sons, James and Charles, attended the public school their father had helped to establish.

There was more to Parker's position than sitting in a courtroom trying cases. He was occasionally called to testify in front of Congress or substitute for other federal judges in the area. He tried several civil cases during his time in Fort Smith as well.

On February 6, 1889, Congress took the circuit court authority from the federal court at Fort Smith and allowed the U.S. Supreme Court to begin reviewing all capital crimes. The latter went into effect on May 1, 1889, and had a very pronounced effect on Parker. Until this time, the president had been the only person with the power to commute sentences; however, now the Supreme Court could overturn cases as well. A month after the Supreme Court's review, Congress passed the Courts Act of 1889, which established a federal court system in the Indian Territory, again decreasing the size of Parker's jurisdiction. The Supreme Court began to reverse the capital crimes tried in Fort Smith, and two-thirds of the cases that were appealed were sent back to Fort Smith for a new trial.

Parker is often called the "Hanging Judge." At the time, capital offenses of rape and murder were punished by death. However, it was not for the judge to decide guilt. Determining guilt was left up to the jury. Parker actually had no say in whether a person was to be hanged; in an interview published on September 1, 1896, in the *St. Louis Republic*, Parker is quoted as saying, "I never hung a man. It is the law." He, in fact, was against capital punishment, adding, "I favor the abolition of capital punishment, too. Provided that there is a certainty of punishment, whatever that punishment may be. In the uncertainty of punishment following crime lies the weakness of our 'halting crime.'" His court did, however, sentence some of the most notorious outlaws to hang. Well-known outlaws such as Cherokee Bill, Colorado Bill, and the Rufus Buck Gang were sentenced to death and executed during Parker's tenure.

On September 1, 1896, another act went into effect, removing the last of Parker's Indian Territory jurisdiction. When the August 1896 term began, however, Parker was too ill to preside. Reporters interviewing Parker about the end of his jurisdiction over Indian Territory had to do so at his bedside. Parker died on November 17, 1896, due to numerous health problems, including degeneration of the heart and Bright's disease. He is buried in the Fort Smith National Cemetery, only blocks from where he once presided as judge. His courtroom is now the Fort Smith National Historic Site.

Maranda Leeper
Waldron, Arkansas

HERE LIES
PARLEY P. PRATT
AND THAT'S THAT

HE GOT ME.

SHOT —

AND STABBED —

BY THE ESTRANGED HUSBAND OF HIS TWELFTH WIFE.

Parley P. Pratt
(Murder of)

Parley Parker Pratt, an original member of the Quorum of the Twelve Apostles of the Church of Jesus Christ of Latter-day Saints (LDS), was murdered in Arkansas in 1857 and buried in the state, despite his wishes to be buried in Utah. The Van Buren (Crawford County) newspaper *Arkansas Intelligencer*, on May 15, 1857, deemed Pratt "a man of note among the Mormons." While another notable event involving Mormons in Arkansas—the massacre of Arkansas emigrants four months later at Mountain Meadows, Utah—was formerly linked to Pratt's murder in Arkansas, more recent inquiry suggests other circumstances may have ignited the violence at Mountain Meadows on September 11, 1857.

Pratt was one of the key figures in the early Church leadership. Pratt's writings, which include pamphlets, hymns, and an entertaining autobiography, helped define early Mormon theology, and his hymns are still widely sung in congregations. Born in Burlington, New York, in 1807, he preached to the Creek and Cherokee nations as a young missionary, as well as to congregations in Canada, England, California, and the Pacific, and he became the first Latter-day Saint missionary to serve in Chile.

Scarcely known in Arkansas during his lifetime, Pratt was murdered on May 13, 1857, in Crawford County by Hector McLean, the estranged husband of Eleanor McComb McLean, who had become Pratt's twelfth plural wife. The murder shocked the Latter-day Saint community and became front-page news throughout the nation. Eleanor McLean portrayed Pratt as a martyr who had rescued her from her alcoholic, abusive husband; however, national accounts, unfavorable to the Mormons' practice of polygamy (discontinued in 1890), reported that Pratt had seduced Eleanor away from her husband.

Pratt and Eleanor McLean had met three years earlier while Pratt was living in San Francisco, California, and presiding over the LDS Church's Pacific mission. Eleanor embraced Mormon principles and was baptized into the Church with her husband's consent. In 1855, following a domestic dispute, Hector McLean secretly sent their children from San Francisco to New Orleans, Louisiana, to live with their maternal grandparents, whereupon Eleanor determined to leave him. She then traveled to New Orleans to get her children.

Eleanor and Pratt had decided to meet at Fort Smith (Sebastian County) and travel back to Utah together. Hector McLean heard of their intended rendezvous and beat them to Arkansas, where he filed charges against them and got warrants for their arrests. Hector caught up with Eleanor and Pratt in Indian Territory (present-day Oklahoma) and again took the children away. Hours later, a state marshal arrested Eleanor on a charge of stealing children's clothing, while a military escort apprehended Pratt. They were first taken to Fort Gibson and then to Van Buren. There, Eleanor was brought before Judge John Ogden, who released her without further charges. Pratt, whose trial was postponed because of public outrage and general hostility, was kept overnight and secretly released early the next day. Hector McLean learned of Pratt's release and caught up with Pratt on the Zealey Wynn property in Fine Springs (Crawford County), some twelve miles northwest of Van Buren, where he shot and stabbed Pratt.

As he lay dying, Pratt requested that his remains be interred with his family in Utah. For many years, family and descendants attempted to locate and remove his remains from the Wynn Cemetery in Fine Springs—north of Alma (Crawford County)—

to the space reserved for him in the family plot in Salt Lake City, Utah. In 2008, the most sophisticated scientific tools available (including ground-penetrating radar) were used to ascertain the location of Pratt's remains. Despite evidence of a burial, no human remains were found.

Today, exiting I-540 east (now I-49) at the Rudy (Crawford County) exit and then turning left at the first road, visitors can find the Pratt grave site in the small Wynn Cemetery. The site is open to the public and is marked by a large granite monument upon which is engraved one of Pratt's most well-known hymns, "The Morning Breaks."

Greg Armstrong
University of Arkansas at Fort Smith

Monument to Parley Parker Pratt, near Rudy; 2008.
Photo by Mike Keckhaver

Prohibition

THERE GOES WHO-HIT-JOHN —

AGAIN!

ARKANSAS HAS HAD ALCOHOL ON THE RUN MANY TIMES.

Prohibition, the effort to limit or ban the sale and consumption of alcohol, has been prevalent since Arkansas's territorial period. The state has attempted to limit use of alcoholic beverages through legal efforts such as establishing "dry" counties, as well as through extra-legal measures such as destroying whiskey distilleries. Since Arkansas's statehood in 1836, prohibition has consistently been a political and public health issue.

As early as the 1760s, European settlers at Arkansas Post (Arkansas County) took steps to limit alcohol use by the Quapaw living in the area. When the area was under Spanish control, British traders successfully maneuvered to trade goods and spirits in Arkansas, plying the Quapaw with rum despite a Spanish law prohibiting the furnishing of alcohol to natives. The Spanish, in turn, often used alcohol as a diplomatic tool for settling disputes with Indians. By the early 1780s, Spanish-controlled Arkansas settled on heavily regulating the production and sale of alcohol, falling just short of outright prohibition.

Control of alcohol initially focused on consumption by Native Americans, but as Arkansas's population began to increase, interest in prohibition began to widen. In the early nineteenth century, as Native Americans began resettling in present-day Oklahoma in accordance with the Indian Removal Act of 1830, a commander at nearby Fort Smith (Sebastian County), Lieutenant Gabriel Rains, organized a sting operation to disrupt the widespread illegal alcohol trade with Indians.

In 1832, a grand jury was empanelled to assess the problem of alcohol in Arkansas Territory. The jury attempted to invoke an outdated Spanish law that prohibited alcohol production and sale, but it could not enforce the ordinance. The emerging Arkansas middle class grew alarmed by the frequent, alcohol-fueled unrest that seemed to surround taverns. There was also a developing sense that alcohol hindered the ability of workers and craftsman to perform their jobs adequately, which some business owners feared would result in lower profits. The rising chorus against alcohol coincided with the sweeping antebellum religious revival known as the Second Great Awakening. A national temperance movement emerged in the 1820s and quickly spread to the drink-sodden South. In Arkansas, drinking was not only an everyday fact of life but also an integral part of state politics, since candidates typically won favor with voters by providing ample amounts of whiskey on Election Day.

The organized temperance movement in Arkansas began in earnest with the formation in 1831 of the Little Rock Temperance Society, which was closely aligned with local churches. Methodists were usually the most ardent in supporting prohibition, while Baptists were not widely involved in opposing alcohol until after the Civil War. At first, Arkansas temperance advocates spoke against whiskey and other "hard" liquors while tacitly condoning beer and wine consumption. Significantly, the Little Rock Temperance Society—unlike other such organizations—allowed women to join its ranks, opening the door for greater female participation in state politics. Women eventually formed the heart of the prohibition movement in Arkansas, opposing alcohol as a threat to the family structure.

In more rustic parts of the state, alcohol consumption was essentially immune to efforts to curb its abuse. Nevertheless, William Woodruff, founder and publisher of the *Arkansas Gazette*, cosponsored an 1841 rally to encourage the state legislature to outlaw liquor sales. In the 1850s, the Arkansas General Assembly moved to ban the manufacture and sale of alcohol, but this measure did little to curtail consumption. Thus, while alcohol use thrived during the decade, so too did efforts to ban or limit its sale. For instance, in 1854, saloons and stills throughout Hempstead County were boarded up and closed by order of local officials. An 1855 law gave municipalities the power to ban alcohol, mandating that prospective taverns be approved by a local majority. This established a precedent that largely still exists today, as counties have been able to hold referendums on whether or not to allow alcohol to be sold within their borders.

The push for prohibition generally came from emerging urban centers such as Little Rock (Pulaski County), where residents worried that the state's economic development would be hampered by Arkansas's reputation as an intemperate frontier. Some of the state's most notorious outposts known for libertine attitudes toward drink, such as Napoleon (Desha County), were subject to attacks from temperance advocates.

The Civil War brought greater efforts by state leaders to prohib-it the sale of liquor. In 1862, under Confederate rule, the state government passed a statewide ban on distilleries in order to save grain for the war effort. This did little to curb backwoods "bootleg" whiskey production, and indeed, many prominent Arkansans openly ignored the law, such as Fayetteville (Washington County) judge David Walker, who proclaimed that he would pay "any price in or out of reason" to acquire whiskey. In 1864, the state's efforts to stop the production of alcohol fell apart when Governor Harris Flanagin signed a bill that allowed distilleries to pay the state for the right to produce alcohol. After the war, amid renewed calls for temperance, the Republican Party embraced the issue as part of a broader platform that endorsed greater government activism on social causes. In an attempt to limit election fraud, Arkansas Republicans passed legislation banning the sale of alcohol on Election Day, while making it illegal to refuse to sell alcohol on the basis of race. In many towns, African Americans were regularly denied alcohol for fear of social unrest.

In the post-war era, farmers found they could earn far greater profits by producing alcohol than by growing corn or other agricultural products. The spread of moonshine stills and the illegal trade in alcohol spurred response from Arkansas law enforcement. Throughout the 1870s, in what became known as the "moonshine wars," federal revenue agents (who assailed moonshine as a violation of the law because it was being sold without paying the requisite liquor tax) fanned out across the hilly terrain of northern Arkansas in search of illegal stills. Raids against moonshiners (also known as "wildcatters") were common, and stories of violent shootouts were vividly recounted in local newspapers. Local officials often sided with wildcatters in opposition to federal authorities, and jury nullification—in which accused wildcatters were given extremely light sentences or acquitted—was commonplace. In the 1890s, John Burris, a deputy revenue collector, personally closed over 150 stills and investigated hundreds more while posing as a timber buyer.

Meanwhile, in communities throughout Arkansas, women were increasingly engaged in urging saloons to close. Local chapters of the Woman's Christian Temperance Union (WCTU), the leading national organ for alcohol reform, emerged across the state. By the late 1880s, over 100 anti-saloon or temperance organizations existed in the state, seeking not only legislative reform but also encouraging young Arkansans to pledge to "abstain from intoxicating liquors." The efforts of temperance proponents culminated in substantial policy reform. In 1871, the General Assembly voted to allow a local referendum to decide whether saloons should be banned within three miles of colleges and schools. Eight years later, the legislature passed a law that called for towns to hold referendums every two years on whether or not to allow the sale of alcohol in quantities less than five gallons. This caused many saloons and stills to go out of business and resulted in gradual, piecemeal prohibition.

The most famous of the state's temperance champions, Carrie Nation, garnered national attention for her efforts to make prohibition a reality. While most of her career was spent outside the state, she settled in Eureka Springs (Carroll County) in 1909. Nation became famous at the turn of the century for attacking saloons in Kansas with a hatchet, and she dubbed her home in Eureka Springs "Hatchet Hall." She had been interested in Arkansas's prohibition movement as early as 1906, when she criticized the leniency toward alcohol exhibited by Governor Jeff Davis, whom she called "the worst governor in the Union." Davis had, while a prosecuting attorney, called for prohibition in 1891, but once he was governor he switched sides, and out of expediency, supported the anti-prohibition movement, which in turn helped fill his campaign coffers.

The prohibition movement gained momentum in the first decade of the twentieth century as Arkansas, and indeed much of the nation, continued to ban saloons. In 1906, sixty percent of American towns had done so, and the Arkansas chapter of the Anti-Saloon League, founded in 1899, urged for more restrictions. In this period, Arkansas governors such as George Donaghey led the way for tighter control of alcohol.

Race played a role in local referendums as in 1913, when the

A moonshine still confiscated in a raid near Quitman (Cleburne County); circa 1930. Courtesy of the Cleburne County Historical Society

legislature passed a bill that required petitions in support of a new saloon to be signed by a majority of white voters. In an era of widespread African-American voter disfranchisement, black opinion on alcohol was simply ignored or suppressed. By 1914, only nine Arkansas counties had managed to keep their saloons open. In 1915, the General Assembly passed the Newberry Act, effectively banning the manufacture and sale of alcohol in the state. In addition, the act failed to exempt the sale of alcohol for medicinal purposes.

In 1916, "wets," or those who favored loosening alcohol restrictions, managed to campaign successfully for a referendum on the issue, but efforts to repeal the Newberry Act—and restore liquor sales—failed by a two-to-one margin. Prohibitionists prevailed, in part because they appealed to prominent African Americans such as Scipio Jones, who urged black Arkansans who were able to vote to support a ban on alcohol. The following year, the legislature made Arkansas one of the first states to pass complete prohibition by outlawing the importation of alcohol. Governor Charles Brough—long a proponent of prohibition—signed the bill at the state Chamber of Commerce. When the United States entered World War I in 1917, the national move toward prohibition gained the final motivation it needed, as the war effort's demand for grain (a key ingredient for producing liquor) outweighed the need for alcohol. As such, Congress passed the Eighteenth Amendment, which Arkansas ratified in January 1919.

During the 1920s, temperance formed an unlikely partnership with the resurgent Ku Klux Klan (KKK), which claimed to have over 50,000 members in Arkansas at its peak. For instance, Lulu Markwell, former president of the Arkansas chapter of the WCTU, was the Imperial Commander of the Women of the Ku Klux Klan. The Klan was particularly active in the oil boom-towns of southern Arkansas, such as those in Union County, where bootleggers and gamblers openly flouted laws prohibiting such activities. In November 1922, a group of Klansmen calling themselves the "Cleanup Committee" launched attacks on liquor and gambling dens, expelling an estimated 2,000 people from the town of Smackover (Union County). By the late 1920s, the assault on liquor was subsequently taken up by Homer Adkins, sheriff of Pulaski County and later governor of Arkansas.

Joseph T. Robinson, longtime Democratic senator from Arkansas, was never a supporter of the prohibition of alcohol, and he used the sweeping Democratic Party victory in the 1932 elections as an opportunity to draft legislation ending Prohibition. The onset of the Great Depression had encouraged many Americans to view repealing the ban on alcohol as economically beneficial. Indeed, by the early 1930s, the public's mood toward alcohol had softened. With the repeal of the Eighteenth Amendment in 1933, the entire state of Arkansas was once again wet. This ushered in a new phase in the state's history of alcohol control, in which prohibition was determined county by county. A 1935 state law mandated that, in order to hold a referendum on the matter, a petition had to be signed by at least thirty-five percent of a county's electorate. This was a formidable hurdle to "dry" advocates, and throughout the 1930s, liquor flowed relatively freely throughout the state.

While the national prohibition movement collapsed following World War II, Arkansas temperance advocates still pushed for dry counties but also had to reconcile with Arkansans' changing attitudes toward consumption. The business community—once stalwart dry proponents—no longer sided with the fading temperance movement. Indeed, from the late 1940s through the 1960s, dries suffered one setback after another. Winthrop Rockefeller, governor of the state during the late 1960s, argued that liquor sales would boost tourism and stimulate the economy.

By the end of the twentieth century, the lines between wet and dry counties had solidified, with forty-three counties dry and thirty-two wet. A 1993 bill essentially updated the 1935 legislation, restricting referendums on county-wide prohibition to once every four years. Yet in order to get on the ballot, thirty-eight percent of the electorate must sign a petition—a high threshold in most counties. In 2003, the state Alcohol Beverage Control (ABC) Board began granting private club licenses (which gave club proprietors in dry counties the right to serve alcohol) in, among other locations, Batesville (Independence County) and Jonesboro (Craighead County). Indeed, throughout nominally dry counties, private clubs that serve alcohol proliferate, the largest number being in Benton County, prior to citizens voting that county wet in 2012. Although governor at the time of the ABC action Mike Huckabee was himself a staunch teetotaler, pleas, largely from religious organizations, for restricting the issuance of private club licenses came to no avail.

Efforts to prohibit the sale and consumption of alcohol have persisted, spanning from before the territorial era to the present day. The peak of the state's prohibition movement, roughly from the 1850s through the 1920s, witnessed a confluence of disparate political forces all aiming to curb the use and abuse of alcohol. And although each of these groups came to support prohibition for different reasons, they found common ground in the belief that alcohol represented a scourge and a threat to the state of Arkansas, a belief that some still hold in the twenty-first century.

Brent E. Riffel
College of the Canyons

Howell A. "Doc" Rayburn (1841?–1865?)

Howell A. "Doc" Rayburn was a Civil War guerrilla chieftain who operated in the area between West Point (White County) and Des Arc (Prairie County). His legacy is a mix of fact and leg-end. His attacks and those of other guerrillas on Union outposts and expeditions tied up countless Union military assets that otherwise could have been used elsewhere.

REBEL GUERRILLA HOWELL "DOC" RAYBURN SNEAKED INTO A UNION OFFICERS' DANCE—

— DISGUISED AS A WOMAN.

Doc Rayburn was born about 1841 in Roane County, Tennessee, one of six children of the farming family of Hodge and Susan Rayburn. A few years later, the family relocated to Texas.

Rayburn joined the Confederate army on October 21, 1861, when he enlisted in Company C, Twelfth Texas Cavalry. The regiment moved to Des Arc in March 1862 and prepared to board steamers that would carry it to Mississippi. When the regiment departed, they left Rayburn behind with a fever. In 1863, after a long recovery from his illness, he began recruiting local youths to form a guerrilla band. For the next two years, Rayburn and his band were a nuisance to Union military authorities, attacking scouting and foraging parties. In at least one such attack near West Point, Rayburn's men all donned Union uniforms and took their enemy by surprise. During Confederate general Sterling Price's 1864 Missouri Raid, Rayburn's command served as Colonel Thomas H. McCray's bodyguard. Numerous expeditions were mounted to capture Rayburn, but none were successful.

The most celebrated legend concerning Rayburn centers upon his activities at DeValls Bluff (Prairie County) in December 1864. He told his men that if he could make it through a Union picket line that evening, he would be their Santa Claus. He had a diminutive stature with long blond hair and blue eyes, and at barely 100 pounds, he passed rather easily for a female. Borrowing a lady's dress and other items, Rayburn made it through the picket line to a Christmas dance hosted by Federal officers. After an evening of dancing, Rayburn made his way to the corral, where he mounted a horse and stampeded enough animals for each man of his command to receive a horse for Christmas.

Rayburn married Martha Booth, the daughter of a prominent resident of West Point, on June 15, 1865, soon after the Civil War ended.

The exact date of Rayburn's death is unknown, but he likely died in late 1865 or 1866. Some state that he died of tuberculosis contracted while he was held by Union authorities in Little Rock (Pulaski County) after the war, while others maintain that he

Howell A. "Doc" Rayburn, a noted Confederate guerrilla leader in White and Prairie counties during the Civil War.
Courtesy of the Arkansas History Commission

was shot by an acquaintance. His gravesite's location is also a mystery, but it is believed to be in the Des Arc area.

Alan Thompson
Prairie Grove, Arkansas

BASS REEVES WAS ONE OF THE FIRST BLACK LAWMEN—

—AND THE TOUGHEST.

HE BROUGHT IN 19 HORSE THIEVES AT ONE TIME.

Bass Reeves
(1838–1910)

Bass Reeves was one of the first black lawmen west of the Mississippi River. As one of the most respected lawmen working in Indian Territory, he achieved legendary status for the number of criminals he captured.

Bass Reeves was born a slave in Crawford County in July 1838. His owners, the William S. Reeves family, moved to Grayson County, Texas, in 1846. During the Civil War, Bass became a fugitive slave and found refuge in Indian Territory (present-day Oklahoma) amongst the Creek and Seminole. Reeves is believed to have served with the irregular or regular Union Indians that fought in Indian Territory during the Civil War.

After the Civil War, Reeves settled in Van Buren (Crawford County) with his wife, Jennie, and children. Oral history states that Reeves served as a scout and guide for deputy U.S. marshals going into Indian Territory on business for the Van Buren federal court. In 1875, Judge Isaac C. Parker became the federal judge for the Western District of Arkansas, which had jurisdiction over Indian Territory. This court had moved to Fort Smith (Sebastian County). In 1875, Reeves was hired as a commissioned deputy U.S. marshal, making him one of the first black federal lawmen west of the Mississippi River.

During his law enforcement career, Reeves stood 6'2" and weighed 180 pounds. He could shoot a pistol or rifle accurately with his right or left hand; settlers said Reeves could whip any two men with his bare hands. Reeves became a legend during his lifetime for his ability to catch criminals under trying circumstances. He brought fugitives by the dozen into the Fort Smith federal jail. Reeves said the largest number of outlaws he ever caught at one time was nineteen horse thieves he captured near Fort Sill, Oklahoma. The noted outlaw Belle Starr turned herself in at Fort Smith when she found out Reeves had the warrant for her arrest.

In 1887, Reeves was tried for murder for the shooting of his trail cook, but he was found innocent. In 1890, Reeves arrested the notorious Seminole outlaw Greenleaf, who had been on the run for eighteen years without capture and had murdered seven people. The same year, Reeves went after the famous Cherokee outlaw Ned Christie. Reeves and his posse burned Christie's cabin, but he eluded capture.

In 1893, Reeves was transferred to the East Texas federal court at Paris, Texas. He was stationed in Calvin in the Choctaw Nation and took his prisoners to the federal commissioner at Pauls Valley in the Chickasaw Nation. While working for the Paris court, Reeves broke up the Tom Story gang of horse thieves that operated in the Red River valley.

In 1897, Reeves was transferred to the Muskogee federal court in Indian Territory. Reeves remarried in 1900 to Winnie Sumter; his first wife had died in Fort Smith in 1896. In 1902, Reeves arrested his own son, Bennie, for domestic murder in Muskogee. Bennie was convicted and sent to the federal prison in Leavenworth, Kansas.

Reeves worked as a marshal until Oklahoma achieved statehood in 1907, at which time he became a city policeman for Muskogee. He died of Bright's disease on January 12, 1910.

On May 26, 2012, a bronze statue depicting Reeves on a horse riding west was dedicated in Fort Smith's Ross Pendergraft Park. The statue, which was designed by sculptor Harold T. Holden and cost more than $300,000, was paid for by donations to the Bass Reeves Legacy Initiative.

Art T. Burton
Harvey, Illinois

Bass Reeves Legacy Monument at Ross Pendergraft Park in Fort Smith.
Photo by Daniel Maher

Tom Slaughter (1896–1921)

Dead before his twenty-fifth birthday, Tom Slaughter was a violent, arrogant, and handsome conman, bank robber, and killer. When he died on December 9, 1921, in Benton (Saline County), Slaughter had been given the death sentence for murder.

Tom Slaughter was born in Bernice, Louisiana, on December 25, 1896, but he lived in the Dallas, Texas, area until he was fourteen. Slaughter then moved to Pope County, Arkansas, where he was convicted of stealing a calf in 1911. Slaughter was sentenced to the Arkansas Boys' Industrial Home. A few months later, he escaped. He returned to Russellville (Pope County), where he paraded before Sheriff Oates, who arrested him. He escaped from jail the second night. For the next ten years, Slaughter broke out of jails in Texas, Oklahoma, Kansas, and Arkansas.

In 1916, Slaughter was arrested for stealing automobiles. He escaped from the Dallas County jail, "one of the…most strongly built in the Southwest, liberating seven other prisoners," according to the December 10, 1921, *Arkansas Gazette*. Sentenced to six years in the Texas penitentiary, he escaped in July 1917, knocking out a guard with a shovel.

Slaughter formed a gang and terrorized the region, robbing banks in Oklahoma, Texas, Arkansas, Kansas, Kentucky, and Pennsylvania. In 1918, Slaughter was being returned to the Texas penitentiary. Inside the prison, he took a "pin and pricked hundreds of holes in his face and body, covered them with croton oil, which brought out a rash, ate two cakes of soap to bring about a fever and reported to the sick bay." Hospital officials diagnosed smallpox and isolated him. Once again, he escaped.

In 1919, the Slaughter gang stole $24,000 in a noon bank robbery in Petty, Texas. Later, Slaughter and Fulton Green, a member of his gang, killed a bank cashier in Pennsylvania. Slaughter enjoyed theatrics. In September 1920, he and his gang robbed a bank in Graham, Texas, on a busy Saturday afternoon when the town was filled with citizens. In October, Slaughter, accompanied by four men and two women, arrived in Hot Springs, where the group went on a drinking spree, disturbing the peace. Hot Springs police went to investigate, a gunfight followed, and Slaughter and Green killed Sheriff Rowe Brown and wounded officer Bill Wilson.

Slaughter fled to Oklahoma, formed a gang, and continued robbing banks. Eventually, Slaughter was caught in Kansas and returned to Arkansas, though Arkansas officials had to bribe a Kansas sheriff before extradition could begin. Citizens in Hot Springs had offered a reward of $5,000 for the capture of Slaughter and Green.

Officials at Slaughter's trial were fearful. A prison trusty claimed he had been approached about wrecking a passenger train behind the prison walls to distract officials while Slaughter escaped. While living at "The Walls," as the prison was called, in Little Rock (Pulaski County), Slaughter asked for a minister to visit him. The Reverend W. B. Hogg of Winfield Memorial Methodist Church responded. Slaughter was converted and baptized into the church by Rev. Hogg, who became an advocate for Slaughter. Laura Connor, the only female member of the penitentiary board, also became an advocate for Slaughter.

In January 1921, Slaughter was sent to Tucker Prison Farm, where Warden Dee Horton tried to break Slaughter, who irritated him with his swaggering independence. The tall and handsome Slaughter had a reputation as a ladies' man, and three women—Myrtle Slaughter of El Dorado (Union County); Nora Brooks of Ponca City, Oklahoma; and Mable Slaughter of Joplin, Missouri—claimed to be his wife. Warden Horton enjoyed whipping and intimidating one of his most illustrious inmates.

On September 18, 1921, Slaughter, attempting to escape, killed inmate Bliss Atkinson. He was tried in Pine Bluff (Jefferson

County) for the killing and sentenced to die. Slaughter was transported to Little Rock and guarded around the clock. One week before his scheduled execution, Slaughter feigned illness, overpowered two guards, unlocked the stockade, and invited everyone to make a break for it. Slaughter marched the nurse ahead of himself and walked to Warden E. H. Dempsey's apartment, where he took the warden and his family as prisoners. For five hours, Slaughter paraded around the prisoners he had "freed," taking the convicts' money and valuables. Then, Slaughter left the prison carrying Jack Howard and five prisoners in Dempsey's automobile. The police at Benton set up a road block. The prisoners abandoned the automobile and camped in the woods. Howard, an inmate from Garland County, shot Slaughter three times, killing him. (Howard later claimed he had escaped with Slaughter to assist in Slaughter's capture.) Slaughter's body was taken to Benton, where "thousands stormed the Healey and Roth funeral home."

The *Arkansas Gazette* on December 13, 1921, reported that the crowds were so large that the funeral home placed Slaughter's body outside and allowed the curious to view him. The Palez Floral Shop of Benton received "several very expensive"

orders from Hot Springs and all over Oklahoma. Three ministers, including Rev. Hogg, officiated at the funeral, and the crowd was estimated at more than 5,000.

Jerry D. Gibbens
Williams Baptist College

Law and Outlaws

Helen Spence
(1912?–1934)

HELEN SPENCE ESCAPED FROM JAIL —

—IN A SUIT SHE MADE OF CHECKERED NAPKINS!

Helen Ruth Spence of Arkansas County was a famous outlaw and prisoner whose story captured the imaginations of many during her life and engendered a body of legend afterward. She was the focus of unprecedented media coverage in her day, up until her death at the hands of Arkansas prison officials.

The July 12, 1934, issues of the *Washington Post* and *New York Times* published accounts of Spence's recent death, but the date of her birth aboard a houseboat on the White River near St. Charles (Arkansas County) remains a mystery. Some accounts claim she was twenty-two years old when she was killed; others say she was eighteen. Arkansas's houseboat-dwelling "river rats" like Spence were eventually expelled from the area as the U.S. Army Corps of Engineers tamed the White River.

Regarded with a mixture of awe and disdain by the "dry-landers" with whom she attended school, Spence gained only a ninth-grade education and married local-boy-turned-moonshiner Buster Eaton. The marriage did not last, and she returned to the White River to live with her father, Cicero Spence, and stepmother (her mother had died years before). During a fishing trip, a man named Jack Worls shot and killed Cicero and assaulted Spence's stepmother, who died in a Memphis, Tennessee, hospital on January 7, 1931.

At Worls's murder trial in DeWitt (Arkansas County), Spence meted out what the locals called "river justice." According to the *New York Times* article published on January 20, 1931 ("Girl Kills Alleged Slayer of Father in Court; Fires as Arkansas Jury is About to Get Case"), the action happened as follows: "Drawing a pistol as the jury rose to decide the fate of the man on trial, Mrs. Ruth Spence Eaton, 18, shot and killed Jack Worls...the only statement the girl would make after the shooting was: 'He killed my daddy.' She showed no remorse." This act culminated in Spence's conviction for manslaughter on October 8, 1932. Due to a wave of public sympathy, however, she was paroled and freed on June 10, 1933.

Prior to her conviction, Spence had worked at a DeWitt café and encountered a man named Jim Bohots.

He allegedly began harassing Spence with unwanted advances and threatening her. In February 1932, Bohots was found dead in a "trysting spot" in the woods, shot with his own gun. Called in for questioning, Spence denied involvement and was released. State Prosecuting Attorney George Hartje, in a letter dated May 31, 1933, had assured the parole board that he was "thoroughly convinced she did not [kill Jim Bohots]," so when Spence walked into a Little Rock (Pulaski County) police station and confessed to the crime, a backlash began against the recently pardoned Spence.

Sentenced to the State Farm for Women in Jacksonville (Pulaski County) for second-degree murder, she began her sentence—ten years of hard labor—on July 3, 1933. She also began a series of daring escapes, the first of which occurred in the fall of that year. The matron of the women's prison routinely transported female prisoners to Memphis to be prostituted. Spence, a proficient seamstress, secretly collected red-checked cloth napkins from the cafeteria and sewed them into the lining of her uniform. Upon arrival in Memphis, she requested to use the restroom. Turning her uniform inside out, Spence simply walked away from the bus station, though she was quickly recaptured.

From September to November 1933, Spence escaped a total of three times, only to be caught and punished by twenty lashes with a leather strap known as the "blacksnake." This method involved stripping a prisoner naked and placing the prisoner over a wooden barrel to be whipped. Afterward, Spence contracted a fever, perhaps due to kidney problems resulting from the beatings. Records show that the petite, five-foot-tall woman was subjected to a round-the-clock series of "high enemas with a colon tube," followed by repeated douches and alternating doses of morphine—a pattern of treatment that was, even by the standards of the time, excessive and which was already out of fashion. Even when her fever dropped below ninety-nine degrees, this ordeal continued for days.

In December 1933, Arkansas's lieutenant governor, Lee Cazort, ordered Spence to the Arkansas State Hospital for "observation." The hospital director concluded that Spence was not insane and should be returned to prison. However, she was held at the asylum for an additional month. During this period, Spence submitted a story to the publication *Liberty Magazine*, but it was rejected. The prosecuting attorney's office confiscated Spence's story. Upon her final escape from prison, it was reported she had written on the magazine's rejection slip: "I will not be taken alive."

Spence escaped from a specially constructed "cage-like cell" on July 10, 1934. Assistant Prison Superintendent V. O. Brockman and prison trusty Frank Martin (himself a convicted murderer) came upon her as she walked down a country road. Martin shot Spence behind the ear, killing her instantly. Brockman was charged with being an accessory to murder for purposely allowing Spence to escape. Brockman was acquitted but lost his position as assistant superintendent. Martin was also acquitted of her killing and eventually paroled.

Newspapers ran wild, with headlines like "Escaped Girl Convict is Trapped and Slain." According to newspaper accounts, hundreds of people appeared at the funeral home to see her body, and she was buried at St. Charles next to her father. However, local legend holds that a young man named John Black led a group who broke into the funeral home during the night before the planned interment and took Spence's body, which they buried in an unmarked grave in St. Charles. Black reportedly planted a cedar tree to mark the spot. For decades, Black tended the secret grave. Before he died, he entrusted this task to their mutual childhood friend, Lemuel Cressie (L. C.) Brown. According to Brown, after parolee Frank Martin later returned to DeWitt and bragged about killing Spence, he "walked into the grocery store to buy a loaf of bread. The lady sold him a different loaf—told him it was just as good, and cost less. Frank Martin ate dinner that night and never woke up the next morning…It was always said that 'the River got him.'"

Denise Parkinson
Hot Springs, Arkansas

Belle Starr (1848–1889)

In the late 1800s, Belle Starr was a notorious female outlaw in America's "Old West." As a resident of Indian Territory, present-day Oklahoma, she came under the jurisdiction of Judge Isaac C. Parker in Fort Smith (Sebastian County). Her close friends included the legendary American outlaws Cole Younger and Frank and Jesse James. Her reputation as a criminal, the novelty her of being a female outlaw, and her violent, mysterious death led to her being called the "Bandit Queen."

Belle Starr was born Myra Maybelle Shirley near Carthage, Missouri, on February 5, 1848. Her father was John R. Shirley, a farmer who later owned a local inn. Her mother, twenty years younger than her husband, was Elizabeth (Eliza) Hatfield Shirley, who was related to the Hatfield family of the infamous Hatfield-McCoy feud. As a child, Shirley attended Carthage Female Academy. She enjoyed the outdoors and horseback riding, becoming a better rider than most women of her time. Among Shirley's childhood friends in Missouri was Cole Younger, who after the Civil War joined neighbors Frank and Jesse James in robbing trains, stagecoaches, and banks. Fleeing the law, they sometimes hid on the Shirley farm, and the teenaged Shirley became influenced by their life of crime.

In 1866, she married another childhood acquaintance, James C. Reed, the son of Solomon Reed, a prosperous local farmer. The couple had two children, daughter Rosie Lee, called "Pearl," and son James Edwin, called "Eddie." After trying unsuccessfully to become a farmer, her husband joined with the Starr clan, an

Notorious outlaw Belle Starr, the "Bandit Queen," who as a resident of Indian Territory, numbered among her friends the likes of Cole Younger and the James brothers.

outlaw Cherokee family in Indian Territory who stole horses, rustled cattle, and bootlegged whiskey. James Reed was accused of robbery in 1874, and Myra Reed was accused of being an accomplice. They fled to Texas, and in 1874, he was killed while trying to escape the authorities.

After his death, Myra Reed joined the Starr clan and lived in Indian Territory west of Fort Smith. She married one of them, Samuel Starr, in 1880, at which point she began calling herself "Belle." She was said to act as a front for bootleggers and to harbor fugitives. With Fort Smith having the nearest court of law, she came to the attention of Judge Isaac Parker, who was known as the "Hanging Judge" for his strict enforcement of the laws of the time. On November 9, 1882, she and Sam Starr were charged in the U.S. Commissioner's Court at Fort Smith with the larceny of two horses. On March 8, 1883, a jury returned a guilty verdict, and Parker sentenced the Starrs to a year in prison. It was a surprisingly lenient sentence; Judge Parker was said to have taken into consideration the fact that it was the first conviction for both, and he expressed hope that they would "decide to become decent citizens." After arranging for the care of her children with friends and relatives, they were transported from Fort Smith to Detroit on a railroad prison car, where Belle was the only woman among nineteen other convicts. The good behavior of the Starrs in prison led to their release within nine months.

After the 1886 death of Sam Starr in a gunfight, Belle and one of his relatives, Jim July Starr (also known as Bill July), began living together and announced their common-law marriage under

Cherokee custom. Some sources say Belle decided to do this to maintain ownership of her property on Cherokee land.

At first, she was suspected whenever neighbors' horses and cattle went missing or when it was believed she was harboring criminals, but she was not convicted. She settled into a relatively quiet life, announcing that fugitives were no longer welcome at her home, and was known to help her neighbors when they were ill. She often visited Fort Smith, where she posed for one of her several photographs. She told the *Fort Smith Elevator*, "I regard myself as a woman who has seen much of life."

Starr's life ended when she was shot in the back as she returned from a general store to her ranch. She died on February 3, 1889. Though suspects included an outlaw with whom she was feuding, a former lover, her husband, and her own son, the killer of Belle Starr was never identified.

She was buried on her ranch near today's Eufaula Dam in Oklahoma. Her tombstone was engraved with a bell, a star, her horse, and a poem by her daughter, Pearl, who lived much of the rest of her life in Fort Smith and Van Buren (Crawford County). Starr became a legend in "dime novels," beginning in 1889 with *Belle Starr, the Bandit Queen, or the Female Jesse James* by reporter Richard K. Fox. She was also the subject of films such as 1941's *Belle Starr* with Gene Tierney and the 1980 television movie *Belle Starr* with Elizabeth Montgomery. While the facts of her life may have been embellished by legend, she was known in her time as a notorious outlaw and a nemesis of Fort Smith's Judge Parker.

Nancy Hendricks
Garland County Historical Society

BELLE STARR WAS KNOWN AS THE *QUEEN* OF THE OUTLAWS.

Law and Outlaws

Texarkana Moonlight Murders

An unidentified assailant often known as the Texarkana Phantom Killer committed a number of murders and assaults in Texarkana (Miller County, Arkansas, and Bowie County, Texas) through the spring of 1946. Five people were killed, and three were wounded. While there was one major suspect, he was never convicted of these crimes. The attacks served partially as the basis for a motion picture, *The Town that Dreaded Sundown*.

On February 22, 1946, two young people, Jimmy Hollis and Mary Jeanne Larey, were parked on a secluded Bowie County road outside Texarkana. They were forced out of the car by an armed man, his face hidden by a burlap sack with two slits for eyes. The assailant beat Hollis with the gun, cracking the young man's skull in two places. He then sexually assaulted Larey before fleeing when he saw the headlights of a car approaching. Both of these victims eventually recovered from the assault.

One month later, on March 24, two more young people, Richard Griffin and Polly Ann Moore, were found on another Bowie County back road, both shot in the back of the head with a .32 revolver. Blood stains on the ground indicated they had been killed outside the car and then put back in it.

The following month, on April 14, teenagers Paul Martin and Betty Jo Booker were found dead in Spring Lake Park on the Texas side of Texarkana, their bodies located some distance away from their car. Again, a .32 was the murder weapon.

The young women in both grisly killings had been tortured and sexually assaulted. Police began patrolling secluded roads and "lovers' lanes."

The next month, on May 3, an isolated farmhouse in Miller County was the scene of another murder. Virgil Starks was shot twice and killed by an attacker standing outside the front window. When the Starks's wife, Katy Starks, heard the shots and ran to the phone, she was shot twice in the face. Nevertheless, she was able to escape and run to a nearby farmhouse for help. Though a .22 pistol had been used in Starks's death, tire tracks similar to those in earlier cases were found at the scene, and the crime was generally attributed to the same killer.

In all, two women and three men were killed. With each new murder, panic rose higher in Texarkana. Citizens bought weapons and stayed in their homes at night, literally dreading sundown. Law enforcement officials on both the Arkansas and Texas sides of the city worked the case. Texas rangers arrived, including the handsome and charismatic Manuel "Lone Wolf" Gonzaullas, and reporters from all over the country flocked to the city, adding a new level of chaos. When neighbors reported seeing strange lights from the Starks farmhouse, local police surrounded the home only to find Gonzaullas and a reporter from *Life* magazine taking photos of the crime scene with flash bulbs.

The murders were soon dubbed the "Moonlight Murders" by the news media, although the first two occurred a week after the full moon and the final attack occurred around the time of the new moon. Because he seemed to strike and vanish, the night stalker was also dubbed the "Phantom Killer" by the local newspaper, the *Texarkana Gazette*.

Numerous individuals claimed to be the Phantom Killer, while other citizens came forward with accusations against various local residents, including an agent of the Internal Revenue Service. One young man, a student at the University of Arkansas (UA) in Fayetteville (Washington County), who came from a prominent Texarkana family, killed himself in his room in Fayetteville, leaving a poem and confession. All turned out to be false leads.

The one suspect who was most often cited as the probable killer was a repeat offender named Youell Swinney, who had a record of car theft, counterfeiting, burglary, and assault. An Arkansas law enforcement official, Max Tackett, had noticed that before each murder, there were reports of a car being stolen and then abandoned. In July 1946, a stakeout of a reported stolen car on the Arkansas side led police to a woman who claimed to be Swinney's girlfriend. She provided details of the murders that had not been released to the public. Subsequently, her story changed, and she married Swinney. Because of the unreliability of her testimony and the fact that she could not be forced to appear as a witness against her husband, law enforcement officials declined to prosecute. In 1947, Youell Swinney was jailed for life as a repeat offender for car theft but was released on appeal in 1973. While some sources say he later died in prison, others say he died in 1994 at a nursing home in Dallas.

In 1977, Arkansan Charles B. Pierce produced an R-rated horror film called *The Town that Dreaded Sundown* with the tagline, "In 1946 this man killed five people....Today he still lurks the streets of Texarkana, Arkansas." It starred Academy Award–winning actor Ben Johnson, Dawn Wells of *Gilligan's Island*, and Andrew Prine. Though it purported to be based on the true story of the Texarkana Moonlight Murders, many people dispute its accuracy. It remains a minor cult classic.

To date, the identity of the Phantom Killer remains unknown. While theoretically still open, it is considered a cold case. In 1996, the *Texarkana Gazette* published a twenty-four-page special section called "The Phantom at 50," and the crime was revisited extensively in 1996 and again in 2003 by the *Dallas Morning News*.

Nancy Hendricks
Garland County Historical Society

Tucker-Parnell Feud

The Tucker-Parnell Feud (or Parnell-Tucker Feud) refers to a series of assaults and shootings in the Union County area between 1902 and 1905, stemming from a shootout in downtown El Dorado (Union County) that left three dead in October 1902. The repercussions of the downtown shootings led to an estimated thirty to forty deaths in Union County over the three-year period.

The dispute began not between the Parnells and the Tuckers, two Union County families, but between two other men over which would marry an El Dorado woman. William Puckett of Texarkana (Miller County) had arranged to marry Jessie Stevenson and arrived in El Dorado on September 17, 1902, to meet her. Stevenson worked for local photographer Bob Mullens, who became enraged when Puckett arrived at his studio trying to find her. He claimed that Stevenson was going to marry him, not Puckett, and allegedly attacked Puckett. Puckett summoned El Dorado city marshal Guy B. Tucker for protection as he located Stevenson and quickly married her. As the newlyweds left El Dorado to board a train back to Texarkana, Tucker accompanied the couple and enlisted El Dorado constable Harrison Dearing to help protect the two. As the couple attempted to board the train, Mullens suddenly appeared and rushed toward them. Dearing arrested Mullens, who was soon released on bail. The next day, Mullens confronted Dearing over the arrest. The fight escalated. Dearing shot Mullens, who died the next day.

The Parnell family had long been close friends with Mullens and at odds with several businessmen and city leaders in El Dorado. Marshall Parnell's eight sons, enraged at the shooting, strongly defended Mullens. The Parnells later claimed that Tucker and Dearing, former business partners, had a vendetta against them arising from a recent dispute over construction at the Parnell store downtown, which had reportedly disrupted the use of a busy sidewalk.

On October 9, the bitterness escalated further. Apparently, a subpoena was to be delivered for another brother, Mat Parnell, to testify before the grand jury at the county courthouse regarding the shooting of Mullins. The subpoena was delayed, enraging the Parnells, who were eager to tell their side of the story. A second brother, Dan Parnell, was able to testify that day. That afternoon at about 4:30 p.m., as Tucker, Dearing, and El Dorado grocer and Parnell rival Frank Newton walked along the east side of the downtown square near the courthouse, they encountered three more of the Parnell brothers: Tom, Walter, and Jim. Heated words were exchanged, and all quickly pulled their guns. Within moments, a confused frenzy of gunfire swept across the street.

Jim Parnell shot at Newton, missing him. Newton returned fire, missing Parnell. Dearing then shot Tom Parnell. Mat Parnell had now arrived and joined the fight as the younger brother of Marshal Guy Tucker, Clarence, arrived. Clarence Tucker and Mat Parnell fought, with Tucker cutting Parnell. Dr. R. A. Hilton arrived and shot Mat Parnell. Jim Parnell then struck Hilton. Dearing, Newton, and Guy Tucker all shot Tom Parnell multiple times, killing him. Constable Dearing and Walter Parnell wildly shot at each other; both were killed. Guy Tucker was shot six times but survived. A crowd quickly gathered to see the aftermath of the carnage, and Union County sheriff H. C. Norris separated the two factions. In the end, Walter Parnell and Tom Parnell lay dead, along with Constable Dearing.

The city was tense in the weeks following the shootings, with factions throughout the county backing either Tucker or the Parnells. Charges were filed against the Parnells in the incident but were dropped on the condition that brothers Mat and Jim Parnell leave Arkansas. The Parnells angrily charged that Tucker had effectively rigged the justice system against them in Union County. Animosity and violence spread across the county in the

THE TUCKER-PARNELL FEUD STARTED OVER A WOMAN— WHEN TWO MEN WANTED TO MARRY HER.

months afterward as attacks began to mount against supporters of either Tucker or Parnell.

In August 1903, Guy Tucker was sent a jug of strychnine-laced whiskey from an unknown assailant. Days after the attempted poisoning, on August 8, Tucker confronted John Parnell on the courthouse square. Parnell had written an angry letter to a local newspaper critical of Tucker and the local justice system just days before the poisoning. After a heated exchange, Tucker shot and killed him. Immediately, rumors of mobs threatening to descend on the town and bomb threats prompted the state militia to be called out to restore order. Tucker was brought up on murder charges for the death of John Parnell but was acquitted in March 1905 after a series of delays.

Tucker resigned as city marshal later in 1905, apparently believing that his resignation would defuse the violence in the area, and began running a saloon in nearby Champagnolle (Union County). Violence continued as two Tucker allies were killed and Tucker himself was later shot by unknown assailants, resulting in the need for amputation of his arm. Tucker then moved to Little Rock (Pulaski County), and the feud gradually subsided. Many of the surviving members of the Parnell family eventually moved away from Union County, but the daughter of Walter Parnell, Blanche Parnell Wade, stayed in El Dorado and became a renowned benefactor in the city. She even had a brief, cordial meeting with Governor Jim Guy Tucker, grandson of Guy Tucker, when he visited the city in 1993.

In the decades since the feud ended, El Dorado has commemorated the incident in a number of ways. Historical markers detailing the events surrounding the violence have been placed in the downtown area. Since the 1980s, re-enactments of the deadly 1902 shootout and the events leading up to it have been held in downtown El Dorado near the site of the violence. The "Showdown at Sunset" has become a popular local attraction and is held every Saturday evening in June, July, and August. The event has been rated as one of the "Top 100 Events in North America" by the American Bus Association.

Kenneth Bridges
South Arkansas Community College

I Left my Heart in GARLAND County

TONY BENNETT FIRST SANG "I LEFT MY HEART IN SAN FRANCISCO" AT THE INFAMOUS VAPORS CLUB IN HOT SPRINGS.

Vapors

The Vapors was a nightclub in Hot Springs (Garland County) during the last era of illegal gambling in the city. Upscale Las Vegas–style entertainment—featuring well-known acts such as Edgar Bergen, the Smothers Brothers, and Tony Bennett—distinguished it from many of the rival clubs in the area.

Dane Harris, who had been a World War II pilot, accumulated money from a stake he had in the Belvedere Country Club and casino during the 1950s and used that money to build the Vapors nightclub. Harris partnered with Owney Madden, owner of the Cotton Club in New York and a noted gangster, to build the nightclub at a site at 315 Park Avenue formerly occupied by the Phillips Drive-In. The club was built in the summer of 1959 and opened in 1960, offering the Vapors' Coffee Shop; the Monte Carlo Room for meetings, events, and luncheons; a large lobby; a dance floor; a theater restaurant with tiered seating and a retractable stage big enough for an orchestra; and a casino that operated late in the evening. Entertainment included two shows every night featuring some of the most popular entertainers in the country.

Tony Bennett notes in his autobiography that he first sang his signature hit "I Left My Heart in San Francisco" at the Vapors. While rehearsing the song there for a later appearance at the Fairmont Hotel in San Francisco, California, Bennett sang the song through once and was told by the only audience member, a bartender setting up for the evening, "If you guys record that song, I'll buy the first copy."

In the late morning of January 4, 1963, an explosion rocked the Vapors, causing extensive damage. Twelve injuries were reported, and three people required hospitalization. Speculation about who was responsible ranged from outside crime syndicates attempting a takeover to local club owners lashing out in response to raids against their own facilities. Such raids were intended to take the public pressure off authorities while leaving more prominent clubs like the Vapors alone. As a result of the bombing, a wall separating the casino from the lobby was demolished, exposing the club's gaming tables and slot machines to the street. Reporters covering the bombing for the *Arkansas Gazette* managed to snap a photograph of the slot machines and craps tables against the orders of police officers securing the area. The photo appeared on the front page of the next day's edition, providing clear proof of illegal gambling in Hot Springs. Illegal gambling would not be completely curtailed in the city, however, until 1967, six months into the first term of reformist Governor Winthrop Rockefeller.

Unlike many former casinos in Hot Springs, the Vapors continued to operate as a nightclub and restaurant after its casino was closed. In 1977, responding to changing tastes in entertainment, Dane Harris began renovations to the club, which would see the addition of the Cockeyed Cowboy and Apollo Disco, as well as an additional showroom completed in 1980.

Harris died in 1981. The Vapors continued to operate as a nightclub into the 1990s but only as a lackluster shadow of its former self. The building was sold in October 1998 to Tower of Strength Ministries for use as a church; in November 2013, the building was again put up for sale.

Michael Hodge
Butler Center for Arkansas Studies

Former location of Vapors in Hot Springs; 2010.
Photo by Mike Keckhaver

Sidney Wallace (1851–1874)

Sidney Wallace was a legendary part of the state's folklore during Arkansas's Reconstruction following the Civil War. Some portrayed him as boldly resisting bushwhackers and carpet-baggers, while, to others, Wallace was a symbol of the lawless frontier life that Arkansas needed to transcend.

Sid Wallace was born on the Wallace family farm near Clarksville (Johnson County) on August 11, 1851, the fifth of seven children of Vincent Wallace, who was a Methodist minister, and his wife, Ruth Suggs Wallace. On December 31, 1863, Wallace's father was murdered in front of his house by three or more men wearing Union army coats. Accounts vary concerning whether the attackers were Union soldiers or local bushwhackers in disguise. Some accounts suggest that Wallace was a witness to his father's murder, but others state that he was sheltered from the sight by the family servant (formerly their slave), Missouri Blackard, and perhaps by his mother. According to folklore, Blackard recognized all the attackers, but she refused to identify them to Wallace until he reached his twenty-first birthday.

Folklore has it that, after learning the identity of his father's killers, Wallace traveled to Kansas to kill one of the attackers. He allegedly shot Joseph T. Dickey on a road outside of Clarksville and beat up Dud Turner, a witness to the Dickey shooting. Wallace is also alleged to have killed a man named Davis in Clarksville, Constable R. W. "Doc" Ward, and Judge Elisha Mears. Finally, from his prison cell in Clarksville, Wallace shot and killed Thomas Paine on November 25, 1873. Paine had testified against Wallace regarding the murder of Ward. Some insist that some or all of these shootings were related in some way to the death of Wallace's father.

Wallace also proved to be a difficult man to keep in prison. When he was first arrested for the shooting of Dickey, he removed the jail window and returned home. Reportedly, when a posse arrived to take Wallace back into custody, he left the house hiding under the skirts of Blackard while she went to the family well. After he was back in his cell in Clarksville, Wallace overpowered his guards, seizing their weapons and shooting Paine, although some claim that a girlfriend had smuggled a gun to Wallace in the prison. The standoff at this time ended after Clarksville authorities threatened to blow up the building containing Wallace and his two younger brothers.

Wallace appealed his conviction for the murder of Ward on the grounds that he was unable to receive a fair trial in Johnson County. He and his family consistently maintained that he had been at home, ill, at the times of the shootings of Ward and Mears. Wallace was held in the state penitentiary in Little Rock (Pulaski County) from February 18 until March 9, the Arkansas Supreme Court having ruled against his appeal on February 5. According to folklore, Wallace was allowed out of prison one evening during this period to accompany the warden's daughter to a social ball. The warden is said to have reversed his feelings about the prisoner when his daughter begged that Wallace be permitted to escape so that the couple could elope. On March 10, the *Arkansas Gazette* reported that 1,068 Johnson County residents had signed a petition requesting that Wallace's sentence be commuted.

According to an article in the March 11, 1874, *Gazette*, Wallace arrived in Clarksville uneventfully, although later accounts paint a dramatic tale involving seizure of the train by Clarksville marshal Bud McConnell to prevent Wallace from being rescued before his hanging. Wallace was hanged in Clarksville on March 14, 1874, in front of hundreds of witnesses. Because his heart was still beating twenty-five minutes after the hanging, he was left suspended for forty minutes, at which point he was declared dead and surrendered to his family for burial. Later accounts state that he may have survived the execution and that the

IN JAIL FOR SHOOTING A MAN —

— SIDNEY WALLACE SHOT *ANOTHER* MAN FROM HIS JAIL CELL.

casket buried by his family contained only bags of sand. Such legendary accounts were believable only long after Wallace was publicly hanged.

Adding more intrigue to the story, the March 15, 1874, *Daily Arkansas Gazette* article about his hanging tells of a mysterious note accompanying a bouquet of flowers and a basket of fruit sent to Wallace by a woman in Little Rock. Other accounts describe a woman from Little Rock, dressed in black, who attended the hanging. The *New York Times* published an account of Wallace's crimes and execution a week after his hanging, sadly concluding that Wallace's mother had encouraged her two younger sons to follow in the footsteps of their martyred brother.

The *Times* article and other descriptions of Arkansas history show Wallace as an example of frontier violence following the Civil War. Books such as C. H. McKennon's *Iron Men*, which details law enforcement in Arkansas and neighboring areas, focus attention on the violence of men like Wallace, often exaggerating their exploits to point to the need for increased law and order. Wallace has become somewhat of a folk hero for others, though, as a symbol of local resistance to Reconstruction. Accounts of his attacking only those who murdered his father are not supported by historical evidence, but they continue to be shared in some circles. Ironically, both those who describe Wallace as a hero and those who emphasize his criminal behavior overlook Wallace's frequent claims that he killed no one except in self-defense and that he had been framed for local crimes.

Steven Teske
Butler Center for Arkansas Studies

The Amazing Adventures of My Dog Sheppy

In an effort to promote economic development and tourism in Stone County, a group of local investors under the leadership of Harold M. Sherman filmed a thirty-minute television pilot titled, *The Amazing Adventures of My Dog Sheppy*. A poor script, inept casting, amateurish acting, and the on-camera killing of a bobcat combined to produce a show that could not be pitched to the national networks. The film is significant, however, for documenting 1950s Stone County before the Ozark Folk Center or Blanchard Springs Caverns opened to the public.

The television pilot was the brainchild of Harold Sherman. This Michigan native was the author of more than sixty books, a motivational speaker, and a Hollywood script writer.

In 1958, television shows involving dogs drew large audiences. Sherman, who had written many scripts in his Hollywood days, worked with his friend Al Pollard, an advertising executive in Little Rock (Pulaski County), to write the script for something similar and then set up Mountain View Productions. A production budget of $20,000 was raised from investors in Mountain View (Stone County) and nearby Batesville (Independence County). Dan Milner of Milner Brothers Productions in Hollywood was hired as director and producer.

The script involved a little girl getting lost in the mountains and being saved by a beautiful white German shepherd—and an equally beautiful female archer who dramatically killed a bobcat that was supposed to be threatening the girl. The archer was Ann P. Marston, the reigning female archer in the country. The male lead was Robert Roark, a minor television and stage actor from Hollywood, who played a game warden. Billy Conner, a

nine-year-old boy from Batesville played the role of Sheppy's master, and after winning a newspaper-sponsored contest, nine-year-old Meredith Lee Ross of Little Rock played the role of the lost girl. Folk musician Jimmy Driftwood was given a cameo role as Uncle Orie. Stone County sheriff Cullen Storey had a few lines of dialogue.

Sherman, a friend and supporter of Governor Orval Faubus, received substantial assistance from the state. Faubus hosted a press event in Little Rock on January 29, 1958, to publicize the film, with Marston performing some archery tricks. On hand to "sign" his contract with a paw print was the German shepherd "Kelly," probably the most experienced actor in the production. Faubus also encouraged the Arkansas Game and Fish Commission to trap nine bobcats for use in the film.

Filming on site in Stone County got off to a poor start in early May 1958, with heavy rains followed by hot, humid conditions. Filming took little more than a week. Sherman went to Hollywood to assist with editing the film, and he seemed enthusiastic at first, telling the *Stone County Leader* that "an expert in the field says that it is equal to if not superior to the Lassie series."

Sherman's hopes were soon dashed by advisors in Hollywood, who believed the pilot would not be of interest to a sponsor. Sherman placed most of the blame on Milner Brothers Productions, claiming they had not adequately rehearsed the actors. He also mentioned that the casting was poor, and that the killing of the bobcat would not be acceptable.

On July 25, 1958, the pilot showed at the Melba Theater in Batesville, the only public showing it received. Sherman continued to promote the idea of filming a TV pilot in Stone County, but he was never successful in doing so. The original film is now part of the archival collections at the University of Central Arkansas (UCA) Torreyson Library in Conway (Faulkner County).

Tom W. Dillard
Glen Rose, Arkansas

Atkins Pickle Company

Atkins Pickle Company was the major industry in the town of Atkins (Pope County) for more than fifty years, and its legacy survives in the annual Picklefest celebration that began in 1992. The building that housed the pickle plant now houses Atkins Prepared Foods. The new company employs more people than the pickle plant did at its end, but it does not provide the same level of recognition for the town once dubbed the "Pickle Capital of the World" and known as the home of the fried dill pickle.

In 1946, a group of citizens led by Lee Cheek raised $17,000 for a loan to the Goldsmith Pickle Company of Chicago, which had agreed to invest $75,000 of its money if $15,000 was raised locally. The company purchased land and erected two buildings. The original facility also contained fifty-seven wooden tanks with a storage capacity of 1,000 bushels each. On July 17, 1946, a test run was made, and the Atkins Pickle Company plant began full operations a few days later with approximately 100 employees. The payroll had increased to 150 by August. The plant grew during the next two years. With W. W. Daugherty

Workers sorting pickles at Atkins Pickle Company; 1955.
Courtesy of Van A. Tyson

as field representative, the plant had contracts with 821 farmers for 1,200 acres of cucumbers. Roy Taylor, a vocational agriculture teacher, succeeded Daugherty as field manager in 1951 and continued in the position for several years.

When the plant failed to make a profit during its first two years, Goldsmith sold it to a group of Arkansas businessmen, including C. Hamilton Moses and Virgil Jackson, both of Little Rock (Pulaski County), and William Forrest Lemley of Russellville (Pope County). On February 28, 1951, it was purchased by a group headed by E. G. Watkins of Little Rock and his wife, who hired Robert Switzer as chemist. He developed many of the products that were important for the company's growth. He developed pickled baby tomatoes, called "Tomolives," and formulated the improved taste and crispness of fresh-packed sweet and dill pickles.

Several other ownership changes came during the 1950s and 1960s, until sales reached $2.4 million in 1962 and totaled $3.1

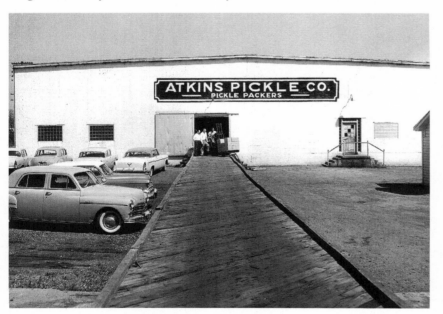

Front view of Atkins Pickle Company; 1955.
Courtesy of Van A. Tyson

million by 1966. Switzer resigned in 1968 to organize a pickle company in New Mexico. Russell Dilks, who joined the company in 1964, was credited with improving sales techniques and the appearance of products. During the 1960s and 1970s, the company continued to buy products from small growers in Arkansas, Mississippi, and Texas, including some grown at the state prison farms. It had sales of $5 million, with major markets in Arkansas, Texas, Missouri, Tennessee, and Colorado.

During the early years, the plant produced specialty items such as Tomolives, as well as pickled okra, peppers, and onions. Gift packs of these items were given to dignitaries visiting Arkansas. However, after Dean Foods bought the plant in 1983, it shifted production to varieties of pickles that could be mass produced, and sales soon reached more than $40 million. Employment was 400 to 500 during the early fresh-pack seasons. In 1992, the Atkins Picklefest was inaugurated, with the pickle plant being a major contributor and providing all the pickles as well as tours of the plant.

Dean Foods closed the plant in 2002 in the midst of a flooded market. Another factor in the plant's closure was the purchase of Dean by Suiza Corporation. The company retained the Atkins trademark at first but has since discontinued its use. In 2004, the plant was turned over to Atkins Prepared Foods, which processes chicken.

Van A. Tyson
The Atkins Chronicle

ATKINS PICKLE PLANT CLOSED IN 2002-

BUT THE TOWN STILL CELEBRATES PICKLEFEST AND FRIED PICKLES.

Black Bears

Black bears (*Ursus americanus*) have a rich and varied history in Arkansas. Once giving the state its unofficial nickname (the "Bear State"), bruins long shaped society and culture in Arkansas and continue to do so. Used for meat, fur, and fat, bears were a valuable commodity in the colonial period. By the early nineteenth century, although bears were still prized for their original uses, the bear-human relationship began to shift toward overt exploitation, and bear hunting became a quest for masculine identity. By the first decades of the twentieth century, Arkansas black bears were at the brink of extirpation, but the population has since been revived.

Native Americans were the first to hunt black bears in the region. Documented evidence of an abundance of bears in what would become Arkansas dates back to early European exploration. Increasingly intense utilization of black bears by the French and Spanish took place from the early eighteenth century onward. By the first decades of the 1700s, large groups of hunters trudged through the hills and deltas seeking all types of available wildlife but were especially interested in bears. Bear fat—more than meat or fur—was prized for its multiple uses, including as fuel for oil lamps, insect repellent, and hair gel. Indeed, through much of the eighteenth and early nineteenth centuries, bear products represented a key segment of the local economy. Before unregulated mass hunting destroyed the bruin population, large numbers of bears were found statewide, centering not only in the Ozark Plateau and Ouachita Mountains but also throughout canebrakes, river valleys, and the Delta.

Arkansas black bears play the starring role in some of the most important and well-known literary pieces of early nineteenth-century literature and folklore. Known throughout the young United States (and through much of Europe) as a hunter's paradise, Arkansas Territory (and, by 1836, the state of Arkansas) was a prime destination for domestic and foreign hunters.

Among the most famous of these was Friedrich Gerstäcker, a German tourist and avid hunter who sought the ultimate experience in Arkansas in the late 1830s. Gerstäcker's exploits while in the company of various Arkansas residents were later published in Europe and the United States, leading to increased interest and hunting in the region. With Gerstäcker's tales came some of the most powerful signs of bear hunting as a masculine endeavor—one in which utilization as the primary goal was replaced by adventure and a sense of reputation. This "honor" through hunting bears as exuded by Gerstäcker and others grew throughout the mid- to late nineteenth century and became a favorite topic for authors and humorists. "Fent" Noland's articles in the *Spirit of the Times* and Thomas Bangs Thorpe's "The Big Bear of Arkansas" further illuminated the close connection between black bears and the culture of nineteenth-century Arkansas.

As Arkansas's population increased following the Civil War, newspapers across the state rang with stories concerning bear attacks or property destruction. The wilderness of Arkansas was slowly becoming populated, and this led to increased bear-human encounters and effectively changed black bears' status in society. Remarkable stories of early hunters crawling into caves after bears turned to less romantic announcements of bears dragging off small children or devouring farmers' pigs. As the latter stories increased, many of which were fanciful, so too did large-scale exploitive hunting of Arkansas bruins by market hunters seeking economic profit. Locals also shot bears on sight and, along with market hunters, used packs of dogs to help chase them down. By 1927, due to over hunting and habitat loss, black bears had become nearly extirpated in the state, with an estimated forty-five bruins remaining in the dense forested wetlands along the lower White and Cache rivers. That same year, the Arkansas Game and Fish Commission (AGFC) officially ended any hunting season for bears. The state nickname was changed as well—with Arkansas being officially recognized as the "Wonder State," then later known as the "Natural State."

Starting in 1959, and throughout the next decade, the AGFC released 256 black bears from Minnesota and Canada into Arkansas. With no hunting allowed until the 1980s, the new bear population thrived. Carefully regulated hunting in the last decades of the twentieth century and into the twenty-first century helped yield a stable bruin population. Although the presence of bears has yet to promote the widespread interest in Arkansas that it once did, their re-emergence throughout the Ozark Plateau and Ouachita Mountains has helped endorse the state's campaign for its naturalness—a tourism movement based on the premise of the "Natural State." In the first part of the twenty-first century, the Arkansas black bear population throughout the state continues to prosper, numbering over 3,000.

Matthew M. Stith
University of Texas at Tyler

COBBITES

- WALKED ON THEIR ROOFS-

BEFORE THEY WENT CRAZIER.

Cobbites

The Cobbites were a religious group that began in White County in 1876 under the leadership of the Reverend Cobb. Their strange behavior eventually culminated in the gruesome murder of a local citizen and several Cobbites. The group did not last past 1876.

Cobb called himself "the walking preacher." Little is known about him, not even his full name, other than that he traveled from Tennessee to White County in 1876. To his followers, he claimed to be God or Jesus Christ. He apparently believed he could perform the works of God, and he used a sycamore pole to command the sun to rise each morning and did the same each evening to command it to set.

His followers were just as fanatical and strange. A common practice among the Cobbites was walking back and forth on the housetop with their eyes shut. They seemed convinced that this proved they were protected and commissioned by God. They believed that the only way to become like Christ was to be sanctified. Sanctification could only come through Cobb to the women, and then through the women to the rest of the group; his idea was based upon 1 Corinthians 7:14, in which Paul writes, "The unbelieving husband is sanctified by the wife." They believed that a person who was sanctified could not sin and could not be harmed. It is unclear exactly what the Cobbites believed beyond sanctification and divine protection.

The Cobbites did not become a large group, consisting mainly of two local families, the Dovers and the Nelsons, led by Cobb. The group settled in a two-story log house a few miles south of Searcy (White County). It was owned by a Preacher Dover (full name unknown). They destroyed all the furniture in the house, killed all the cats and dogs, and tore down the fences to let the cattle roam free. A few of the Cobbites would stand near the road, drag passersby from their buggies and horses, and make them pray inside the house. Local citizens became alarmed by the bizarre behavior of the Cobbites. Others who heard the strange tales traveled to the settlement to satisfy their curiosity.

One such curious citizen, a Searcy (White County) bartender named Carter Humphries, along with his friend Rufus Blake, traveled to the Cobbite settlement to see what all the fuss was about. When the Cobbites saw the men, they came toward them, telling Humphries and Blake that "God is here" and "come in and see God." Humphries made a sarcastic remark, and the Cobbites dragged the men from their wagon with shouts of "Kill them!" and "Cut their heads off!" A dull axe was brought out, and Humphries's neck was stretched over a nearby tree root. His body was held still, and Dover proceeded to chop off Humphries's head. When Blake saw what was in store for him, he escaped from the Cobbites and rushed back to town.

An armed mob formed and rushed to the Cobbite settlement. The Cobbites claimed that the mob's guns would not go off, but after an initial misfire, several did, and Dover and his son-in-law were killed. The rest of the Cobbites were arrested; several later became ill and died in prison. Reverend Cobb disappeared soon after, and the rest of the Cobbites dispersed.

Shelby Watkins
Little Rock, Arkansas

Crater of Diamonds State Park

Located on State Highway 301 in Pike County, the Crater of Diamonds State Park contains the world's only diamond mine that is open to the public.

John Wesley Huddleston, a farmer and sometime prospector, first found diamonds on the site in 1906. Huddleston's discovery sparked a diamond rush in Pike County. Diamond-bearing soil was also found on Millard M. Mauney's property that was adjacent to Huddleston's. Prospectors and fortune hunters rushed to the area, and soon the town of Kimberly developed to accommodate the influx of people.

Within a few years of the discovery, all the land on top of Prairie Creek Pipe was in the hands of two rival companies: Arkansas

Searching for diamonds at Crater of Diamonds State Park near Murfreesboro (Pike County).
Courtesy of the Arkansas Department of Parks and Tourism

Diamond Company and Ozark Diamond Mines Corporation. The two companies maintained mining operations sporadically over the next forty years but operated under constant financial strain, poor management, lawsuits, and sabotage.

In 1924, a 40.23-carat diamond was found by Wesley Oley Basham, a workman for the Arkansas Diamond Company. The diamond was dubbed with Basham's nickname, and the "Uncle Sam," as it is called, still holds the record as the largest diamond ever found in the United States.

The owners of the rival companies formed a partnership in 1952 and opened the property to the public as a tourist attraction called the Crater of Diamonds. For a nominal fee, visitors were allowed to search for diamonds and keep what they found. The venture was a modest success from the start. Well-known diamonds found during this time included the 15.33-carat Star of Arkansas (1956), the 6.42-carat Gary Moore diamond (1960), and the 34.25-carat Star of Murfreesboro (1964).

The Crater of Diamonds was purchased by the State of Arkansas in 1972 and established as Crater of Diamonds State Park. Each year, the park hosts thousands of visitors and averages two diamonds found daily. Crater diamonds are usually less than a carat in size and come in all colors, with white, yellow, and brown being the most common. They are usually smooth and rounded in appearance and have an almost metallic luster. In addition to diamonds, the search field also yields agate, jasper, quartz, and amethyst.

The most well-known diamond found since the area became a state park is probably the Strawn-Wagner. Shirley Strawn of Murfreesboro found this 3.03-carat diamond in 1990. It was cut to a 1.09-carat brilliant shape and certified as a perfect D flawless diamond, the highest quality diamond ever graded by the American Gemological Society. Strawn gave the diamond her name and that of her great-great-grandfather, Lee Wagner. The diamond is on display at the park.

In the early 1990s, Governor Bill Clinton signed a bill to authorize a lease for commercial exploration and mining at the park. Four companies participated in a cooperative project to explore the possibility of mining the area. By 1994, the land had not yielded enough return to make a full-scale mining operation viable, and the companies withdrew. Since 1996, additional tests and sampling have resulted in minimal yields.

The park encompasses 911 acres of woodlands along the Little Missouri River, including a 37-acre search field visitors can access for a small admission fee. The search field sits atop an ancient volcanic vent called the Prairie Creek Pipe. The volcanic explosion that formed this pipe more than 100 million years ago brought diamonds from deep within the earth's mantle to the surface.

Staff of the Arkansas Department of Parks and Tourism

ANYBODY CAN DIG FOR THE STATE GEM AT CRATER OF DIAMONDS STATE PARK.

Crescent Hotel

The Crescent Hotel was built in 1886 in Eureka Springs (Carroll County) by the Eureka Springs Investment Company, the president of which was former governor Powell Clayton. The organization purchased twenty-seven acres of wooded land for the site of the hotel and hired Isaac S. Taylor from St. Louis, Missouri, as architect for the project. The massive eighteen-inch-thick stones used for the body of the hotel were made of limestone, hand-carved from a quarry on the White River near Beaver (Carroll County) by a crew of Irish workers. These stones were hauled to the site of the hotel on trains and specially constructed wagons, and were placed in such a fashion that no mortar was needed.

The hotel boasted every modern convenience, from electricity to elevators, and was well known for its location near the springs and their supposedly healing waters. The cost for this hotel, declared America's most opulent resort, was $294,000. The hotel

The Historic Crescent Hotel in Eureka Springs.
Courtesy of the Arkansas Department of Parks and Tourism

opened its doors to the public on May 1, 1886, with an open house two weeks later. On May 20, a banquet was held for guest of honor James G. Blaine, the 1884 Republican presidential nominee. A gala ball was held for the 400 attendants, with Harry Barton's orchestra entertaining, followed by a speech from Blaine.

The Crescent enjoyed great success for many years, but as the economy worsened in the 1900s, the hotel opened for business only during the summer months. The Eureka Springs Investment Company formulated a plan to use the facility year-round and, in 1908, opened the hotel as an elite girls' boarding school called Crescent College and Conservatory for Young Women. The college operated from September through June, converting into a hotel during the summer months. The college remained open for sixteen years but was forced to close its doors in 1924 due to lack of funding, although it reopened for a time.

In 1925, the Crescent was sold, and its new owners advertised the hotel for its exquisite cuisine and special weekly rates. By 1929, the hotel had changed hands again and was open only seasonally. Business was further slowed by the onset of the Depression, and the Crescent closed its doors in 1933. In 1937, the hotel was purchased by Norman Baker, who opened the Baker Hospital and Health Resort in 1938 to serve cancer patients. The lobby of the hotel was remodeled and painted bright purple. It featured large geometric designs, which reflected the character and wardrobe of its owner. This venture, however, was short lived; Baker was convicted of mail fraud in 1940, and the hospital closed. The Crescent fell into disrepair for six years, and not until 1946 was the property purchased again and renovated to its original look, reopening on July 4, 1946, as "A Castle in the Air High Atop the Ozarks."

The hotel has enjoyed a long period of success, despite a fire on the fourth floor in 1967, which damaged some of the building. In 1973, restorations began, and the hotel was again open to the public by May of that year. Renovations came again in 1980 to restore the original luxury to the hotel, and improvements continued to be made until 2002. The hotel remains open, with the addition of the New Moon Spa to the basement level, which reflects the original purpose of the hotel as a destination for relaxation and healing.

The hotel is also a member of the National Trust Historic Hotels of America and has been featured on the Discovery Channel for its historic Victorian beauty.

The hotel has also had many reported ghost sightings (stemming primarily from its time as a hospital), including the ghost of Dr. Baker and the ghost of a nurse pushing a gurney. An apparition called Theodora, who was a patient of Dr. Baker, is said to haunt room 419, and rooms 414 and 218 are also supposedly haunted.

Jenny Vego
Millington, Tennessee

Dardanelle Pontoon Bridge

The Dardanelle Pontoon Bridge was the largest pontoon bridge in existence in the United States, crossing the Arkansas River between Dardanelle (Yell County) and Russellville (Pope County). A toll bridge, it opened for traffic in 1891 and lasted until the construction of a steel bridge replacement in 1929.

The bridge cost $25,000, financed by a group of stockholders and built by Roberts and Sons of Independence, Missouri. Construction started in 1889, and the bridge opened for traffic on April 1, 1891. It was over 2,200 feet long and eighteen feet wide, with a load limit of 9,000 pounds. Originally, each end of the bridge was anchored to a piling, and only the center actually floated.

The Dardanelle Pontoon Bridge, spanning the Arkansas River between Dardanelle and Russellville.
Courtesy of the U.S. Army Corps of Engineers

However, the fluctuation of the river level led to the removal of the pilings, so that the bridge floated entirely upon seventy-two boats, held in place by a steel cable connected to a series of seven towers that stretched along the length of the bridge. A special steamboat was kept on hand to assist in removing the bridge, which could be disassembled into thirteen separate sections in the event of high water or to open the way for river traffic. The steamboat was then used to ferry passengers and freight across the river.

One month after its opening, the bridge almost washed out, and its owners sold it to a company of Dardanelle residents. In 1892, it was purchased by the Dardanelle Railroad Company. It was later sold to the McAlester Fuel Company.

The initial toll rates were as follows: five cents for a person walking, fifteen cents for a person on horseback, five cents per horse or cow, twenty-five cents for a single buggy, and thirty-five cents for a double buggy. When automobiles were introduced to the area, they were charged fifty cents per car and seventy-five cents per truck or five-passenger car.

In early 1928, a rise in the river level tore the bridge from its moorings, and more than forty of the seventy-two pontoons were swept downstream. The owners wanted to abandon the bridge, given that a new steel bridge had begun construction nearby on November 30, 1927. However, the State Highway Department, recognizing the need for the pontoon bridge in the interim, provided aid for the replacement of the lost pontoons, and the bridge was back in commission by late February, though it served the local population for less than a year after it was rebuilt. The new Highway 22 bridge was dedicated on January 17, 1929, and the Dardanelle Pontoon Bridge was removed.

Guy Lancaster
Encyclopedia of Arkansas History & Culture

BALLOON?-NO! SPITTOON?-NO!

PONTOON?-YES!

THE DARDANELLE PONTOON BRIDGE WAS THE LONGEST OF ITS KIND.

Eureka Springs Baby

The 1880 discovery of a fossilized human child in Eureka Springs (Carroll County) was not revealed as a hoax until 1948. The find was exhibited locally and then around the state. Within a year, the carving—known variously as the "Eureka Baby," the "Petrified Indian Baby," or as a Hindu idol—had been exhibited in St. Louis, Missouri; Galveston, Texas; and New Orleans, Louisiana. It was also reportedly en route to the Smithsonian Institution in Washington DC at the time of its disappearance.

This hoax was the brainchild of Henry Johnson, a Scottsville (Pope County) merchant who closely modeled his deception on the nationally famous Cardiff Giant. This massive stone man was "discovered" in 1869 in Cardiff, New York, and publicly acknowledged as a hoax the following year in a lawsuit that pitted its originator against showman P. T. Barnum. In both the Cardiff and Eureka Springs hoaxes, the stone likenesses were created by tombstone carvers, buried, and then unearthed by well diggers. Both hoaxes made money for the owners.

In 1880, many newspaper writers appeared convinced of the validity of the Eureka Springs find, calling it "proof of pre-Adamic generations" or predicting that it would "revolutionize geology." There were some skeptics, however. L. J. Kalklosch, Eureka Springs's earliest historian, while never claiming to have viewed the baby, agreed with those who called it "a humbug." Other newspapers expressed doubts, but most telling of all was the *Arkansas Gazette*, which opined of the "petrified Indian baby" that "there has never been such a thing before. Indian blood was never claimed for the Cardiff giant."

T. J. Rowbotham at about ninety years old—around the time he revealed the Eureka Springs Baby as a hoax. Courtesy of the Rowbotham family

Henry Johnson had the means and the connections to undertake such a scam, as he was related to Marcus Lafayette Kelly, a Fayetteville (Washington County) tombstone carver. Kelly created the eighty-five-pound, twenty-six-inch-long statue of a child, which was later encased in a thick coating of clay and ash, aging the marble to a mottled blue-gray color. Around the time it was being carved, Thomas Campbell (also of Pope County) and J. B. Hallum of Texas arrived in Eureka Springs. Hallum bought a piece of land near town and hired Campbell to dig a well on it. On October 1, Campbell, working alone, supposedly dug up the baby at a depth of four feet.

In 1880, Eureka Springs was just a year old, but belief in the curative powers of the town's many springs had attracted hundreds of health-seekers. Thus, in addition to the townspeople, there was a large audience of invalids eager to see the latest attraction. Johnson (who established his claim by supposedly buying a share in the baby's ownership), Hallum, and Campbell charged ten cents to view the find, later raising the rate to thirty-five cents. Within three months, having exhausted local interest, the men took their creation to Clarksville (Johnson County) and then Russellville (Pope County) before selling out to two Little Rock (Pulaski County) investors for a reported $4,600. The baby changed owners again over the course of its travels.

In 1948, after all of the participants were dead, T. J. Rowbotham gave an interview to the *Arkansas Democrat*, revealing the connections between the participants. Rowbotham's brother John lived in Eureka Springs in 1880 and rented a room to Henry Johnson; Hallum was the Rowbothams' brother-in-law and lived nearby. Campbell surely knew Johnson back in Pope County because he used Johnson's business partner as a character witness when making a sworn statement concerning his "find."

T. J. Rowbotham also revealed that Johnson and Kelly were related by marriage, and he stated that the baby had been seen in an unidentified Chicago, Illinois, museum, complete with information on its origins.

To date, the carving has not been located, but it is known that it did not end up at the Smithsonian. However, a similar stone baby of unknown origin is held by the Museum of Discovery in Little Rock.

Abby Burnett
Kingston, Arkansas

"The Fayetteville Polka"

"The Fayetteville Polka" was written by Austrian immigrant Ferdinand Zellner in honor of his adopted hometown of Fayetteville (Washington County). It was accepted for publication in 1856, becoming what is said to be the first published piece of sheet music by an Arkansan.

Ferdinand Zellner came to the United States in 1850, when the showman P. T. Barnum brought Swedish soprano Jenny Lind from Europe to the United States on a concert tour that ran through 1852. Called the "Swedish Nightingale," she was one of the greatest coloratura sopranos of the nineteenth century, possessing a voice of outstanding range and quality. Zellner, a young Austrian violinist, accompanied her on her prestigious U.S. tour.

At the end of Lind's U.S. tour in 1852, she returned to Europe, but Zellner stayed in Arkansas. By 1854, he was professor of music at Sophia Sawyer's Fayetteville Female Seminary. In her journal, Marian Tebbetts of Fayetteville, a student at the time, noted that while he was so educated in music as to have been

Lind's violinist, he could not sing. Therefore, he concentrated on teaching, performing on the violin, and writing music.

In 1856, Zellner traveled to St. Louis, Missouri, and visited the noted musical publishing house of Balmer and Weber. That year, Balmer and Weber published his composition, "The Fayetteville Polka," written in honor of his adopted town. The lively three-part polka was dedicated to Katy Smith, a student at Sawyer's school who came from a prominent local family. According to the Old State House Museum in Little Rock (Pulaski County), "The Fayetteville Polka" was the first piece of sheet music by an Arkansan to be published.

The song was well received at the time of its publication and is still performed by regional musicians at events sponsored by the Washington County Historical Society and other local organizations. It was the theme song for the play *Second to None*, which was presented at the Walton Arts Center in 1999.

Nancy Hendricks
Garland County Historical Society

Sheet music for "The Fayetteville Polka"; 1856.
Courtesy of Special Collections, University of Arkansas Libraries, Fayetteville

Fouke Monster

Fouke (Miller County) is a small town in southwest Arkansas that attracted attention in the early 1970s when a resident of Texarkana (Miller County) reported being attacked by a mysterious creature there. A reporter for the *Texarkana Gazette* wrote an article about the events, and from that small publication, a legend was born. Fouke and its monster became famous and were featured in a 1973 movie.

In May 1971, Bobby Ford reported to the Fouke constable that he was attacked at his house by a hairy creature that breathed heavily, had red eyes, and moved very fast. Ford said the man-like creature, which was about seven feet tall and three feet across the chest, put its arm around his shoulder and grabbed him. Ford broke free from the creature and ran, reporting that he ran so fast that he did not stop to open the front door but barreled right through it. He was treated at a local hospital for minor scratches and shock.

Ford said the being had been around his house for several days and that there were other eyewitnesses, including his brother and a hunting companion. Ford's wife, Elizabeth, claimed that she was asleep in the front room when she saw a hairy arm with claws coming in the window. She also saw the creature's red eyes. On the night of the attack, Ford claimed, he and his

hunting companions spotted the creature at the back of Ford's house with the aid of a flashlight. They shot at it and thought they saw it fall. The men started out toward it, but Bobby Ford ran back to the house when the group heard women screaming. Upon Ford's return to the house, he was attacked. The men shot at the creature several more times, but investigators never found blood. The sheriff's department searched the area, and the officers found only a set of strange tracks and claw scratches on the Fords' porch.

Jim Powell, then a reporter for the *Texarkana Gazette* and the *Texarkana Daily News*, and Dave Hall, then the director of Texarkana radio station KTFS, went to the Ford Place and found a terrified family moving out of the house it had owned less than a week. Powell wrote an article that appeared in the newspaper, outlining the family's alleged sighting and attack. The next day, both the *Texarkana Gazette* and the *Texarkana Daily* published the same follow-up story. It contained the first reference to the name "Fouke Monster." The Associated Press and United Press International wire services transmitted the article to newspapers across the nation.

In 1973, the incident was made into a low-budget movie, *The Legend of Boggy Creek*, which perpetuated the story to an even larger audience. The movie, filmed in Fouke, is a pseudo-documentary thriller about the creature and the town, and it stars some of the eyewitnesses and residents of Fouke. Reported sightings of the Fouke Monster date back as far as 1946, when a resident reported to Miller County sheriff Leslie Greer that she had seen a strange creature near her home. Sightings of a creature have been reported throughout Fouke history, but no sighting has been as famous as the one that gained national attention in 1971.

Amy Michelle Thompson
North Little Rock, Arkansas

Ghost Legends

Arkansas is rife with legends of ghosts and haunted places. Some of these legends, such as those surrounding the nationally famous Gurdon Light or the historic Crescent Hotel, are unique to the state, though Arkansas has also been one of the locations cited in well-known, widely reported legends, such as that of the "vanishing hitchhiker," which has been ascribed to localities across the country.

The Crescent Hotel in Eureka Springs (Carroll County) is one of Arkansas's most famous haunted locations. The ghost of former owner Dr. Norman Baker, who turned the hotel into a health resort and hospital in the 1930s, is said to wander around the old recreation room by the foot of the stairs leading to the first floor. In July 1987, a woman reported having seen a ghost of a nurse pushing a gurney down a hallway in the middle of the night. Another ghost believed to haunt the Crescent Hotel is a man named Michael, who died during the hotel's initial construction. Sources disagree on whether he is Swedish or Irish. Another ghost, usually seen in the lobby or the bar, whose identity is unknown, is described as a dignified, bearded man in formal clothing. The ghost of a cancer patient of Dr. Baker is said to haunt room 419, and people report seeing ghosts in other rooms as well. It is uncertain when these ghost stories began, but reports of ghost sightings increased dramatically in the 1990s.

A famous Arkansas haunted house is the Allen House in Monticello (Drew County). It was built in 1905 by Joe Lee Allen, who lived there with his wife, Caddye, and his children, Ladelle, Lonnie Lee, and Louis. Pictures of them still hang in the front hall. Joe Lee Allen died in 1917. Sometime later, Ladelle committed suicide in the south bedroom by drinking potassium cyanide. Caddye Allen had the room sealed off until 1986, when new owners opened it up and found the bottle of cyanide still sitting on a shelf in a closet. The house is said to be haunted by Ladelle and her son, Allen Bonner. Since the 1950s, tenants of the Allen House have heard footsteps and moans and have reported other supernatural incidents. One couple, seeing a closet door ajar, tried to close it but felt someone pushing back on the other side. When they opened the door, they saw no one.

Several places in the natural world are the sites of their own ghost legends, usually connected to murders. Lorance Creek in Saline County is said to be haunted by a girl, her name unknown, who was apparently murdered by being pushed into the creek; she was buried at Cockman Cemetery near the creek a few days later on December 24, 1863. By the 1920s, her wooden grave marker was entirely weathered away. The first reported sightings of her ghost were in 1920, when workers started drilling for oil near the creek and cemetery. Some workers said they heard a girl's scream, and one worker reported seeing her on Halloween. She was crying and was heard cry out, "Why?" She then walked to the creek and disappeared. She was seen several times later that year, reportedly appearing in the white dress she was buried in. After the workers left, her ghost was seldom seen.

The famous Gurdon Light has spawned its own ghost story. The phenomenon consists of a light floating above the railroad tracks near the town of Gurdon (Clark County). A variety of scientific explanations have been advanced to explain the light, but local legend connects it to a murder. In December 1931, a railway worker attacked his foreman with a shovel and then beat him with a spike maul, killing him. Other stories attached to the Gurdon Light include those of a miner looking for his wife or his daughter, or a man looking for his head because it was cut off by robbers or by a train. The light is, in all the stories, said to be the light of a lantern held by the ghost. Similar stories exist in Stamps (Lafayette County) regarding a dangerous railroad crossing where several people have died.

Of course, Arkansas is home to "migratory" ghost legends—stories that are widely known across the country and happen to have been reported with Arkansas connections. In one community, several men report having seen a headless man who wanders on or near a certain ridge on dark, drizzly nights, crying out and looking for his head. Another legend reports that a woman and her baby were killed in a car crash on a bridge over Faulkner Lake in Pulaski County and that, if a person stands on the bank and yells, "Mama Lou, come and get me," three times, the ghost of the mother will drag the person into the lake, thinking that person is her baby. Such legends are common across the United States, each with its own local variation.

One of the most famous migratory legends reported in Arkansas is that of the "vanishing hitchhiker." One version reports that a man driving from Batesville (Independence County) to Little Rock (Pulaski County) sees a girl by the side of the road. She is wearing white and has a torn dress and a cut above her eye. The man stops to offer her a ride, and she gives him her address, explaining that she has been in an accident. When he arrives at her place, he realizes that she is no longer in the car with him. Confused, he gets out of his car and knocks on the front door. An older man answers; he is not surprised to hear about the incident and explains that the girl is the ghost of his daughter, who had died in a car crash two months before. At midnight, she appears at the place she died and asks the driver of a passing car to take her back home. Other versions of this story take place near Redfield (Jefferson County) or Woodson (Pulaski County).

Of course, this by no means constitutes a full accounting of ghost legends in Arkansas. Most communities can cite at least one haunted place linked to a specific past incident. Others, such as the cemetery of Keller's Chapel in Jonesboro (Craighead County), have dozens of legends associated with them. Ghost legends continue to proliferate in Arkansas, as they do elsewhere, with new stories being told every day.

Magdalena Teske
North Little Rock, Arkansas

Gowrow

The gowrow, one of several monsters reported in Arkansas popular lore, may owe its origins more to journalism than to traditional narrative and folk belief. The principal documentation of the creature's existence is a story that appeared in the *Arkansas Gazette* on January 31, 1897, apparently written by Elbert Smithee. Elmer Burrus provided an illustration, allegedly based on a photograph, to accompany the piece.

Fred W. Allsopp, who edited the *Gazette* at the time, recounted the circumstances that led to Smithee's story. William Miller, a Little Rock businessman who had been traveling in the Ozarks of northwest Arkansas, told Smithee of a "horrible monster" known as the gowrow. Its name came from the noise it made during its nocturnal depredations. The creature had been slaughtering livestock and pets near Blanco (Searcy County) in Calf Creek Township. Miller formed a posse that tracked the gowrow to its lair, a cave littered with animal skeletons and even some human remains. As they waited to ambush the monster, they heard it emerge from a nearby lake, causing the earth to tremble as it made its way toward them. The gowrow perished after several volleys from the posse. Before its death, it ripped up several trees and tore off the leg of one of the posse members.

An examination of the remains revealed a creature twenty feet in length with two tusks, large webbed feet ending in claws, a row of short horns along its back, and a long thin tail with a blade on the end. Williams claimed to have sent the body to the Smithsonian Institution, but it never arrived at the Washington DC museum. Allsopp dismissed the account: "It was a great fake, probably without foundation in fact."

The Ozark research conducted by folklore collector Vance Randolph revealed additional details about the gowrow, which he believed had been reported as early as the 1880s. Randolph's sources suggested that the gowrow was a species of creature rather than an individual monstrosity. The young hatched from soft-shelled eggs as large as beer kegs, and the mother carried newly hatched infants in a pouch. Randolph related a story about an encounter with a gowrow by a spelunker exploring Devil's Hole in Boone County. He also told of someone from Mena (Polk County) who claimed to have captured a gowrow by inducing the creature to eat so many dried apples that it swelled to a size that prevented its escaping into its burrow. The gowrow's captor was exhibiting his catch to anyone who would pay a quarter. Once he had a sufficient audience, the man would stagger from behind a curtain with his clothes in rags announcing that the gowrow had escaped. This sent the crowd into a panic without his having to produce an actual gowrow.

Creatures such as the gowrow abound in the folklore of exaggeration that is often associated with the frontier. Though sometimes stories about them may be told as true, more frequently they are tall tales or "lies," as some storytellers classify them. In fact, Randolph presented his material on the gowrow in his collection of tall tales titled *We Always Lie to Strangers.*

William M. Clements
Arkansas State University

Oddities

Gurdon Light

The Gurdon Light is a mysterious floating light above the railroad tracks near Gurdon (Clark County) that was first sighted during the 1930s. Many theories and stories exist to explain the light, including one that connects it the 1931 murder of William McClain, a railroad foreman. The popular local legend drew national attention in December 1994, when NBC's *Unsolved Mysteries* television show documented the phenomenon.

Gurdon is located approximately eighty-five miles south of Little Rock (Pulaski County) on Interstate 30, just east of the interstate on Highway 67. The light appears along a stretch of railroad tracks outside of the town. Some people believe the light originates from the reflection of headlights from cars on Interstate 30.

WHAT— IS THE EERIE GURDON LIGHT?

SOME SAY A GHOST WITH NO HEAD!

However, the site is more than two miles from the highway, and people began seeing the light several decades before Interstate 30 was built in the 1970s. Others believe that swamp gas creates the light, though the light appears in all kinds of weather. Still others believe that pressure on the quartz crystal underneath Gurdon causes them to let off electricity and produce the light.

Many trace the Gurdon Light legend to a murder that took place near the railroad tracks in December 1931. William McClain, a railroad foreman with the Missouri Pacific, was involved in an argument with one of his employees, Louis McBride, regarding how many days McBride was being allowed to work. Since it was during the Depression, the company did not have the option of giving McBride more hours on the job. McBride became very angry, hit McClain on the head with a shovel, and beat him to death with a railroad spike maul or a spike hammer. The Gurdon Light was first sighted shortly after this murder, and many have come to believe that the light is actually McClain's ghostly lantern glowing.

Another somewhat popular story is that a railroad worker was working outside of town one night when he accidentally fell into the path of the train and was killed. Since his head was severed from his body, many locals say that the light is the lantern his ghost uses while looking for his head.

The local legends made the area near Gurdon a very popular place, especially around Halloween. The story became so well known that, in October 1994, NBC's *Unsolved Mysteries* television show traveled to the Gurdon area to film a re-creation of the 1931 murder. The program aired on December 16, 1994, documenting the phenomenon of the Gurdon Light and describing the legend behind it.

Staci Nicole Morrow
Ouachita Baptist University

140

Harmonial Vegetarian Society

The Harmonial Vegetarian Society was an experiment in communal living in Benton County, along the lines of the famed Oneida Community of New York, whose members practiced a strict vegetarian diet and shared all property in common. Though it was in existence for only four years, it has the distinction of being the only utopian commune in nineteenth-century Arkansas.

Historical records regarding the Harmonial Vegetarian Society are sketchy at best. The community started in about 1857 when Dr. James E. Spencer, a Connecticut physician, moved to Arkansas and purchased a large tract of land in Benton County. He named this land Harmony Springs and settled a group of vegetarian "Reform Christians" on his property later that year. This group, for which Spencer served as a spokesperson, seems to have held beliefs similar to those of the Oneida Community—namely, an emphasis on humankind's ability to achieve illumination and perfection on earth through works rather than faith. They set aside no specific day for worship; thus, they were all accused of breaking the Sabbath in April 1859 and later convicted. A history of the area put out by Goodspeed Publishing Company in 1889 asserts that the society also renounced marriage and instead chose mates by lots, though there is no direct evidence of this.

It is unknown how large the community was at its apex, but thirty-eight members of the group responded to the 1860 census. In the spring of 1859, the vegetarians began building a large mansion to house the Harmonial Healing Institute, which, Spencer announced, would make available to people the "Hydro-Electrical system of medical application." In a July 27, 1859, letter to the *Arkansas True Democrat*, Spencer also announced the opening of a post office at Harmony Springs. The society began publishing a monthly paper, the *Theocrat*, in August 1859. By fall of the next year, the group was formally chartered as the Har-

monial Vegetarian Society and bought the original acreage and a separate parcel of land from Spencer for $6,000.

Soon after receiving this payment, Spencer exited the state with what is only described as a female companion—perhaps his wife or someone else—thus depriving the society's Harmonial Healing Institute, from which the group anticipated a steady stream of revenue, of its only physician. Several other residents left soon thereafter. By May 2, 1861, those who remained authorized two of the trustees to sell all the lands owned by the group. However, the real deathblow to the community came later that year when Brigadier General Nicholas Bartlett Pearce commandeered the society's lands for a Confederate training camp. On the basis of certain letters, Kim Allen Scott and Robert Myers speculate that society members might actually have been arrested and later released, but their exact fate remains unknown.

Guy Lancaster
Encyclopedia of Arkansas History & Culture

THE HARMONIAL VEGETARIAN SOCIETY PLANNED TO LIVE IN A MANSION—

HOME SWEET HOME.

POTATO SWEET POTATO.

Incoming Kingdom Missionary Unit

One of Arkansas's quirkiest religious groups, the Incoming Kingdom Missionary Unit, located at Gilbert (Searcy County), was founded shortly after World War I. A midwestern clergyman, the Reverend John Adams Battenfield (1876–1952), taught that the world would end "shortly" amid "a great world-wide war between Catholics and Protestants." Therefore, the faithful—those who heeded Rev. Battenfield's message—needed to prepare for this event by fleeing their present communities and establishing themselves in completely self-sufficient communities, or "Kingdom Units," in scattered remote mountain areas across the nation. From here, they would emerge after the holocaust and establish the Millennial Kingdom of God. In each community, all property was to be communally owned, government was to be in the hands of the church elders, and those who refused to work ("shirkers") faced eviction from the community. All members would also learn Hebrew, the language of the incoming kingdom. Because of its remoteness in the Ozark Mountains, Gilbert was chosen as the location of one of these units.

Rev. Battenfield was born in Napoleon, Ohio, on September 8, 1876. He became fascinated with religion, especially with Bible prophecy, at an early age; by fourteen, he had memorized the book of Revelation and, by sixteen, was already preaching. Before he was twenty, he was ordained as a minister in the Christian Church (Disciples of Christ). Soon after beginning his formal ministry, he claimed to have discovered within the Hebrew text of the Old Testament "patterns of sevens" that provided him with an infallible technique for distinguishing its "true readings from interpolations." Shortly before the beginning of World War I in Europe, he published the first of a series of pamphlets called "The Great Demonstration" announcing that the world as it existed would end soon, perhaps in 1923.

About the same time, he left his denomination's formal ministry and became a traveling religious lecturer on a divinely appointed mission to prepare the world for this great, apocalyptic event. In 1919, the first issue of his defining religious newspaper, the *Incoming Kingdom Harbinger*, was published in Olney, Illinois. However, after initial acceptance from denominational leaders, his extremely complex theology and his speculations concerning the imminent end of the age soon met with increasing skepticism. Eventually, his views were denounced as "weighed in the balances and found wanting."

Battenfield, believing that he had a divinely appointed mission, proceeded with plans to build his "economic self-sufficient colonies" across the country, with Gilbert as the first. Subsequent colonies were established in Elkton, Oregon, and Buffalo Ridge, Virginia. His movement attracted followers from urban and rural working classes, many of whom were dissatisfied with established churches. The Gilbert Kingdom Unit was launched in September 1920 when C. E. Jordan, a wealthy Illinois farmer and a firm believer in Battenfield's vision, bought land at the site and divided it into lots for the incoming "colonists." Within a few months, seventy people made their homes in the community. A church, schoolhouse, and printing plant were quickly built. The *Incoming Kingdom Harbinger* was printed and mailed out nationwide from Gilbert. The new citizens of Gilbert also began mission outreaches in the nearby communities of Bruno (Marion County), St. Joe (Searcy County), and Witts Springs (Searcy County). A cooperative store was opened at Bruno, and a manufacturing cooperative, Water Creek Christian Industries, was organized at Maumee (Searcy County). However, all of these efforts were short lived.

Battenfield's utopian vision soon ran afoul of the individuality of his colonists, with many of his followers reluctant to share their possessions or resources freely with others. Other problems arose when Battenfield began to abandon traditional Christian teachings on the holy trinity and other subjects. The year of 1923 passed without the appearance of the Messiah and his kingdom. In 1925, after several failed public attempts to bring a deceased parishioner back to life, Battenfield suffered a nervous breakdown. His publication was immediately suspended, and he and his family left Gilbert. Shortly afterward, his remaining Gilbert followers renounced his prophesies and teachings.

By 1930, Battenfield and his family were living in Olney, Illinois, where he was again pastoring Christian Churches. He died in Holmes County, Ohio, on January 3, 1952.

Russell P. Baker
Mabelvale, Arkansas

Ivory-billed Woodpeckers

Long believed to be extinct, the ivory-billed woodpecker (*Campephilus principalis*) was rediscovered in the Big Woods of east Arkansas in 2004. More than sixty years after the last confirmed sighting in the United States, a research team announced on April 28, 2005, that at least one male ivory-billed woodpecker survived in the vast bottomland swamp forest. Published in the journal *Science*, the findings included multiple sightings of the elusive woodpecker and frame-by-frame analyses of brief video footage. The evidence was gathered during an intensive year-long search in the Cache River and White River National Wildlife Refuges in eastern Arkansas, involving a team of more than fifty experts and field biologists working as part of the Big Woods Conservation Partnership, led by the Cornell Laboratory of Ornithology and the Nature Conservancy.

Ivory-billed woodpeckers were once found in mature bottomland hardwood forests of the southeast United States and Cuba. Because of their specialized diet of beetle larvae, they require an extensive habitat of mature forests with many recently dead, but still standing, trees. To reach the larvae, the birds strip the still-tight bark from the trees using their large ivory-colored bills, made of bone covered with keratin. The birds were probably never common, but by the 1930s, nearly all of their habitat had been destroyed.

The ivory-billed woodpecker is the third-largest woodpecker in the world and the largest north of Mexico. At eighteen to twenty inches tall, it has a wingspan of thirty to thirty-one inches and weighs sixteen to twenty ounces. It has a black body with large white patches on the wings. A white stripe extends from below each eye down the sides of the neck and onto the sides of the back. When the wings are folded, a large patch of white is visible on the lower back. The male has bright red on its crest, which curves backward; the female's black crest curves forward. Because the ivory-billed woodpecker looks similar to the slightly smaller, more common pileated woodpecker (*Dryocopus pileatus*), identification requires knowledge of the field marks of both species.

Ivory-billed woodpeckers do not have the undulating flight characteristic of many woodpeckers. Their flight is strong and direct. When traveling long distances, they typically fly above the trees. Their call is a nasal-sounding "kent," which sounds like the toot of a tin horn. They are known for the unique double-knock they make when striking a tree with their beaks. Ornithologists believe that this is used to announce the bird's presence or establish territory. Most woodpeckers in the ivory-billed's genus (*Campephilus*) make a similar double-knock, but the other species live in Latin America.

Ivory-billed woodpecker at nest.
Courtesy of the U.S. Fish and Wildlife Service

Knowledge about ivory-billed woodpeckers is limited because there have been so few in-depth studies of the species. Some ornithologists believe they are nomadic, continually searching for habitat. In the 1930s, Cornell University researcher James T. Tanner estimated that each pair of the birds required a territory of at least six square miles. Ivory-billed woodpeckers excavate trees for nesting cavities and roosts. They begin breeding in January, laying an average of three eggs per clutch. Both parents care for the young, which fledge at about five weeks and may depend on their parents for a year or more. Ornithologists speculate that they may live twenty to thirty years.

Under the Endangered Species Act, the U.S. Fish and Wildlife Service is required to establish a recovery team to prepare a comprehensive recovery plan for the ivory-billed woodpecker and to advise agencies, stakeholders, and the public on conservation proposals. Many issues remain for the recovery team to sort out, including the compatibility of traditional uses such as hunting and fishing in the region's wildlife refuges, public accessibility for bird watching, and forest management to enhance the chances of the ivory-billed woodpecker's survival. The director of the Cornell lab, Dr. John W. Fitzpatrick, noted that the tangible evidence of the ivory-billed woodpecker's existence "ought to be sufficient to compel a long-overdue national effort to locate any remaining individuals and populations, and simultaneously to launch conservation and recovery planning that prepares us for potential new discoveries."

Jane Jones-Schulz
Arkansas Natural Heritage Commission

King Crowley

King Crowley is the most famous archaeological fake produced in Arkansas and was originally part of a collection "found" in Jonesboro (Craighead County) along Crowley's Ridge in the 1920s and 1930s. Despite the discoverer's claim that the collection was an important archaeological find, present-day researchers now refer to King Crowley and its companions as folk art instead of forgeries, as the pieces did not reproduce prehistoric artifacts.

Dentler Rowland, a gunsmith and jeweler from Jonesboro, began selling these artifacts of a "lost" civilization in 1923, and he continued to do so until the 1930s. Rowland claimed to have discovered them while digging along Crowley's Ridge, an erosional remnant within the Mississippi River Delta upon which the city of Jonesboro was founded. Approximately eighty statues and other objects, ranging from crude to expertly crafted human figures or animal caricatures, survive today. All of the figures seem to be crafted of sandstone and artificially stained to appear old. They are embellished with the brass, silver, and steel parts of a horse harness. Though the artifacts are unique and valuable as folk art, they are neither remnants of a "lost" civilization, as Rowland claimed, nor are they representative of any other Native American culture.

The most popular artifact Rowland "discovered" was a small statue later dubbed King Crowley by Bernie Babcock, the founder of the Museum of Discovery in Little Rock (Pulaski County). Along with Jonesboro historian Harry Lee Williams, Babcock argued for the authenticity of the find, though experts elsewhere in the state and the nation, including archaeologists at the Smithsonian Institution, never believed the find to be valid. There is reason to believe that by the 1930s even Babcock had relented in her defense of the artifacts. Nonetheless, news of the excavation of King Crowley, which appeared in Arkansas schoolbooks, spread quickly. The discovery, which was controversial from the beginning, made its way throughout the Mid-South, eventually wending its way into newspapers as far north as St. Louis, Missouri. Speculation that King Crowley was four or five thousand years old and had been made by Aztecs generated much excitement because the statue would have been one of the most ancient artifacts of its kind found in North America.

The bust of King Crowley is of a stern-looking young male with hair swept back, metal eyes, metal ear ornaments, and a metal heart set into the chest. The statue is about twelve to fourteen inches tall and weighs about forty pounds, based on observations made before it disappeared with all of Babcock's correspondence into a collection in California shortly after World War II. This collection of at least thirty-five to forty objects has been relocated, but the present owner remains anonymous. The only other large collection (of thirty-six objects) is in the Arkansas State University museum in Jonesboro.

The reason for the faking of these artifacts remains unknown, and while there seems to be some disagreement over Rowland's full role in the fiasco, he more than likely at least aided in the creation of the site's finds. Rowland himself was a fine craftsman whose home stood where a sandstone boulder, identical to the sandstone used to make many of the statues, was found. There is reason to believe that the excitement surrounding the archaeological discoveries in Egypt at the time led Rowland to fake his own discovery of an early civilization—among the animals depicted in the collection were a camel and a hippopotamus, which are not native to North America but are found in Egypt.

Dan Morse
University of Arkansas, Fayetteville

Old Mike (?–1911)

Old Mike is the name given to a traveling salesman who died in 1911 in Prescott (Nevada County). The people of Prescott only knew him by his first name, Mike. After his death, he was embalmed and publicly displayed for over sixty years.

Mike visited Prescott about once a month to sell pens, paper, and thread to homes and businesses near the railroad tracks in the center of town. He would arrive on the southbound 3:00 p.m. train and stay overnight. The next day, he would re-board the 3:00 p.m. train and continue his journey.

On April 11, 1911, Mike probably attended an outdoor revival in the city park. The next day, his body was found underneath a tree in the park, where he had apparently died of a heart attack or stroke.

The body was taken to the Cornish Funeral Home, where it was embalmed. A search of Mike's belongings did not turn up any identification. What was known about Mike was that he was forty to forty-five years old; spoke English with little accent; was probably Italian; had suffered some type of injury to his right arm and left leg, possibly the effects of a stroke; and had had very elaborate dental work done. The body was placed on display at the funeral home in hopes of someone identifying it. No one came forward to identify or claim the body.

As the years passed, it became more and more unlikely that Mike would ever be identified. The body turned into somewhat of a tourist attraction, and people traveled from surrounding areas to view the remains.

In 1975, the Arkansas Attorney General's Office asked Cornish Funeral Home to bury the body. On May 12,

1975, a quiet ceremony was held at the DeAnn Cemetery, and Old Mike was put to rest.

David Sesser
Henderson State University

Tarantulas

Tarantulas are the largest spiders in Arkansas and are among the most recognizable. Tarantulas are relative newcomers to Arkansas, having arrived in the state about 8,000 years ago. At that time, the climate of North America was much warmer and drier than it is today. Because of higher temperatures and lower amounts of rainfall, habitats more typical of the southwestern United States and the Great Plains expanded eastward into Arkansas and Missouri. Along with drier habitats came many of the animals associated with them, such as tarantulas and scorpions. As the climate became cooler and wetter about 4,000 years ago, these species did not retreat west. Instead, they became isolated within suitable patches of open, dry habitat surrounded by increasing amounts of forest.

In Arkansas, tarantulas are known to range from the Ozark Mountains southward across the Arkansas River Valley and Ouachita Mountains, into the West Gulf Coastal Plain. While a few records of tarantulas in Crowley's Ridge exist, these spiders appear to be largely absent from most of the Mississippi Alluvial Plain.

The lifespan of a tarantula is uncommonly long by spider standards. Sexual maturity is reached at about ten years of age, and although males die shortly after mating, females can live for up to twenty years. The majority of these years are spent in underground burrows, which can be ten to twenty-four inches deep.

Tarantulas are not active, roaming hunters; instead, they sit in or near the opening of their burrow and wait for potential prey to pass by. Once prey is detected, the tarantula rushes forward, seizing its prey, inserting its fangs, and injecting venom to immobilize its captive. Beetles, grasshoppers, crickets, and other spiders make up the typical diet of a tarantula.

Fall is tarantula mating season in Arkansas, and males search out females. Mature males generally leave their burrows sometime between August and October. These wandering males account for most sightings of tarantulas in Arkansas. Males may wander long distances, up to one and a half miles, in search of a mate. After mating, male tarantulas typically die from starvation with the coming of winter, while the females spend the winter in their burrows. The following year, sometime in early summer, fertilized females begin to create silken egg sacs, into which 200 to 800 eggs are deposited. Once finished, the egg sac is vigorously guarded and tended by the doting mother. Eggs typically hatch during July and August.

Tarantulas possess mild venom that is used to subdue prey. The bite of an Arkansas tarantula has been described as being about as painful as a bee sting.

Much of what we now know about tarantulas in Arkansas is due to the work of William J. Baerg, the father of North American tarantula research. In 2004, the Arkansas Natural Heritage Commission contributed to this knowledge base with the first ever statewide citizen-science effort to map tarantula distribution: the Arkansas Tarantula Survey.

Michael D. Warriner
Arkansas Natural Heritage Commission

Turkey Trot Festival

Turkey Trot is an annual festival held in Yellville (Marion County) on the second weekend in October, all day Friday and Saturday. Like many Arkansas festivals, Turkey Trot was founded to draw attention to local natural resources as well as to provide community entertainment.

The festival originated just before Thanksgiving in 1946, when Yellville's American Legion post, with help from local businessmen and professionals, sponsored the National Turkey Calling Contest and Turkey Trot. The day's activities were intended to be a wild turkey–conservation activity, calling attention to Arkansas's dwindling turkey population, which by the mid-1940s had dropped to only 7,000, very few of which remained in the Ozarks.

The "Turkey Trot" portion of the event originally referred to an activity in which event organizers dropped live turkeys from the courthouse roof. Festival attendees could chase and attempt to capture the birds, and those who caught birds could keep them for Thanksgiving dinner. In 1948, a local pilot began dropping the turkeys for the Turkey Trot from an airplane. This portion of the festival was so popular that the name was eventually adopted for the entire weekend's activities.

In its early years, the festival included educational conservation programs, political speakers, turkey dinners, archery and other sporting demonstrations, square dances, and live music. Later, the American Legion post handed over organization of the festival to the Yellville Area Chamber of Commerce. The Chamber of Commerce added a parade, street dance, 5K run/walk, a lip-syncing contest, and the Miss Turkey Trot pageant, which includes a Miss Drumsticks division, in which participants are judged on the beauty of their legs alone.

A December 1989 article in the *National Enquirer* brought notoriety to the festival. The article, which referred to the festival as "sick" and "bizarre," featured graphic photographs of the turkey drops, which inspired outrage from people all over the country. Event organizers defended the drops, arguing that wild turkeys are able to use their wings to glide gently to the ground. In response to the criticism, the Yellville Chamber of Commerce officially stopped sponsoring the airplane drops, but the tradition was continued by an unidentified private citizen, popularly known as the "phantom pilot." The turkey drops came under further scrutiny in 2011, when the organization People for the Ethical Treatment of Animals (PETA) offered a $5,000 reward for the arrest of the phantom pilot. The Federal Aviation Administration (FAA) has also weighed in on the issue, saying that pilots caught releasing birds from an airplane risk losing their license.

Mary Buchman
Powhatan Historic State Park

THE PHANTOM PILOT DROPPED LIVE TURKEYS OVER YELL COUNTY—

FLAP FLAP FLAP FLUP!

SOME FOLKS CALLED IT "BIZARRE."

White River Monster

The White River Monster is one of Arkansas's premier mysteries. Since 1915, along the White River near Newport (Jackson County), the monster has supposedly appeared several times and has become a local legend.

Sightings of "Whitey" began in 1915 but were sporadic until 1937. On July 1 of that year, Bramlett Bateman, owner of a plantation near the river, saw the monster. He reported it as having gray skin and being "as wide as a car and three cars long."

As news spread, construction of a huge rope net to capture the monster began. The monster had been seen in an eddy, so a diver was brought in to search for it. However, Whitey was not captured, and construction of the net stopped because of the lack of money and materials.

In 1971, the sightings began again when someone reported seeing a gray creature with a horn sticking out from its forehead. Other witnesses described it as having a spiny back twenty feet long. Later, a trail of three-toed, fourteen-inch prints was found in the White River area. Crushed vegetation and broken trees were evidence that something large had passed by, and it was assumed that the tracks were Whitey's.

In 1973, the legislature signed into law a bill by Arkansas state senator Robert Harvey, creating the White River Monster Refuge along the White River. The area is located between "the southern point on the river known as Old Grand Glaize and a northern point on White River known as Rosie." It is illegal to harm the monster inside the refuge.

While there have been no recent sightings, theories about Whitey abound. The monster is hypothesized to be anything from a huge fish to an elephant seal, though none of the theories fully explain Whitey.

Conor J. Hennelly
Roland, Arkansas

THE *WHITE RIVER MONSTER* IS ONE OF THE OLDEST MYSTERIES IN ARKANSAS-

PEOPLE HAVE CLAIMED TO SEE "*WHITEY*" SINCE 1915. BUT HE MIGHT NOT BE REAL.

NO HUNTING!

REAL OR NOT, THE *MONSTER* HAS A REFUGE CLOSE TO NEWPORT!

Oddities

Julie Adams (1926–)

Julie Adams is an actress who has made more than fifty films and appeared in numerous television series. She was raised in Little Rock (Pulaski County) and attended Little Rock Junior College, now the University of Arkansas at Little Rock (UALR). She may be best remembered for her role in the 3-D thriller and cult classic *Creature from the Black Lagoon*. She also had a recurring role on the popular TV series *Murder, She Wrote*.

Julie Adams was born Betty May Adams on October 17, 1926, in Waterloo, Iowa, but grew up in Little Rock, where she began acting in elementary school. After attending Little Rock Junior College, she left in 1946 to live with an aunt in Hollywood, California, where she studied dramatics and worked part time as a secretary.

Her first movie role was a small, uncredited appearance as a starlet in Paramount's *Red, Hot and Blue* (1949). Next came a series of low-budget westerns for Lippert Studios, with her billed as Betty Adams. In 1951, after helping on a screen test with an actor under consideration, she was signed to a contract with Universal Studios, where her first name was changed to Julia and, in 1955, to Julie.

Around this time, Universal made a publicity splash by insuring her legs. In 1954, still billed as Julia, she was cast in the role for which she is often remembered, as Kay Lawrence in the 3-D thriller *Creature from the Black Lagoon*. Her role was described as "not only lovely, but an intelligent researcher who is both feminine and strong-willed."

Notable movies include the film noir *Slaughter on Tenth Avenue* (1957), *Tickle Me* (1965) with Elvis Presley, and the TV movie *Go Ask Alice* (1973). In 1954, she married actor Ray Danton, with whom she had two sons. Danton rose to fame in the 1950s playing smooth operators and gangster types, gaining notice for his role in *I'll Cry Tomorrow* (1955) as well as two gangster films, *The Rise and Fall of Legs Diamond* (1960),

Publicity still of Julie Adams of Little Rock, from the 1954 3-D thriller Creature from the Black Lagoon.
Courtesy of Julie Adams

and *Portrait of a Mobster* (1961). She and Danton divorced in 1981.

She was cast in a leading role as Jimmy Stewart's wife on *The Jimmy Stewart Show*, a 1971 family situation comedy television series. From 1987 to 1993, she had a recurring role as flirtatious real estate agent Eve Simpson on the popular TV mystery series *Murder, She Wrote*. Adams continues to appear occasionally in episodes of television shows, including *Cold Case* and *CSI:NY*. She lives in California. In 2011, she published her autobiography, *The Lucky Southern Star: Reflections from the Black Lagoon*. In 2012, Adams won the Rondo Award for the Monster Kid Hall of Fame at the annual Wonderfest in Louisville, Kentucky. In 2013, she was honored with UALR's Distinguished Alumni Award.

Nancy Hendricks
Garland County Historical Society

LITTLE ROCK ACTRESS JULIE ADAMS GOT CARRIED AWAY BY THE *CREATURE FROM THE BLACK LAGOON.*

WHICH WAY TO ARKANSAS?

Celebrities

"Broncho Billy" Anderson (1880–1971)

"Broncho Billy" Anderson was the stage name of Gilbert Maxwell Aronson, America's first cowboy movie star. Anderson pioneered the genre that eventually produced stars such as John Wayne, Gary Cooper, Roy Rogers, Buck Jones, and Tom Mix. Anderson also worked behind the camera as a director and producer and developed production techniques still in use today. He was awarded a special Oscar by the Academy of Motion Picture Arts and Sciences in 1958.

Max Aronson was born in 1880 in Little Rock (Pulaski County). His parents were Henry, who was a traveling salesman, and Esther Aronson. The Aronsons had seven children. Most of the children were born in Texas, but Max was born in Arkansas.

Aronson moved to Pine Bluff (Jefferson County) in the 1890s to work for his brother-in-law, Louis Roth, who had married Aronson's sister, Gertrude, and who worked as a cotton broker. He left Arkansas around the turn of the century for New York, where he became involved with the old Vitagraph Company, a theatrical group.

From 1900 until 1926, Aronson produced, directed, or appeared in more than 600 motion pictures—everything from the one reelers, which were movies that consisted of approximately 400 feet of film, to full-length motion pictures that consisted of approximately 2,000 feet of film, produced later in his career.

In 1903, Aronson was cast in Edwin S. Porter's film *The Great Train Robbery*, a classic silent western. In his early films, he played various roles under the name G. M. Anderson, as in the movie *Raffles, the Amateur Cracksman* for Vitagraph in 1904, the first film he directed.

In 1907, Anderson moved to Chicago to produce films. There, he developed the idea that the public would pay to see good western movies. The era of "cowboy" films, that is, films based on marketing the name of the cowboy, had begun.

For a short time, he produced films in Colorado, but William Selig, an early movie producer for whom Anderson was working, could not see the advantage of western scenery in their releases. Anderson's contribution was to develop the western-looking film. Techniques he devised, including the "long shot," "medium shot," "close up," and "reestablishment scene," have become standard techniques present even in modern westerns.

Back in Chicago, Anderson partnered with George K. Spoor, a theatrical booking agent. The two of them established Essanay Studios in 1907, the name being derived from a phonetic spelling of their initials, S and A. Anderson married Molly Louise Schabbleman in 1908, and the couple had one child, Maxine.

From 1908 to 1915, Anderson made 375 westerns. The most famous of these was the *Broncho Billy* series. Anderson read a story in the *Saturday Evening Post* about a character called Broncho Billy. He liked the idea of a series character and developed Broncho Billy into a franchise of films that became extremely popular with the American public.

Anderson established a studio at Niles, California, in 1912, where he turned out a two-reel *Broncho Billy* story approximately every two weeks. The films cost approximately $800 per movie to produce, and each grossed approximately $50,000. The Essanay Studios were in their heyday.

Many legendary Hollywood stars worked at Essanay, such as Francis X. Bushman, one of the leading stars of his day; Gloria Swanson; and Charlie Chaplin. Anderson signed Chaplin for the unheard of salary of $1,250 per week, plus a bonus of $10,000, but neither Spoor nor Chaplin were happy with the arrangement. Spoor was shocked by the salary, and Chaplin was not happy with either the Chicago or Niles studios and their regimented way of mass-producing films. At Niles, Anderson and Chaplin appeared together in Chaplin's thirty-eighth film, *The Champion,* released in March 1915, the only film in which the two stars appeared together.

The Bushman, Chaplin, and Anderson movies produced substantial profits for Essanay, but the studio began to experience problems. First, Chaplin was hired away by Mutual for $10,000 a week and a $150,000 signing bonus. Then, Anderson began to realize that the public was demanding more than simple two-reelers.

He approached Spoor about producing longer, more involved features. Spoor did not want to incur more expense for longer productions, so Anderson eventually sold his interest in Essanay in 1916. The separation contract stipulated that Anderson could not engage in motion picture production for two years and that the Broncho Billy character would remain the property of Essanay.

For all practical purposes, Anderson retired. Essanay finally dropped out of the film production business. In 1918, Anderson attempted producing westerns again, but the public had new heroes on the silver screen, and the franchise ceased.

In 1958, Anderson was awarded an honorary Oscar by the Academy of Motion Picture Arts and Sciences for his contribution to the development of motion pictures as entertainment. He lived in quiet retirement for most of his remaining years but was seen again in the publicity of receiving his honorary Oscar. He died in Pasadena, California, on January 20, 1971, of a heart attack.

Dave Wallis
Pine Bluff, Arkansas

"BRONCHO BILLY" ANDERSON WAS THE FIRST MOVIE COWBOY.

Rodger Bumpass (1951–)

Rodger Bumpass is an actor and voice performer who was born in Little Rock (Pulaski County) and attended Arkansas State University (ASU) in Jonesboro (Craighead County). Along with numerous television and film roles, he has achieved fame as the voice of the character Squidward in the popular *SpongeBob SquarePants* film and TV series.

Rodger Bumpass was born on November 20, 1951, in Little Rock to Carroll C. Bumpass and Virginia Cathey Bumpass, owners of Bumpass Cleaners and Dyers in Little Rock. He grew up with two siblings, Leonard and Cathey, and attended Little Rock Central High School, where he had his first experience in theater, primarily in the area of comedy. In high school, he attended a radio–TV competition at ASU, where he won the announcing contest. Upon graduation from Central High School in 1970, he decided to attend ASU, where he majored in radio–TV and minored in theater. He worked at the campus radio station and later found a job at Jonesboro's ABC television affiliate, KAIT-TV.

At KAIT, he worked as an announcer, film processor, cameraman, audio technician, and technical director. He also had his own late-night comedy program called *Mid-Century Nonsense Festival Featuring Kumquat Theater*, for which he wrote and performed. After acting in a theatrical competition and being encouraged by an ASU professor to consider professional theater, he graduated from ASU in 1976 and left for New York City in June 1977.

Among his early jobs in Manhattan was selling carpet cleaner on the sidewalk outside Woolworth's. He auditioned and won a role in *National Lampoon*'s music and comedy road show titled, *That's Not Funny, That's Sick* (1977–78).

The show toured forty-five states and played at the University of Arkansas (UA) in Fayetteville (Washington County). Bumpass was often singled out for special praise in reviews of the show. In 1979, *National Lampoon* began producing its next movie in Hollywood, to be called *Jaws III–People 0*. Bumpass moved to California and was awarded the leading role, in which he would have a love scene with Bo Derrick. However, the film was canceled due to objections by the creators of the movie *Jaws*.

Bumpass remained in Los Angeles, found an agent, and soon began appearing in movies such as *Escape from New York* (1981) and TV shows including *Hart to Hart* and *Silk Stalkings*. He also became greatly in demand for his voice work. He has voiced characters in films such as *Heavy Metal* (1981), *Hercules* (1997), *A Bug's Life* (1998), *Tarzan* (1999), *The Emperor's New Groove* (2000), *Monsters, Inc.* (2001), *Spirited Away* (2002), *Treasure Planet* (2002), *Shrek II* (2004), and *Ice Age: The Meltdown* (2006).

His TV voice work includes *The New Adventures of Mighty Mouse*, *Where in the World Is Carmen Sandiego?*, *Batman: The Animated Series*, *Invader ZIM* (as Professor Membrane), and beginning in 1999, the hit Nickelodeon TV show *SpongeBob SquarePants* as Squidward Tentacles, a squid who seems annoyed by almost everything in the fictitious undersea world of Bikini Bottom in the Pacific Ocean.

In November 2004, *The SpongeBob SquarePants Movie* was released. Bumpass again portrayed Squidward. Fellow cast members included Alec Baldwin, Jeffrey Tambor, Scarlett Johansson, and David Hasselhoff. He has also done voice work for the TV shows *Chuggington* (2010), *Gravity Falls* (2012), and *Teen Titans Go!* (2013), among others, as well as for the movie *Monsters University* (2013).

On-camera roles in TV movies include *Santa Jr.* (2002), *A Boyfriend for Christmas* (2004), *Just Desserts* (2004), *Murder Without Conviction* (2004), and the two-part mini-series *Marco Polo: Discovery of the World*. He also had a film role in the theatrical release *Cars* (2006) and has done voice work for such video games as *Infamous* (2009) and *Dead to Rights: Retribution* (2010).

In 2012, he was nominated for a Daytime Emmy Award for Outstanding Performer in an Animated Program.

Bumpass continues to be in demand for both on-camera and voice work. He resides in Burbank, California.

Nancy Hendricks
Garland County Historical Society

Johnny Cash (1932–2003)

Johnny Cash was a world-renowned singer/songwriter of country music. With his deep, rich voice and sometimes dark, sometimes uplifting lyrics, he created a body of work that will be heard and remembered for generations to come.

J. R. Cash was born on February 26, 1932, in Kingsland (Cleveland County) to Ray and Carrie Cash. He had six siblings: Roy, Louise, Jack, Reba, Joanne, and Tommy. In 1935, the family moved to Dyess (Mississippi County), where they lived modestly and worked the land. The tragic death of Jack Cash in a 1944 sawmill accident haunted young J. R. for the remainder of his life. His mother introduced him to the guitar, and the local Church of God introduced him to music. He acquired a fascination for the guitar and a love for singing. Cash first sang on the radio at station KLCN in Blytheville (Mississippi County) while attending Dyess High School. Upon graduation in 1950, he enlisted in the U.S. Air Force after a brief search for work in Michigan.

Cash was stationed in Germany, where he bought his first guitar for five dollars and formed his first band, the Landsberg Barbarians. After receiving an honorable discharge in 1954, Cash moved to San Antonio, Texas, where he married Vivian Liberto, whom he had met while in basic training four years earlier. The couple settled in Memphis, Tennessee, where Cash took radio broadcasting classes at Keegan's School of Broadcasting and worked as an appliance salesman for the Home Equipment Company.

In Memphis, Cash met bass player Marshall Grant and guitarist Luther Perkins. They formed a band and soon were hired to perform once a week on Memphis radio station KWEM, which had recently moved from West Memphis (Crittenden County). In 1954, Cash and his band auditioned for Sam Phillips at Sun Records in Memphis. After several sessions, the trio recorded their first record, 78 rpm and 45 rpm, "Hey Porter" and "Cry, Cry, Cry" in 1955. It was Phillips who gave Cash the name Johnny and labeled his band "Johnny Cash and the Tennessee Two." The release was successful and sold more than 100,000 copies. Cash toured feverishly, primarily through the tri-state area of Arkansas, Mississippi, and Tennessee—often with other Sun artists, such as Elvis Presley and Carl Perkins. When Sun Records released his second 78 rpm and 45 rpm record, "Folsom Prison Blues" and "So Doggone Lonesome" (1955), Cash was already a performing member on Shreveport's weekly radio program *Louisiana Hayride*. Around this time, Cash quit his job as a part-time appliance salesman and pursued music full time. In mid-1956, Cash left *Louisiana Hayride* to perform at the Grand Ole Opry, but his stint at the Opry was short because Cash preferred not to appear in Nashville every Saturday night.

With his third release, "I Walk the Line" and "Get Rhythm" (1956), Cash established himself as a rising star. The recording peaked at No. 2 on the country charts and No. 19 on the pop charts. In 1957, Cash signed a lucrative recording contract with Columbia Records, taking effect the following year. At the end of 1957, Cash was the third-best-selling country artist in America and began appearing on national television programs such as *The Jackie Gleason Show*.

Sun Records continued to release Cash singles and albums until 1964, including his first No. 1 country single "Ballad of a Teenage Queen" (1958), just a few months before his Columbia record "Don't Take Your Guns to Town" (1958) reached the No. 1 spot. During the next decade, Columbia Records sold more than twenty million Cash albums worldwide.

Cash moved his family to California in 1961, which allowed him to pursue a limited acting career. He appeared on the television program *Wagon Train* (1959) and in the movie *Five Minutes to Live* (1961). He continued acting throughout his career, appearing in a total of four theatrical movies, including *A Gunfight* (1971), as well as seven television movies.

The long tours and endless one-night gigs took a toll on many a performer, and in 1957, on a long road trip to Jacksonville, Florida, Cash began taking amphetamines to stay awake. Members of his touring party were using them and were happy to share these "bennies" with Cash and his band. This was the start of an addiction that would plague Cash

for the next decade. A bottle of 100 or so pills cost less than ten dollars, and on the road, they were as important to Cash as his guitar.

During the 1960s, Cash maintained a hectic international touring schedule. His drug abuse increased, and his persona of the Man in Black took shape. Cash scored No. 1 country hits with "Ring of Fire" (1963) and "Understand Your Man" (1964). Cash was also releasing theme albums such as his acclaimed album titled *Bitter Tears* (1964), which recounted the plight of the American Indian. Cash was branching out of country music and finding a whole new "folk" audience. He performed at the Newport Folk Festival in 1964, and it was around this time that Cash wrote a scathing letter to *Billboard* magazine blasting the country music establishment for ignoring his "new" music.

Cash's drug abuse continued. While on stage at the Grand Ole Opry, he used a microphone stand to smash footlights along the front of the stage. Months later, he was arrested in El Paso, Texas, for illegally purchasing hundreds of pills in Juarez, Mexico. Two years later, when Cash was again arrested in Lafayette, Georgia, he realized he needed help. However, that same year, Cash attempted to kill himself by driving alone to Chattanooga, Tennessee, and getting himself lost in a series of dark caves. He felt so despondent over his drug addiction and broken promises that he wanted to disappear. However, once deep inside the caves, he became religiously inspired and realized he had much more to live for. He found his way out of the caves and, at that point, decided to seek help for his drug addiction and renew himself religiously. June Carter, who had toured with Cash since the early 1960s, was instrumental in breaking his addiction by constantly reassuring him and never giving up on him. In early 1968, Vivian Cash was granted a divorce from her husband, and Cash promptly married June Carter.

On February 4, 1968, Cash triumphantly returned to Arkansas for a special "Johnny Cash Homecoming Show" at the Dyess High School gymnasium. Later that year, long-time friend and guitarist Luther Perkins died. Arkansan Bob Wootton, born in the small town of Paris (Logan County), joined Cash's band as a permanent replacement after literally coming out of the audience to play guitar during a concert in Fayetteville (Washington County) on September 17, 1968.

The year 1969 was a remarkable one for Cash. He was clean and sober, and he sold six and a half million albums. Cash toured the Far East; his album *Johnny Cash at San Quentin* went to No. 1 on the country and pop charts; he had two No. 1 country singles, "A Boy Named Sue" and "Daddy Sang Bass"; he recorded with Bob Dylan on Dylan's *Nashville Skyline* album; and ABC launched *The Johnny Cash Show,* which was filmed at the Grand Ole Opry and aired in prime time through 1971. On April 10, 1969, Cash returned to Arkansas for a much-anticipated concert at Cummins Prison in Lincoln County.

Cash began the 1970s with another No. 1 country song, "Sunday Morning Coming Down" (1970). He would not have another country No. 1 hit until 1976, when Columbia Records released "One Piece at a Time." Cash began spending time with his evangelist friend Billy Graham, and in 1971 and 1972, he produced and filmed a movie in Israel about the life of Jesus Christ, titled *Gospel Road* (1973). Cash and Graham's friendship grew over the next thirty years, and Cash often appeared at Billy Graham Crusades held around the world. One such appearance was in Little Rock (Pulaski County) at War Memorial Stadium in September 1989. In 1975, Cash published his autobiography, *Man in Black,* which sold more than one million copies. He briefly returned to television with *The Johnny Cash Show* as a 1976 summer replacement series and continued to tour the world throughout the 1970s and 1980s.

In 1980, Cash became the youngest person ever elected to the Country Music Hall of Fame. A year later, Cash found himself in Stuttgart, Germany, at the same time as old friends Carl Perkins and Jerry Lee Lewis. They went on stage together and recorded a live album titled *The Survivors* (1982).

In the early 1980s, Cash had eye surgery, broke several ribs, and damaged a kneecap, all on separate occasions, and again became addicted to pills. He was hospitalized in 1983 with internal bleeding that almost killed him. Upon regaining strength, he checked into the Betty Ford Clinic and remained clean until his death.

In 1985, Cash joined several of his friends for a couple of albums. *The Highwaymen* reached No. 1 on the country charts and featured Cash with Willie Nelson, Waylon Jennings, and Kris Kristofferson. Later that year, Cash returned to Sun Records in Memphis to record the album *Class of '55* with Carl Perkins, Roy Orbison, and Jerry Lee Lewis.

Cash published his second book, *Man in White*, in 1986. It chronicled the life of Paul the Apostle. That same year, Cash was dropped from Columbia Records, and he signed with Mercury/Polygram Records, with which he recorded four albums: *Johnny Cash Is Coming to Town* (1987), *Water from the Wells of Home* (1988), *Boom Chicka Boom* (1989), and *The Mystery of Life* (1991). In 1989, Cash was elected to the Songwriters Hall of Fame.

The second Highwaymen collection, titled *Highwaymen II*, was released in 1990. It peaked in the top five on the country charts. During the 1990s, Cash received recognition from many organizations: the Rock and Roll Hall of Fame (1992), the Kennedy Center Honors for Lifetime Contribution to American Culture (1996), and the Arkansas Entertainers Hall of Fame (1996), as well as receiving the Grammy Award for Lifetime Achievement (2000)—one of his numerous Grammy Awards.

In 1994, Cash signed an unlikely contract with rap producer Rick Rubin and American Recordings and released the successful album *American Recordings*. Cash's popularity soared. This release began a new series of acclaimed albums: *Unchained* (1996), *American III: Solitary Man* (2000), and *American IV: The Man Comes Around* (2002). These featured Cash recording songs written by such alternative rock performers as Soundgarden,

Beck, and Nine Inch Nails. In March 2003, Country Music Television proclaimed Johnny Cash the "Greatest Man in Country Music."

In 1997, Cash published a new version of his autobiography, titled *Cash: The Autobiography*. That same year, he announced he had been diagnosed with a rare form of Parkinson's disease and was forced to give up touring. In 2001, the diagnosis was corrected when he learned he had autonomic neuropathy, which is not a disease but a group of symptoms affecting the central nervous system. Throughout the final years of his life, Cash was frequently admitted to the hospital, suffering primarily from various stages of pneumonia.

On May 15, 2003, June Carter Cash died of complications from heart surgery. Almost four months later, on September 12, 2003, Johnny Cash died at Baptist Hospital in Nashville from respiratory failure brought on by complications from diabetes—one of the many physical ailments Cash had been facing over the years. Johnny Cash is buried near his wife at Hendersonville Memory Gardens in Hendersonville, Tennessee.

In 2005, a major motion picture documenting the first half of his life, *Walk the Line*, was released and garnered both critical and commercial success. Several posthumous albums of Cash's material have been released, including the "lost album" recorded in the early 1980s: *Out Among the Stars* (2014) on Columbia Records.

Tourists continue to visit Dyess to see the place that was home to Cash during his youth. In 2011, Arkansas State University in Jonesboro (Craighead County) purchased Cash's boyhood home for a reported $100,000 and is working to restore the house to serve as a museum. In 2013, the United States Postal Service released a memorial stamp in honor of Cash.

Eric Lensing
Memphis, Tennessee

Gail Davis (1925–1997)

ARKANSAN GAIL DAVIS-

SHOT TO THE TOP AS TV'S PIG-TAILED *ANNIE OAKLEY.*

Gail Davis was an Arkansas-born actress who starred as the legendary sharpshooter in the groundbreaking western series *Annie Oakley*, which ran from 1954 through 1956. She appeared in thirty-two feature films, was guest on a number of TV shows, received a star on the Hollywood Walk of Fame, was inducted into the National Cowgirl Hall of Fame, and was a role model for young women.

Gail Davis was born Betty Jeanne Grayson on October 5, 1925. Her mother was a homemaker and her father, W. B. Grayson, was a physician in McGehee (Desha County). McGehee did not have a hospital, so her birth took place in Little Rock (Pulaski County). When her father became the state health officer, the family moved from McGehee to Little Rock, where Grayson attended Little Rock Senior High School. As a child, Grayson rode horses and was a tomboy. Grayson also held various beauty titles in high school and college, and she sang and danced in local shows from the time she was eight.

While studying dramatics at the University of Texas in Austin, she married Robert Davis in 1945, with whom she had a daughter, Terrie. After World War II, they moved to Hollywood, where she worked as a hat-check girl until being discovered by an agent who obtained an MGM screen test for her. She was signed to a contract, with her first appearance in 1947's *The Romance of Rosy Ridge,* starring Van Johnson. Robert and Gail Davis divorced in 1952.

She worked steadily in movies, including fourteen films with Gene Autry in the late 1940s and early 1950s. He changed her name to Gail Davis and cast her as the star of the *Annie Oakley* TV show, which he produced through his company, Flying A Productions. The show ran for eighty-one episodes from 1954 through 1956.

At just over five feet tall and under 100 pounds, Davis was a charming heroine on *Annie Oakley* who wore pigtails and stopped criminals by outsmarting them or shooting the guns out of their hands. She rode horses and did many of her own stunts. She was the first woman to star in a TV western. Many young women later said they were influenced by watching Gail Davis as Annie Oakley, a female character in a traditionally male role. In the show, Davis took care of her younger brother, Tagg, in the fictional town of Diablo and solved crimes with handsome deputy sheriff Lofty Craig.

More young women probably saw her on TV than in her thirty-two movies, which included *In Room 303* (1947), *Merton of the Movies* (1947), *The Far Frontier* (1948), *Law of the Golden West* (1949), *West of Wyoming* (1950), *Texans Never Cry* (1951), *Flying Leathernecks* (1951), *The Old West* (1952), and *Winning of the West* (1953). After her TV series ended, she appeared as Annie Oakley in the 1959 film *Alias Jesse James* starring Bob Hope. In that film, she appeared in an uncredited role along with such other stars, also uncredited, as Gary Cooper, Bing Crosby, Roy Rogers, James Garner (as Bret Maverick), and Fess Parker (as Davy Crockett).

Her television appearances include guest roles on *The Lone Ranger*, *The Gene Autry Show*, *The Cisco Kid*, and *Death Valley Days*, as well as a 1961 episode of the *Andy Griffith Show* (Episode 37, "The Perfect Female"), her final appearance as a performer and in which she demonstrated her trademark sharpshooting.

Gail toured with Gene Autry's Wild West show and made appearances as herself on TV programs such as *Wide, Wide World: "The Western"* (1958) with fellow Arkansan Ben Piazza. For her work in television, she was awarded a star on the Hollywood Walk of Fame and, in 2004, she was inducted posthumously into the National Cowgirl Hall of Fame.

In the latter part of her life, Davis married auto dealer Carl Guerriero, who died in 1982. She retired to California's San Fernando Valley but still participated in film festivals, such as 1989's Knoxville Film Festival and certain collector shows. Her last public acceptance of an award came in 1994, when she received the Golden Boot Award from the Motion Picture and Television Fund for positive portrayals in the western tradition.

Gail Davis died of cancer in Los Angeles on March 15, 1997, and is buried in Hollywood's Forest Lawn Cemetery. According to the National Cowgirl Museum and Hall of Fame, Gene Autry said she was the perfect western actress.

Nancy Hendricks
Garland County Historical Society

Bob Dorough (1923–)

Robert Lrod Dorough is a composer, lyricist, and musician best known for his jazz compositions and 1970s *Schoolhouse Rock!* shorts on ABC Saturday morning television.

Bob Dorough was born on December 12, 1923, in Cherry Hill (Polk County), the oldest of four children of Robert Lee Dorough, who was an automobile and insurance salesman, and Alma Audrey Lewis, who was a housewife and Singer sewing machine instructor. Dorough's unusual middle name was suggested by his aunt. He attended elementary schools in De Queen (Sevier County), Mena (Polk County), and Texarkana (Miller County) and graduated from Plainview High School in Plainview, Texas, where the family moved in 1934. The Plainview High School bandmaster inspired Dorough musically and gave him free lessons in harmony and the clarinet to complement his previous training in violin, piano, and voice.

Dorough attended three semesters at Texas Tech University before being drafted into the U.S. Army in February 1943. Because of a punctured eardrum, present since childhood, he was placed in limited service and was never sent overseas. He received a medical discharge in December 1945. While in a military Special Services band, Dorough wrote many arrangements and played in various musical groups. Dorough returned to school after his discharge and earned a Bachelor of Music degree from North Texas State Teachers College (now University of North Texas) in 1949. He moved to New York City after graduation to pursue a master's degree from Columbia University but dropped out before completion after his GI Bill funds were depleted.

Dorough married Jacqueline Wright in 1945. They divorced in 1953. He married Ruth Corine Meinert in 1960; they had one daughter. Meinert died of cancer in 1986. Dorough married Sally Shanley in 1994.

After leaving Columbia University, Dorough supported himself as a piano player. In 1952, he met boxing champion Sugar Ray Robinson, who was learning a tap routine at the Henry LeTang Dance School. The retired boxer hired Dorough to be his music director in his new career in show business, and they toured Canada and the United States, with Dorough either at the piano or conducting big bands for Robinson's act. They went to Paris, France, where Dorough remained after Robinson decided to return to the boxing ring, playing nightly at the Mars Club, a famous Right Bank boîte, for six months (1954–1955).

Dorough's first song to be recorded was "Devil May Care," written with Terrell Kirk. It was recorded in 1953 by the Les Elgart Band. His first full-length album, also titled *Devil May Care*, was a jazz album issued by Bethlehem Records in 1956. He has recorded and released more than fifteen solo albums and has been featured on more than twenty albums by different artists, including Miles Davis and Blossom Dearie. Dorough also has dabbled in acting, appearing in one episode of the television series *Have Gun, Will Travel* (1959), in the movie *Chasers* (1994), as well as voicing (uncredited) a character for the animated television series *Drawn Together* (2005).

In 1971, Dorough was commissioned by David B. McCall, president of a New York advertising company, to set the multiplication tables to music to make learning numbers easier. He wrote and recorded eleven songs for McCall, including "Three Is a Magic Number." McCall approved the release of the songs for a commercial album, titled *Multiplication Rock*, which was issued by Capitol Records in 1973.

The advertising executives considered ideas for tie-ins with the album, settling finally on an animated adaptation, drawn by Tom Yohe. The idea was pitched to the television network ABC, which at the time was looking for more kid-friendly materials for the Saturday morning schedule. The network's head of children's programming approved the three-minute skits, which the General Mills company sponsored. The first four segments of *Schoolhouse Rock!* premiered on ABC on January 6, 1973, with "My Hero Zero," "Elementary, My Dear," "Three Is a Magic Number," and "The Four-Legged Zoo." Following "Multiplication Rock" came "Grammar Rock," which featured songs such as "Lolly, Lolly, Lolly, Get Your Adverbs Here"; "History Rock" (originally known as "America Rock"), featuring "Mother Necessity"; and "Science Rock." Dorough wrote twenty-two of the fifty-two songs for the series, including the series theme song "Schoolhouse Rocky." He served as musical director for the series, which ran on ABC's Saturday morning lineup from 1973 to 1985. The network began re-running the series in 1993.

Dorough continues to produce jazz albums and perform around the world. He and his wife live in Pennsylvania.

Timothy G. Nutt
University of Arkansas Libraries

APOLOGIES TO "BILL" ON ABC.

PASSED!

BILL

BOB

BOB DOROUGH CREATED TV'S *SCHOOLHOUSE ROCK*.

"Aunt Caroline" Dye (1843?–1918)

Caroline Tracy Dye, better known as "Aunt Caroline," was a highly respected seer whose name was recognized in Arkansas and the Mid-South in the early years of the twentieth century. The fact that she was an uneducated African American made her popularity at the time all the more unusual.

Caroline Tracy's parents' names are unknown, and there has been an abundance of conflicting information through the years about her date of birth and early life. She was born into slavery in Spartanburg, South Carolina, about 1843, shortly after the death of her parents' master, William Tracy. His widow, Nancy, later moved with her family and slaves to Arkansas, settling near present-day Rosie (Independence County). Caroline Tracy had an infant daughter, Hannah, before the death of Nancy Tracy in 1861. All of the slaves, including Caroline Tracy, were the property of the Tracy estate until they were freed after the Civil War.

Caroline Tracy had became aware of her abilities as a seer as a young child. She could reportedly see things outside her line of vision that others could not. Among several early examples is a story that, during the Civil War, she foretold a visit by a member of Tracy family, someone thought dead in the early years of the war.

Tracy later moved to Elgin (Jackson County), where she married Martin Dye on June 16, 1867. They had one child, a girl named Mary, who died at the age of eleven months. Through the years, they raised several children who were not their own, including one or more children who were Martin's but not Caroline's.

Caroline Dye's gravestone at Gum Grove Cemetery in Jackson County; 2008.
Photo by Wes Goodner

It was after Dye moved to Newport (Jackson County) that her reputation began to grow. She never claimed to be a fortune teller; that title was given to her by others. Historian John Quincy Wolf wrote that, in a 400-mile radius from Newport, "Aunt Caroline" was as well known as President Woodrow Wilson. She enjoyed a large clientele from all over the Mid-South, with an especially strong following from Memphis, Tennessee. So many arrived in Newport from Memphis that one train was known locally as the "Caroline Dye Special." Her clients were both black and white, and most showed their appreciation by paying her a few dollars for a reading, although payment was not required. Dye reported that she received twenty to thirty letters a day, with most including money for her services. It was said that some prominent white businessmen of Jackson County would not make important decisions before consulting her. All day long, people crowded into her home in Newport waiting for a reading. She took advantage of the large number of visitors and sold meals from her house.

While she invested in farmland and rental property with the money she earned, she also purchased Liberty Loan Bonds to support the war effort. In later years, many people searched for the gold that she was purported to have buried around Newport.

Dye reportedly used only a deck of cards to help her concentration and would not give readings about love or the outcome of World War I; she did, however, tell many people the location of strayed or stolen livestock, sometimes giving specific directions, and she helped people locate missing jewelry. She revealed visions of the future for her clients and offered advice on missing persons. In one case, she was consulted about the guilt of a man arrested for assault near Austin (Lonoke County). She enjoyed confronting skeptics before they uttered a word and many times told them of situations about themselves that she could not have previously known. It was said that she even predicted Newport's future great fire of 1926, which wiped out a large part of the town some eight years after her death.

Several incorrect predictions brought her reputation into question. She predicted that the tail of Halley's Comet would strike the earth in 1910, causing major damage. Also, it was reported that she claimed Searcy (White County), Kensett (White County), Bald Knob (White County), and Beebe (White County) would be destroyed by tornadoes in 1915; she later denied saying this. These predictions caused great excitement in the days leading up to the projected dates, but the disasters never occurred.

Dye died on September 26, 1918, in Newport. After her death, large amounts of cash were reportedly found in her house. She is buried in Gum Grove Cemetery in Newport next to her husband, who had died in 1907.

Dye's reputation lives on in two songs written by Memphis bluesman W. C. Handy. He said the gypsy mentioned in "St. Louis Blues" (1914) was Dye. In "Sundown Blues" (1923), he named the fortune teller as Aunt Caroline

AUNT CAROLINE DYE FORETOLD THAT HALLEY'S COMET WOULD HIT THE EARTH.

HEY!

HOW RUDE!

OTHER THINGS, SHE GOT RIGHT.

Dye of Newport, Arkansas. Through the years, the legend of Dye has been distorted and stretched, identifying her as a fortune teller, a "hoodoo" woman, or a "two-headed doctor" (or psychic).

Robert D. Craig
Kennett, Missouri

Celebrities

Gil Gerard (1943–)

TV'S *BUCK ROGERS* GIL GERARD WENT TO TEACHERS COLLEGE IN CONWAY TO BE A CHEMIST.

Actor/producer Gil Gerard is best known for his role of Buck Rogers in the 1979 movie *Buck Rogers in the 25th Century* and the spin-off television series that followed. He was raised in Little Rock (Pulaski County) and attended Arkansas State Teachers College (now the University of Central Arkansas in Conway in Faulkner County), where he pursued a career in chemistry.

Gil Gerard was born on January 23, 1943, in Little Rock, the youngest of three sons. He gave up a promising business career as an industrial chemist to pursue his dream of acting, moving at the age of twenty-six to New York, where he attended the American Music and Dramatic Academy (AMDA) for two semesters. To make ends meet while studying, he got a job driving a cab at night. Gerard appeared on stage in plays such as *Stalag 17* and *Oklahoma*, and while he was driving his cab, a passenger suggested that he audition as an extra for the film *Love Story* (1970), in which he made a brief appearance in a scene in the background behind Ryan O'Neal.

Gerard went on to appear in more than 400 commercials over a period of six years and, in 1974, starred as Dr. Allen Stewart in the daytime soap opera *The Doctors*. He played the role for two years before moving to Hollywood. It was around this time that Gerard formed his own production company, Prudhomme Productions. He then went on to produce and star in his first film, *Hooch* (1976). He soon landed guest-starring roles in an episode of *Little House on the Prairie* called "The Handyman," an episode of *Hawaii Five-0* called "The Ninth Step," and an episode of *Baretta* called "Dear Tony." He also starred in the TV movies *Ransom for Alice* (1977) and *Killing Stone* (1978). Then, in 1979, he landed the leading role in the movie and TV series *Buck Rogers in the 25th Century*.

After the cancellation of *Buck Rogers* in 1981, Gerard went on to star in TV movies such as *Not Just Another Affair*(1982) and *Stormin' Home* (1985), as well as the TV series *Sidekicks* (1986) and *E.A.R.T.H. Force* (1990); he was also the host of the reality show *Code 3* (1993–1994). In 1983, he produced the musical *The Amen Corner*, which opened in the Nederlander Theater in New York.

Gerard has been involved in many charities over the years. He was on the board for the national Make-a-Wish Foundation and on the celebrity advisory board for the Childhood Leukemia Foundation. He has also been active with the Special Olympics for many years.

In October 2005, Gerard appeared on the show *Action Hero Makeover* on the Discovery Health Channel, which documented his year-long progress after undergoing life-saving mini-gastric bypass surgery. According to the show, he had been struggling with his weight for forty years.

Still acting, Gerard had a starring role in TV movies *Beyond* (2006) and *Reptisaurus* (2009), and appeared in TV movies *Nuclear Hurricane* (2007), *Bone Eater* (2007), *Ghost Turn* (2009), and *The Lost Valentine* (2011). He also starred in the film *Blood Fare* (2012). In 2013, he was a guest star on the TV series *Star Trek New Voyages: Phase II*. Since approximately 1997, he has been attending science fiction conventions, meeting fans in the United States and internationally.

Rebecca Evans
Wolverhampton, England

Celebrities

Kenny Johnson (1942–)

GO GREEN!

KENNY JOHNSON CREATED TV'S "THE INCREDIBLE HULK."

Kenneth (Kenny) Culver Johnson Jr. is a television writer, producer, and director. He is the creator of numerous Emmy-winning projects including *The Bionic Woman*, *The Incredible Hulk*, the original TV miniseries *V*, and *Alien Nation*.

Kenny Johnson was born on October 26, 1942, in Pine Bluff (Jefferson County) to Kenneth Culver Johnson Sr. and Helene Maye Brown Johnson. His father was an electrical engineer in the U.S. Army Corps of Engineers who helped build the Pine Bluff Arsenal. Johnson and his family left Pine Bluff after his father was transferred to the Pentagon near the end of World War II, and he was raised in Washington DC. His parents divorced in 1946, and his father moved to Little Rock (Pulaski County). Johnson spent his summers in Arkansas with his father and other family members. At Sherwood High School in Sandy Spring, Maryland, Johnson became interested in theater.

Johnson attended college at Carnegie Tech, now Carnegie Mellon University, in Pittsburgh, Pennsylvania. At Carnegie, he met Bill Pence, leader of the school's film society, and television writer and producer Steven Bochco. Later, Johnson took over the film society and financed his college education by setting up film societies for colleges across the country.

He married Bonnie Hollaway on February 2, 1963, and they had three children. The couple divorced in 1975. On June 19, 1977, he married Susan (Susie) Appling, and they had one child.

After graduating from Carnegie's Department of Drama in 1964, he moved to New York, where he soon became a producer and director. In 1966, he joined *The Mike Douglas Show* in Philadelphia, Pennsylvania, as a producer and directed much of the show's film work. In 1967, when he was only twenty-four, he replaced Roger Ailes as executive producer of the show.

In 1970, he moved to California and worked on several game shows, including *The Joker's Wild*; he also produced the killer whale shows at SeaWorld. With the encouragement of Steven Bochco, he began writing. Bochco introduced him to the producer of *The Six Million Dollar Man*, and Johnson's first idea was to create a show about a bionic woman. He gave her the name of Jaime Sommers after a water-skier he had met while producing at SeaWorld. He joined Universal Studios as a producer, and, in 1976, he created *The Bionic Woman* series. In one episode, he named a character Carleton Harris after the Arkansas Supreme Court chief justice and family friend. In 1978, he created the television version of *The Incredible Hulk*, though he moved it away from its comic book origin.

In 1983, he created *V*. Inspired by Sinclair Lewis's anti-fascist novel *It Can't Happen Here*, the miniseries tells the story of an alien race that, under the guise of friendship, seeks to take over Earth. The character of Ruby on *V* is named after Johnson's maternal grandmother, Ruby Piper Brown. The miniseries was the number-one TV show in America, drawing 80 million viewers for both nights it was on the air. Johnson's later projects include *Alien Nation*, winner of the prestigious Viewers for Quality Television Award, and the motion picture *Short Circuit 2* (1988). Johnson has also created screenplays for *Cliffhangers* (1978), *Hot Pursuit* (1984), *V: The Final Battle* (1984), and *Shadow Chasers* (1984–1986).

Johnson directed and/or produced *Bride of the Incredible Hulk* (1978), *Steel* (1997), *An Evening of Edgar Allan Poe* (1970), *Senior Trip* (1981), *The Liberators* (1987), *Sherlock Holmes Returns* (1993), *Alien Nation: Body and Soul* (1995), and *Alien Nation: The Udara Legacy* (1997).

Johnson is the only producer/creator with three shows on "TV Guide's 25 Greatest Sci-Fi Legends": *The Six Million Dollar Man*, *The Bionic Woman*, and *V*. In addition to producing and directing, he is a published novelist and teaches filmmaking seminars at major film schools in the United States and Europe.

Gwendolyn Shelton
Little Rock, Arkansas

Louis Jordan
(1908–1975)

Louis Thomas Jordan—vocalist, bandleader, and saxophonist—ruled the charts, stage, screen, and airwaves of the 1940s and profoundly influenced the creators of rhythm and blues (R&B), rock and roll, and post–World War II blues.

Louis Jordan was born on July 8, 1908, in Brinkley (Monroe County). His father, James Aaron Jordan, led the Brinkley Brass Band; his mother, Adell, died when Jordan was young. Jordan studied music under his father and showed promise in horn playing, especially clarinet and saxophone. Due to World War I vacancies, young Jordan joined his father's band and soon joined his father in a professional traveling show—touring Arkansas, Tennessee, and Missouri by train.

Jordan briefly attended Arkansas Baptist College in Little Rock (Pulaski County) in the late 1920s and was later a benefactor to the school. He played saxophone and clarinet with Jimmy Pryor's Imperial Serenaders in Little Rock and Bob Alexander's Harmony Kings in Union County during the boom lumber and oil eras, getting twice the going five-dollars-per-gig rate in Little Rock. The Harmony Kings then took a job at Wilson's Tell-'Em-'Bout-Me Cafe in Hot Springs (Garland County); Jordan also performed at the Eastman Hotel and Woodmen of the Union Hall and with the band of Ruby "Junie Bug" Williams at the Green Gables Club on the Malvern Highway near Hot Springs, as well as at the Club Belvedere near Little Rock.

The lengths and legitimacy of his marriages are in some dispute. He first married Arkadelphia (Clark County) native Julia/Julie (surname unknown). He met Texas native singer and dancer Ida Fields at a Hot Springs cakewalk and married her in 1932, though he may have still been married to his first wife. He and Fields divorced in the early 1940s, and he married childhood sweetheart Fleecie Moore in 1942. Moore is listed as co-com-

poser on many hit Jordan songs, such as "Buzz Me," "Caldonia Boogie," and "Let the Good Times Roll." Jordan worked with an additional music publisher using her name; he had cause to regret it later after she stabbed him during an argument. They briefly reconciled before divorcing. Jordan married dancer Vicky Hayes in 1951 (and separated from her in 1960), then singer and dancer Martha Weaver in 1966.

In the 1930s, in Philadelphia, Pennsylvania, Jordan found work in the Charlie Gaines band, which recorded and toured with Louis Armstrong. The two Louises would later play duets when Jordan became a solo star. Jordan learned baritone sax during this period. In 1936, he joined Chick Webb's Savoy Ballroom Band. Ella Fitzgerald was the band's featured singer; Jordan played sax and got the occasional vocal, such as "Rusty Hinge," recorded in March 1937. In 1938, Jordan was fired by Webb for trying to convince Fitzgerald and others to join his new band.

Jordan's band was always called the Tympany Five, regardless of the number of pieces. The band's small size made it innovative structurally and musically in the Big Band era. Among the first to join electric guitar and bass with horns, Jordan set the framework for decades of future R&B and rock combos. Endless rehearsals, matching suits, dance moves, and routines built around songs made up the band's stage show. Jordan's humorous, over-the-beat monologues and depictions of black life are a prototype of rap, and his crossover appeal to whites calcified his popularity. Jordan charted dozens of hits from the early 1940s to the early 1950s—up-tempo songs like "Choo Choo Ch'Boogie" (number one for eighteen weeks) and "Ain't Nobody Here But Us Chickens" (number one for seventeen weeks), and ballads like "Is You Is or Is You Ain't (My Baby)."

He could play a solo and delve into a rapid-fire vocal or routine without missing a beat. Although Jordan's songs could depict drunken, raucous scenes—like "Saturday Night Fish Fry" (number one for twelve weeks) and "What's the Use of Gettin' Sober?"—he did not drink or smoke and could be quiet and aloof. Jordan was also a fine ballad singer—as songs such as "Don't Let the Sun Catch You Crying" and "I'll Never Be Free," sung with Ella Fitzgerald, exemplify. He helped introduce calypso music to America and toured the Caribbean in the early 1950s, fooling natives with his faux West Indian singing accent.

Jordan also starred in early examples of music video—"soundies," introduced in 1940—and longer films based around his songs, such as *Beware!* (1946), *Reet, Petite, and Gone* (1947), and *Look Out Sister* (1948). He cameoed in movies such as *Follow the Boys* (1944) and *Swing Parade of 1946* (1946). Loved by World War II GIs and selected to record wartime "V-discs," he remains known overseas today.

The sounds Jordan pioneered eventually led to slow record sales as R&B and rock and roll emerged. His more than fifteen years on Decca—not counting his time there with Webb—ended in 1954; he had sold millions of records for the company and performed duets with Armstrong, Bing Crosby, and Fitzgerald. During the late 1950s and early 1960s, Jordan released consis-

tently engaging material, but for a variety of labels (Aladdin, Black Lion, RCA's X, Vik, and Ray Charles's Tangerine) and to decreasing sales. Jordan continued to tour, including in Europe and Asia in the late 1960s. He returned to Brinkley in 1957 for Louis Jordan Day. He spent much of the late 1960s and early 1970s without a recording contract. In 1973, Jordan issued a final LP, *I Believe in Music*, on the Black & Blue label.

Just over a year later, on February 4, 1975, he died in Los Angeles, California. Jordan is buried in St. Louis, Missouri, hometown of his widow, Martha.

A host of prominent musicians claim his influence, including Ray Charles, James Brown, Bo Diddley, and Chuck Berry. His songs have appeared in commercials, on TV, and in movies, and have been recorded by dozens of popular artists. Tribute albums include Clarence "Gatemouth" Brown's *Sings Louis Jordan* (1973), Joe Jackson's *Jumpin' Jive* (1981), and B. B. King's *Let the Good Times Roll* (1999).

Jordan was inducted into the Rock and Roll Hall of Fame in 1987 and named an American Music Master by the Hall in 1999. A musical revue of Jordan's songs, *Five Guys Named Moe*, played on London's West End and on Broadway in the 1990s. A nine-CD Decca retrospective was released by Germany's Bear Family in 1992. In Little Rock, the first Louis Jordan Tribute concert was held in 1997, with proceeds benefiting a Jordan bust in Brinkley by artist John Deering. Jordan was inducted into the Arkansas Entertainers Hall of Fame in 1998 and the Arkansas Black Hall of Fame in 2005. In 2008, the U.S. Postal Service released a stamp featuring Jordan as he appeared in the 1945 short film *Caldonia*.

Stephen Koch
Arkansongs

This entry, originally published in *Arkansas Biography: A Collection of Notable Lives*, appears here in an altered form. *Arkansas Biography* is available from the University of Arkansas Press.

Lum and Abner

From 1931 to 1955, the *Lum and Abner* radio show brought the town of Pine Ridge (Montgomery County) into the homes of millions of listeners across the country. During World War II, Armed Forces Radio took *Lum and Abner* around the world. Their humor was clean and honest, reflecting small-town life and human nature. The stories had universal themes that have not become dated, and therefore *Lum and Abner* continues to be popular with old-time radio fans.

Chester "Chet" Lauck and Findley Norris "Tuffy" Goff, two young comedians from Mena (Polk County), created the characters when they were invited to appear on a statewide flood relief broadcast over KTHS radio in Hot Springs (Garland County) on April 26, 1931. Seconds before being introduced, they created the names Lum Edwards (pronounced "Eddards") for Lauck and Abner Peabody for Goff.

The two old codgers (Lauck and Goff were actually in their late twenties) ran the Jot 'Em Down General Store in Pine Ridge. Lum was a bachelor with an eye for women, and his ego usually got in the way of common sense. Abner was a hen-pecked married man, and his gullibility was enormous. They were civic-minded merchants who never seemed to have any money in the cash register. Their schemes for grandeur always brought them to the brink of tragedy.

Additional characters were created for later broadcasts. Lauck portrayed Cedric Wehunt, and nosey Grandpappy Spears, while Goff became Dick Huddleston (the real store keeper in Waters, the town upon which Pine Ridge was based), schemer Squire Skimp, shy Mousey Gray, Mose Moots the barber, town-meany Snake Hogan, and many others. Each character was based on a composite of old friends from Waters and Mena.

As the *Lum and Abner* show was set in the Jot 'Em Down Store in

Pine Ridge, on April 26, 1936, the citizens of Waters changed the town's name to Pine Ridge in honor of *Lum and Abner*.

KTHS groomed the young talent on Sunday broadcasts for just a few months, and then they auditioned in Chicago for a network show on NBC radio. *Lum and Abner* was picked up immediately and continued for almost twenty-five years, including 5,800 daily live fifteen-minute programs. A series of contracts saw them on the air for four radio networks (NBC, ABC, CBS, and Mutual), sponsored by such major companies as Quaker Oats, Ford Motor Company, Horlick's Malted Milk, Alka Seltzer, General Foods, and General Mills.

Lum and Abner was the first network program broadcast from Radio City in New York in 1933, the first to do a marathon charity broadcast, and the first to make a transatlantic "simulcast," with Lauck in London and Goff in Chicago. Their promotions of war effort causes during World War II were especially successful. Their sponsors offered premiums that are now collectibles.

As a result of their radio popularity, *Lum and Abner* broadcasts moved to Hollywood studios in 1939 in order for the actors to pursue careers in motion pictures. The pair made six movies during the 1940s: *Dreaming Out Loud* (1940), *The Bashful Bachelor* (1942), *So This Is Washington* (1943), *Two Weeks to Live* (1943), *Going to Town* (1944), and *Partners in Time* (1946). *Lum and Abner Abroad* (1956) was made in Europe as a television pilot, with the two characters as Hollywood personalities. Lauck and Goff did not like the result, and it was not released to theaters; it is now sought-after piece of Lum and Abner history.

Lum and Abner had begun as a lark in Mena, traveled to Hot Springs, and grown in Chicago and Hollywood. Early broadcasts were carried by local sponsors, but later nationwide sponsors carried the show into millions of homes. After nearly twenty-five years of radio, television had made inroads into audiences, and the programs were again locally sponsored. By 1955, the two were ready to quit, as Norris Goff had been in poor health for many years. Their humor and style has been copied on such programs as *The Beverly Hillbillies* and by the comic strip *Li'l Abner*, which is often confused with *Lum and Abner*.

Lum and Abner made a small town in Arkansas world famous. Today, Pine Ridge is home to the Lum and Abner Museum. The National Lum and Abner Association was founded in 1984 and has 600 members nationwide.

Kathryn Moore Stucker
Lum and Abner Museum

Douglas MacArthur (1880–1964)

General of the Army Douglas MacArthur, one of the six men to attain that rank, was born in Little Rock (Pulaski County). MacArthur Park and the MacArthur Museum of Arkansas Military History in Little Rock bear his name.

Douglas MacArthur was born in the Tower Building of the Little Rock Barracks (previously called the Little Rock Arsenal) on January 26, 1880, the third son of Captain Arthur MacArthur and his wife, Mary Pinkney Hardy MacArthur. Arthur MacArthur had served in the Wisconsin Twenty-fourth Volunteer Infantry Regiment during the Civil War and was stationed at the Little Rock Barracks. The MacArthurs remained in Arkansas only six months before the captain was reassigned to New Mexico. Before departing Little Rock, Douglas MacArthur was baptized at Christ Episcopal Church, a site he visited when he returned to Little Rock for a visit in 1952.

MacArthur received countless awards and recognitions throughout his lifetime. He was first in his graduating class at West Point in 1903 and was one of the most highly decorated American soldiers in World War I. In 1928, he headed the American Olympic Committee for the Amsterdam games. He served as chief of staff of the army under two presidents. In 1937, he retired and became field marshal of the Philippine Army only to return to active duty in 1941. During World War II, he served as general of U.S. Army Forces–Far East and was later appointed Supreme Al-

lied Commander of the Southwest Pacific Theater, reaching the rank of a five-star General of the Army. For his actions, he was awarded the Congressional Medal of Honor. He accepted the surrender of Japan and served as Supreme Commander of the Allied Powers in the occupation of Japan. Later, he was made commander of United Nations forces in the Korean War but was relieved of command after making public statements that were inconsistent with those of President Harry S. Truman. He delivered the keynote speech at the 1952 Republican National Convention.

MacArthur married Louise Cromwell Brooks in 1922; they divorced seven years later. He married Jean Marie Faircloth in 1937, and they had one son.

The preserved Tower Building stands today in MacArthur Park in downtown Little Rock and currently houses the MacArthur Museum of Arkansas Military History. MacArthur returned to the Little Rock site in 1952 for ceremonies commemorating the park in his name. The site was designated a National Historic Landmark in 1994.

Douglas MacArthur; circa 1945.
Courtesy of the National Archives and Records Administration

MacArthur died on April 5, 1964, at the U.S. Army Hospital Walter Reed in Washington DC from complications following surgery. He is interred along with his wife in a museum dedicated to his memory in downtown Norfolk, Virginia.

John Spurgeon
Bella Vista, Arkansas

Robert McFerrin Sr. (1921–2006)

Robert McFerrin Sr. was an African-American baritone opera and concert singer who became the first black male to appear in an opera at the Metropolitan Opera house in New York City, his debut following by less than three weeks the well-publicized breaking of the color barrier by contralto Marian Anderson. However, McFerrin's career at the Met was brief, being limited to ten performances in three seasons over three years. Although he sang in European opera houses and performed concerts extensively, he failed to attain major prominence. He is best remembered as the father of singer and conductor Bobby McFerrin, with whom he sometimes performed.

Robert McFerrin was born on March 19, 1921, in Marianna (Lee County) to Melvin McFerrin, who was a minister, and Mary McKinney McFerrin. He had seven siblings. McFerrin showed musical talent at an early age. The family moved to Memphis, Tennessee, when he was two, and he completed eight grades there. A talented siffleur (whistler), he joined a family gospel-singing trio at age thirteen. His father arranged for him to attend Sumner High School in St. Louis, Missouri. McFerrin intended to become an English teacher but changed his career plans after he joined the high school choir and received his first formal music instruction under chorus director Wirt Walton.

After graduation from high school in 1940, McFerrin was accepted at Fisk University in Nashville, Tennessee, but stayed only one year. In 1941, after winning a singing contest, he entered Chicago Musical College, where he studied under George Graham. In 1942, he won first prize in the Chicagoland Music Festival. After being drafted and serving in the army, he returned to college. In 1948, he moved to New York, where he became a student of Hall Johnson, a prominent figure in Afro-American music. He married Sara Copper in 1949; she was a Howard University graduate and singer who gave up her career to further his. She was also a polio victim and was in an iron lung while pregnant with their son, Robert Jr. (Bobby), one of their two children.

McFerrin's New York career began in 1949 with a small part in Kurt Weill's *Lost in the Stars*. His performance attracted the attention of Boris Goldovsky, who gave him a scholarship to study at the Tanglewood Opera Theatre outside Boston. There, in 1949, he made his operatic debut in Giuseppe Verdi's *Rigoletto*. He then joined Goldovsky's touring company, where he added roles in Charles Gounod's *Faust* and Christoph Willibald Gluck's *Iphigenie en Tauride*. In addition, he sang with the National Negro Opera company in Verdi's *Aida* and at the New York City Center Opera Company in the world premiere of fellow Arkansan William Grant Still's *Troubled Island*. Finally, he returned to Broadway for a revival of *Green Pastures* in 1951 and the following year for some performances in *My Darlin' Aida*, an updated version of the Verdi opera set in Memphis in 1861.

In 1953, urged on by his manager, he entered the Metropolitan Opera's "Auditions of the Air," which he won. Usually, the winner received a contract and six months of training. In McFerrin's case, he received no contract, and his training lasted for thirteen months. McFerrin did not object and later lauded the program for teaching him fencing, ballet, and other aspects of stage deportment.

The second African American and first black male to sing at the Metropolitan Opera, McFerrin debuted on January 27, 1955, when he was cast as Amonasro in *Aida*. Racial politics rather than sound musical values dictated his being cast as Amonasro. The black Ethiopian king (and father of Aida) has no love duets to sing with white women. At five foot seven inches tall and 140 pounds, the young McFerrin was hardly prepossessing on stage as an evil father-figure. His even but not large voice was not displayed to its best advantage. In addition, prior to the performance, he had never met the evening's female leads, Aida (Herva Nelli) or Amneris (Blanche Thebom).

A Town Hall recital found him in more congenial circumstances. McFerrin eventually sang only ten performances at the Metropolitan Opera. He did, however, record excerpts from *Rigoletto* in 1956 for the Metropolitan Opera Club. In addition, there exists a 1956 recording taken from a live broadcast of *Aida* from Naples, Italy. In 1958, he went to Hollywood to supply the vocals for Sidney Poitier's Porgy in the motion picture version of George Gershwin's *Porgy and Bess*. McFerrin and his wife decided to stay in California, where they became music teachers. In 1973, following their divorce, McFerrin moved back to St. Louis, where he lived until his death. In 1989, he suffered a stroke that affected his speaking but not his singing. He occasionally performed with his son, Bobby, and his daughter, Brenda. In 1994, he and fellow Arkansan William Warfield, who was also African American, appeared in a Schiller Institute concert.

"I am not attempting to carry the load for all Negro singers," McFerrin had told the *New York Post* prior to his debut, but in reality the load he had to carry transcended vocal concerns. One major reason for his truncated career was management's fear of the reaction of

ARIA OR ARIA NOT FROM ARKANSAS? —

ROBERT McFERRIN SR. OF MARIANNA SANG AT THE MET.

audiences to seeing black men on stage as husbands or lovers of white women.

McFerrin died on November 24, 2006, in St. Louis. He is buried in Jefferson Barracks National Cemetery.

Michael B. Dougan
Jonesboro, Arkansas

Patsy Montana (1908–1996)

Patsy Montana was a pioneering country and western music singer whose signature song, "I Want to Be a Cowboy's Sweetheart," was the first record by a female country artist to sell a million copies.

Patsy Montana was born Ruby Blevins on October 30, 1908, near Hot Springs (Garland County). She was the eleventh child and only daughter of farmer Augustus Blevins and his wife, Victoria Blevins. By the 1920 census, the family was living in Hempstead County. Raised on church songs, fiddle music, and the music of country star Jimmie Rodgers, Blevins headed to Los Angeles with her brother and sister-in-law in 1930; hoping to catch the public's eye, she changed the spelling of her first name to Rubye. She studied violin at the University of the West (now the University of California at Los Angeles—UCLA) until a victory in a talent contest in 1931—she yodeled and sang Jimmie Rodgers songs—led to her own show on KMIC radio. Initially billed as "The Yodeling Cowgirl From San Antone," Blevins soon became Patsy Montana, a name given to her by singer/songwriter Stuart Hamblen while she was performing with the Montana Cowgirls on a KMIC show Hamblen hosted with cowboy star Monte Montana.

In 1932, after two years spent breaking into the music business in Los Angeles, Montana returned to Arkansas, where country singer Jimmie Davis heard her on KWKH in Shreveport, Louisiana, and invited her to sing backup for him at his next recording session. She recorded four debut songs on that trip. A bigger break came in 1933 when she accompanied two of her brothers carrying a watermelon to the

Patsy Montana attired in western garb.
Courtesy of the UALR Center for Arkansas History and Culture

Chicago World's Fair and landed a job as vocalist for the Prairie Ramblers, a hugely successful Kentucky string band that appeared on radio station WLS. She then appeared regularly on the enormously popular *National Barn Dance*, a pioneering country-themed broadcast that started before the *Grand Ole Opry* show, and recorded for the American Record Corporation. Montana also toured steadily, even after her marriage on July 4, 1934, to Paul Rose, who worked with WLS's touring shows. Her biggest hit, "I Want to Be a Cowboy's Sweetheart," composed by Montana herself, was recorded in 1935.

By this time, Montana was an established star with a clearly defined image as a "cowboy pal" who yodeled and dressed in the full western regalia favored by 1930s country stars, complete with gun and holster. Other songs followed in the same vein—"Sweetheart of the Saddle" (1936) and "I Wanna Be a Western Cowgirl" (1939), among others. Even more spirited were numbers such as "The She-Buckaroo" (1936) and "A Rip-Snortin' Two-Gun Gal" (1939)—in the former she portrays herself as a "man-hatin' lassie." In the 1940s, Montana contributed "Goodnight, Soldier" to the war effort and also recorded with such well-known groups as the Sons of the Pioneers and the Light Crust Doughboys.

Montana also appeared in several films, the best known being *Colorado Sunset* (1939) with Gene Autry. From 1946 to 1947, she had her own network radio show, *Wake Up and Smile*, on ABC, which featured her trademark greeting, "Hi, pardner! It's Patsy Montana," accompanied by the thunder of horses' hooves.

Montana returned to Arkansas in 1947, raising her two daughters, Beverly and Judy; doing radio shows on KTHS in Hot Springs; and appearing on Shreveport's *Louisiana Hayride*. Her husband's work eventually took the family to San Jacinto,

California, but Montana continued to tour and make records into the 1990s, adding to her reputation as a hard-working professional entertainer. Between 1934 and 1992, she made more than 7,000 personal appearances in the United States, Canada, and Europe. In the fall of 1995, just before her eighty-seventh birthday, Montana played concerts in Hope (Hempstead County) and Little Rock (Pulaski County). She was frail and tiny in her boots and cowboy hat, but she sang and yodeled vigorously, closing as always with "I Want to Be a Cowboy's Sweetheart."

Patsy Montana died in San Jacinto on May 3, 1996. Later that same year, she was inducted into the Country Music Hall of Fame. As long as women sing country songs in cowgirl outfits, Montana's niche in the pantheon of groundbreaking female country music stars is secure.

Robert Cochran
University of Arkansas, Fayetteville

PATSY MONTANA SANG "*I WANT TO BE A COWBOY'S SWEETHEART.*"

Hal Needham (1931–2013)

Hal Needham was an American stuntman, stunt coordinator, writer, and director who performed stunts in many films and television shows. The director of hit movies such as *Smokey and the Bandit*, *Smokey and the Bandit II*, *Stroker Ace*, *Cannonball Run*, *Cannonball Run II*, and *Hooper*, Needham was considered a

pioneer in the stunt industry, having introduced techniques and safety equipment still in use today.

Harold Brett "Hal" Needham was born on March 6, 1931, in Memphis, Tennessee, the third of three children of Howard and

MOVIE STUNTMAN HAL NEEDHAM GREW UP
ALL AROUND ARKANSAS-

182

Edith Needham. Needham's father left the family soon after he was born. Eventually, Needham's mother married a sharecropper named Corbett, who moved the family to Arkansas when Needham was four. She and Corbett had two children of their own. Due to his stepfather's transient and desperately poor livelihood following the crops, Needham and his four siblings lived all over the state during his childhood, including El Dorado (Union County), Georgetown (White County), Pangburn (White County), and West Helena (Phillips County), usually moving from place to place by wagon.

After the outbreak of World War II, Needham's stepfather moved to St. Louis, Missouri, to work in war materiel plants, and his family soon followed. As a teenager living in St. Louis, Needham worked as a bowling pin setter and tree trimmer. After a stint in the military as a paratrooper during the Korean War, Needham moved to California, where he was approached by a former paratrooper friend about helping perform a stunt for the television show *You Asked For It!*, in which Needham would jump from a low-flying airplane onto the back of a galloping horse. After successfully completing the stunt, Needham was hooked and set his sights on becoming a professional stuntman. Eventually, he broke into the business. During his career, he performed stunts on more than 4,500 episodes of television shows, including *Have Gun, Will Travel*, *Gunsmoke*, *Charlie's Angels*, and the original *Star Trek*. He also worked extensively in film during his career, performing and coordinating stunts and directing in more than 310 films, including *Little Big Man*, *Stagecoach*, *McClintock*, *How the West Was Won*, *White Lightning*, and *Shenandoah*.

While speaking at a college campus in the early 1960s, Needham saw pole vaulters jumping into a large, air-filled bag and got the idea to use a similar bag to allow stuntmen to safely fall from high buildings—an innovation that revolutionized how high-fall stunts were performed. Later, after a filmmaker asked him to develop a way to flip a moving car without a ramp, Needham designed a trunk-mounted, car-flipping cannon still used in film-making today—though Needham's first test of the system snapped the car in half and landed him in the hospital with a broken back.

In 1961, he married Marie Arlene Wheeler. They were divorced in about 1973. While having no children together, Needham adopted Wheeler's three children from a previous marriage. In 1981, Needham married actress Dani Janssen. They divorced in 1987.

A friend and house guest of the actor Burt Reynolds in the 1970s (he was Reynolds's stunt double for the 1973 movie *White Lightning*, filmed in Arkansas), Needham conceived the story for his first motion picture, 1977's *Smokey and the Bandit*, after hearing someone at a party mention that bringing Coors beer east of the Mississippi River was considered bootlegging. Needham went on to direct Reynolds in the wildly popular film and its sequel, which have since become classics.

Needham founded the Skoal Bandit NASCAR team, drove a high-horsepower ambulance cross country in an illegal coast-to-coast rally race (an experience later dramatized in Needham's 1981 film, *Cannonball Run*), and tried to break the sound barrier on land in a rocket car.

After retirement, he lived in West Hollywood, California, with his third wife, Ellyn Wynne Williams, whom he married in 1996. In 2011, he published his autobiography, *Stuntman!: My Car-Crashing, Plane-Jumping, Bone-Breaking, Death-Defying Hollywood Life*. Needham received an honorary Academy Award in 2012.

Needham died on October 25, 2013.

David Koon
Little Rock, Arkansas

Kate Phillips (1913–2008)

Mary Katherine (Kay) Linaker (a.k.a. Kate Phillips) was a veteran stage and screen actress who went on to become a writer of television and movie screenplays. She achieved her greatest notoriety as a writer on the 1958 horror/science fiction classic *The Blob*.

Kay Linaker was born on July 19, 1913, in Pine Bluff (Jefferson County). Her father owned C. A. Linaker and Company and was

KAY LINAKER (KATE PHILLIPS) OF PINE BLUFF WROTE *THE BLOB*.

a wholesaler for Armour Food Company. Linaker's father died when she was eleven. When she was twelve, she entered the Hillside School in Norwalk, Connecticut, a boarding school from which she graduated at sixteen. She had already expressed an interest in theater and planned to attend Wellesley College, but the exercise treatments for the polio she had contracted were in New York, so she took night classes at New York University and studied during the day at the American Academy of Dramatic Arts.

After graduating, she got a film contract with Warner Bros., having attracted the attention of screen scouts with her work in several Broadway roles. Her first film was *The Murder of Dr. Harrigan* (1936). She said she got the role when movie star Mary Astor got into trouble with the studio; thereafter, Linaker often got leading roles, while Astor had to settle for smaller parts. Among her acting credits are five *Charlie Chan* movies, and she worked with actors from Tyrone Power to Henry Fonda to Claudette Colbert.

Linaker's acting work connected her to other noteworthy Arkansans when she signed to play opposite Lum and Abner (Chester Lauck and Norris Goff) in 1943's *Two Weeks to Live*. As she later recalled, "We were sitting around talking, waiting between takes, when we realized that our parents had known one another. My father had also introduced rice to Arkansas—and this is how he got to know the fathers of the men who started that small Jot 'Em Down Store. Their father ran a small mom and pop place, which was the inspiration for the show."

Linaker's film career came to a halt during World War II when she joined the Red Cross, serving as a USO hostess at clubs run by the army. She met her future husband, Howard Phillips, when he was "supposedly setting up groups of singers to entertain GIs, but he really was checking on security leaks!" A singer

in the U.S. Army Air Forces, Howard Phillips was having some moderate success with writing, and after they were married, they teamed up to write for television. (He later became an NBC television executive.) Kay Phillips herself had previously done some writing for a radio show called *Voice of America*, a military sponsored show, and had lived among writers and actors in a colony in Malibu.

The couple moved to New Hampshire. Phillips then garnered her most famous credit—she wrote *The Blob* (1958). The movie came about after the meeting of Irvine H. Milligate, the head of visual aids for the Boy Scouts of America, and Jack H. Harris, a distributor who dreamed of producing films. While the two traveled the country promoting a film Milligate had done, they had the idea to make a monster movie. With the help of Irvin S. Yeaworth's company, Valley Forge Films, Harris and Milligate began work on *The Blob*, then under the title *The Molten Meteor*, with Milligate coming up with the story. Later, Kay Phillips (listed as Kate Phillips) and Theodore Simonson finished the screenplay. Despite the success of the film, which starred Steve McQueen in his first major role, she received very little remuneration, later recalling, "Both Steve McQueen and I were to receive $150 plus ten percent of the gross. Neither one of us got the percentage—and the film (and its remake) have earned millions—but I got an important writing credit, and Steve became a star!"

After *The Blob*, Phillips had very few writing credits and went on to teach acting and screenwriting at the college level. She taught in Canada (where she started a performing arts center in Ontario) and at Keene State College in Keene, New Hampshire.

Phillips died on April 18, 2008.

Michael G. Fitzgerald
El Dorado, Arkansas

Anita Pointer (1948–)

Anita Marie Pointer, who has strong ties to Arkansas, is an original member of the singing group the Pointer Sisters. She started singing gospel in her father's church in West Oakland, California, and went on to attain pop/R&B stardom. The group's top-ten hits include the songs "Fire," "Slow Hand," "He's So Shy," "Jump (For My Love)," "Automatic," "Neutron Dance," and "I'm So Excited."

Anita Pointer was born on January 23, 1948, in Oakland, California, the fourth of six children (four of them daughters) of Elton Pointer and Sarah Elizabeth Silas Pointer. Her parents were Arkansas natives, and Pointer's two older brothers, Fritz and Aaron, were born in Little Rock (Pulaski County). Shortly thereafter, their parents moved the family to Oakland. The family traveled by car almost yearly from California to Arkansas to visit Pointer's grandparents. Usually, the trip was related to her father's ministry.

As a child, Pointer loved Arkansas so much that she did not want to leave one year, so her mother allowed her to stay in Prescott (Nevada County) with her grandparents to attend fifth grade. She went back to Arkansas again for seventh grade and tenth grade. Pointer still owns the land on which sat the two-story house her grandfather built.

Pointer noticed the differences between Oakland and racially segregated Prescott: "Going to school in the segregated South is an experience that will bring history to life. The 'colored only' and 'white only' signs, I never saw in Oakland, even though there were places we knew not to go just because. Only being allowed to sit in the balcony of the movie theatre, picking up food from the back door of the restaurant because you can't go inside, picking cotton, I did all that and then some."

Pointer attended McRae Elementary, McRae Jr. High, and McRae High School, which were all-black schools at the time. She was a member of the McRae High School Band, playing alto sax. She did not get to listen to much radio, but she was able to listen to broadcasts from the Grand Ole Opry and sneak out to juke joints a few times.

Pointer and her sisters began singing gospel in their father's church, the West Oakland Church of God. Before long, their interest in music expanded and proved too strong for their parents to corral. Bonnie and June Pointer began performing as a duo in the Bay Area, calling themselves Pointers—A Pair. Shortly thereafter, Anita Pointer quit her job at a law office to join the fold, and the Pointer Sisters were officially born. The group started singing back-up in clubs and in studio sessions for such acts as Taj Mahal, Grace Slick, Boz Scaggs, Elvin Bishop, and others. Ruth Pointer later joined the group, and they released their debut album in 1973. Critics called the Pointer Sisters "the most exciting thing to hit show business in years." The Pointer Sisters were the first black female group ever to perform at the Grand Ole Opry, and their song "Fairytale," written by Anita and Bonnie Pointer, won the sisters their first Grammy Award in 1975 for Best Country Performance by a Duo or Group; Elvis Presley later did his own recording of "Fairytale."

With her sisters, Pointer has performed in front of millions around the world and recorded eighteen albums and one solo album. She has performed in diverse settings from Disneyland and the San Francisco Opera House to Roseland Ballroom, Carnegie Hall, and the White House. She has also performed on television shows such as *American Bandstand*, *Soul Train*, *The Flip Wilson Show*, *The Carol Burnett Show*, *The Tonight Show*, and *Arsenio Hall*. The Pointer Sisters were one of the first black acts to be played in heavy rotation on MTV. Pointer also participated in the recording of "We Are the World," the 1985 charity single that raised funds to help famine-relief efforts in Africa. Her act-

ing roles have included the movie *Car Wash* (1976) with Richard Pryor, as well as *The Love Boat*, *Gimme a Break*, and the Pointer Sisters' NBC Special *Up All Night*.

In 1998, Anita Pointer was inducted into the Arkansas Black Hall of Fame. The Pointer Sisters are the recipients of many music awards, including three Grammys and three American Music Awards. They have five gold records, one platinum record, and one multi-platinum record. They were presented with a star on the Hollywood Walk of Fame in 1994. That same day, it was an-

nounced that Pointer and her sisters would embark on a national tour of the Tony-winning musical *Ain't Misbehavin'*.

Pointer, who had married at age seventeen, is divorced; she had one daughter, who was born in 1966 and died in 2003. She has said of Arkansas: "I do feel like home is where the heart is, and my heart feels at home in Arkansas. I love the South."

Paul Ciulla
Everett, Massachusetts

Jimmy Wakely (1914–1982)

Jimmy Wakely, an American country and western singer and actor from the 1930s through the 1950s, made several recordings and appeared in B-western movies with most major studios as a "singing cowboy." Wakely was one of the last singing cowboys after World War II and also appeared on radio and television; he even had his own series of comic books. He has a star on the Hollywood Walk of Fame.

Jimmy Wakely was born James Clarence Wakeley on February 16, 1914, in Mineola (Howard County) to Major Anderson Wakeley, who was a farmer, and Caroline (or Carolin) "Cali" Burgess Wakeley. As a teenager, he changed "James" to "Jimmy" and dropped the second "e" in his last name, making it Wakely.

Wakely married Dora Inez Miser on December 13, 1935. They had four children.

In 1937 in Oklahoma City, Oklahoma, Wakely formed a country singing group named the Bell Boys after their Bell Clothing sponsor. The group performed locally and made recordings and frequent radio broadcasts on Oklahoma City's WKY. The name of the band changed over time, becoming the Jimmy Wakely Trio.

Wakely was discovered by western movie star Gene Autry while Autry was on a tour through Oklahoma. Autry invited Wakely to play on his new *Melody Ranch* radio show, which debuted on CBS in January 1940. The Jimmy Wakely Trio joined the show in mid-1940. After a couple of years, Wakely left to pursue movie work and a recording contract with Decca Records that ran from 1941 through 1947.

Wakely made his screen debut with the Jimmy Wakely Trio in a 1939 Roy Rogers western called *Saga at Death Valley*. In the 1940s, he provided songs and musical support for many B-westerns and appeared alongside many notable performers, including Hopalong Cassidy, Johnny Mack Brown, and Tex Ritter. He appeared in one Autry film, *Heart of the Rio Grande*, in 1942. Wakely also appeared in non-westerns, including *I'm from Arkansas* (1944), a showcase for country performers. He also had his own comic book series from 1949 to 1952, published by DC Comics and titled *Hollywood's Sensational Cowboy Star!*

Wakely was sometimes referred to as a "low-budget Gene Autry." In response, he declared, "Everybody reminds somebody of someone else until they are somebody. And I had rather be compared to Gene Autry than anyone else. Through the grace of God and Gene Autry, I got a career."

Wakely recorded several country albums throughout his career, but some crossed over to the pop charts, notably collaborations with singers Margaret Whiting and Karen Chandler, as well as the Christmas song "Silver Bells."

In addition to appearing on Autry's radio program, Wakely had his own radio show on CBS, *The Jimmy Wakely Show* (1952–1958), and he co-hosted others. He appeared on several television variety shows including hosting the NBC-TV program *Five Star Jubilee*. Wakely developed Shasta records in the 1960s and owned two music publishing companies. Working from a studio converted from part of his California ranch, he produced recordings for himself as well as for other notable country performers, including Tex Williams, Merle Travis, Eddie Dean, Tex Ritter, and Rex Allen.

In his later years, Wakely performed at the Grand Ole Opry and on the *National Barn Dance*. His nightclub act visited Las Vegas, Nevada; Reno, Nevada; and elsewhere. He did a Christmas USO tour with Bob Hope. He also made appearances at western film nostalgia conventions and continued with personal appearances

JIMMY WAKELY WAS ONE OF THE LAST SINGING COWBOYS.

and stage shows, often performing with his daughter Linda and son Johnny.

After being diagnosed with emphysema, Wakely died on September 23, 1982, in Mission Hills, California. He was inducted into the Nashville Songwriters Hall of Fame in 1971 and the Western Music Association Hall of Fame in 1991.

C. L. Bledsoe
Wynne, Arkansas

Elton and Betty White

In the mid- to late 1980s, Elton and Betty White were highly visible Little Rock (Pulaski County) street musicians and eccentrics, recognized for their sexually explicit ukulele songs and their flamboyant wardrobe of sombreros and skimpy swimwear.

Betty White was born Betty Crandall in 1927 in Mabelvale (Pulaski County), one of seven children of the town's postmaster and his wife. In 1946, after graduating as valedictorian of Mabelvale High School, she married air force sergeant Scotty White, with whom she had a son, Sammy. Together, they traveled the nation and the world. After returning to Arkansas, she found secretarial work with the law firm of Wright, Lindsey & Jennings, for whom Bill Clinton was then practicing. Following a diagnosis of schizophrenia, though, Betty divorced her husband and lost her job.

Elton White was born in 1958 in Dumas (Desha County). A high school basketball star, he played four years of college ball at Westark Community College (now the University of Arkansas at Fort Smith) and the University of the Ozarks. He tried out with the Atlanta Hawks, but his professional prospects were eradicated by a knee injury. He moved to Little Rock, finding work as a day laborer, until the night someone "put something in his drink," as he often told the story, and he fell on hard times.

Elton and Betty met in 1984 at Little Rock's Union Rescue Mission, and despite the thirty-year age difference between the white woman and the black man, "It was love at first sight," Betty later recalled, adding, "There was a real magnetism." The two of them began delivering newspapers and writing music together, renting an apartment at the Albert Pike Residence Hotel. They married in 1989.

From 1986 to 1989, with the assistance of producer Jerry Colburn, they released three albums—*The Best of Elton and Betty*, *Sex Beyond the Door*, and *Hard Deep Sex Explosion*—and recorded some 250 songs, many of them frank celebrations of their sex life, both raunchy and tender, with titles such as "A Jelly Behind Woman Blows My Mind," "Lady, Your Breast, I Love to Caress(t)," "My Three-Feet Red-Hot Tongue Is Sweet as Sugar," "Menopause Mama," and "America, We Are Sexy." During these years, they also dabbled in politics, with Elton running for Congress and Betty for governor in 1986, and Elton for governor and Betty for the U.S. Senate in 1990.

In 1991, *The Arsenio Hall Show* aired a recording of the couple performing Elton's "I'm in Love with Your Behind" in the aisles of Little Rock's RAO Video. That same year, the couple moved to Venice Beach, California, where they began performing on the boardwalk as "The Married Couple" and launched a public-access television show, *Husband and Wife Time*. Their jubilant outlandishness led to television appearances on *Sally Jessy Raphael*, *Maury Povich*, and *The Daily Show*, as well as articles in *Variety*, *LA Weekly*, and the French *Agence de Presse Photographique*. The *Philadelphia Inquirer* said of Betty, "She's 72, a former coworker of Bill Clinton's, wears a beaded bikini, plays the ukulele, and freely offers advice on love, marriage and sex," and of Elton, "He's 41, a onetime NBA prospect, wears a Speedo stuffed with socks, plays a toy keyboard, and holds the umbrella they perform behind."

Betty White died on August 20, 2003, at age seventy-six. Elton White continues to reside in the beachfront apartment the couple once shared on Venice Beach.

While much of their music has become scarce, their album *Hard Deep Sex Explosion* is available on iTunes through Rural War Room Records.

Kevin Brockmeier
Little Rock, Arkansas

ELTON AND BETTY PUT OUT
RAUNCHY UKULELE MUSIC.

TWO BEARDED GENTLEMEN OF RENOWN:

RON WOLFE *is a cartoonist and features writer for the* Arkansas Democrat-Gazette, *as well as author of the graphic novel* Knights of the Living Dead. *He and his puppeteer wife, Jan Wolfe, live in Little Rock.*

GUY LANCASTER *is the editor of the online Encyclopedia of Arkansas History & Culture, a project of the Butler Center for Arkansas Studies at the Central Arkansas Library System. He lives in Little Rock with his wife and Butler Center colleague, Anna Lancaster.*